AUG 3 1 2004

On the Viking Trail

On the Viking Trail

Travels in Scandinavian America

by Don Lago

University of Iowa Press
Iowa City

University of Iowa Press, Iowa City 52242
Printed in the United States of America

Design by Omega Clay

http://www.uiowa.edu/uiowapress

The publication of this book was generously supported by
the University of Iowa Foundation.

Printed on acid-free paper

Library of Congress Cataloging-in-Publication Data
Lago, Don, 1956–.
  On the Viking trail: travels in Scandinavian America / by Don Lago.
    p. cm.
  Includes bibliographical references (p.) and index.
  ISBN 0-87745-892-8 (cloth)
    1. Swedish Americans. 2. Lago, Don, 1956– —Journeys. 3. Swedish
Americans—Biography. I. Title.
E184.S23L345 2004
305.83'97073—dc22   2003063416

04 05 06 07 08 C 5 4 3 2 1

CONTENTS

ACKNOWLEDGMENTS

One advantage of a personal memoir is that many of the people who guided me along the way have been acknowledged in the text. Of those who weren't, foremost thanks goes to my long-lost cousin Cheri Fuller-Olson, whose enthusiastic research into our family history was an inspiration not just to me but to my uncles Orlan and Nils. I'd also like to thank Orlan and Nils, both my aunt Marys, and my cousins Cissie, Larry, Phil, and Diane for their hospitality and support throughout my father's ordeal. Several friends in Flagstaff, Arizona, were always happy to hear about my travels, including Marilyn Anderson, Anna Mattson, Lea Parker, Joanne Tallarovic, and, most of all, the Stilley family, whose ancestor Olof Stille arrived in the New Sweden colony in 1641 and who have been the best possible neighbors.

On the Viking Trail

The Swedish Prayer

wasn't much interested in my Scandinavian roots until my father developed Alzheimer's disease, and I discovered the importance of memory and the cost of forgetting.

One hundred and five years after my great-grandfather left Sweden for America, my father arrived in the Swedish town that for him and his father had been merely a name: Gränna. My great-grandfather hadn't maintained contact with anyone there, and as far as my father knew, we had no family left there. But my father had always been interested in history, and he hoped that merely by walking down the street that had been home for his grandfather, he could acquire a better sense of family history. He looked at the main street and thought Gränna was a pleasant town. Then he looked more specifically at the names of the shops. He was startled by the sign over the door of one shop. It was our name: Lago. He walked to the door and looked inside. It was a clothing and tailor's shop. His grandfather had been a tailor. He looked at the man inside. The man looked familiar. My father stepped inside and introduced himself as a Lago from America. The shop owner was astounded. He introduced himself as a Lago from Sweden. The Lagos in Gränna had long known that in 1869 a Lago had left for America, but they had never heard from him again. For all they knew he had perished soon afterward and left only a grave. Now, a century of silence and forgetting had come to an end.

For people from many nations, immigrating to America was often an act of forgetting. Some wanted to forget their personal past. Some wanted to forget their society, where they were peasants without hope of ever being anything more than peasants. Even if they only wanted to be farmers like their fathers before them, they needed to forget a homeland where they had little chance of acquiring land or homes of their own. Some wanted to forget a church or a government that had mistreated them. Perhaps they didn't want to forget their parents, friends, and childhood homes, but preserving sanity in a strange new land required them to forget even good memories. This act of forgetting was passed on to the immigrants' children. The children often heard very little about the old homeland. They were discouraged from learning their parents' language. They were pushed to be completely American and proud of it. The forgetting of history in favor of a self-created ideal future became part of American psychology and public policy. When, in the second half of the twentieth century, America became responsible for the Old World, our forgetting of history did not always serve us well.

Not everyone could forget. My great-grandfather, August Lago, had sailed for America with his older brother, Israel. Israel later decided to return to Sweden. This was not unusual; about one fifth of the Swedes who immigrated to America eventually returned home. Many never intended to stay in America, wanting only to earn enough money to buy land back home. Others were disillusioned to find not streets paved with gold but years of challenges. Others became homesick.

One cure for homesickness was to persuade those you missed to join you in America. One reason my great-grandfather immigrated was a woman he had known in Gränna, Gustava Carlson, who had immigrated the year before. He headed straight for the Indiana town where Gustava had settled and married her a few months later. Gustava was one of nine siblings, eight of whom followed one another to America. When their mother missed her children, she too immigrated.

In her old age, Gustava followed her son to Oklahoma, where she spent her last years living in his house with his three sons, one of whom was my father. Thus for several years my father lived with a grandmother who had been born in Sweden and could still speak Swedish. He heard some of her stories and could identify with Sweden not as history but as home. My grandfather, who never saw Sweden, encouraged his sons to remember Sweden. He gave my father, on his seventh birthday, a 182-page book about Sweden. It was published by the Swedish American Steamship Line, no doubt intended to encourage Swedish Americans to visit the old homeland. Among other things, the book mentions a promising new institution called the Nobel Prize, and it has a graph showing that as of 1914, Stockholm had more telephones per capita than London, Paris, or Berlin. At the dinner table every night, Gustava or her son repeated a prayer in Swedish.

On the wall of my father's nursing home room, in 1995, I placed photos of his parents and of Gränna. Sometimes I took down these photos and held them before my father and explained them. I pointed out the main street of Gränna and the shop with our name over the door. I reminded him that he had gone there many years ago and been delighted to meet our relatives, that from church records and a local genealogist he had learned a lot about our family history. The Lagos had been the tailors in Gränna since 1795, but in America our family had become teachers. I told him that his father was a teacher and he was a teacher and his brother Nils was a history teacher and Nils's children were teachers. For a time my father could remember visiting Sweden, but eventually he showed no more recognition of it. Then he could no longer recognize his parents. As his memory failed, I tried to serve as his memory for him, but I realized that in one respect I couldn't do this. In one realm I had no memories to share. My father held the very last personal memories of our Swedish past. I had never heard his grandmother's stories of Sweden. I was the first person in the history of our family to grow up never hearing a word of Swedish. For centuries, this had been the only language we had known. Perhaps our Viking ancestors had orally passed sagas from one generation to the next. But somehow memory had failed, and I had received nothing. Memories of places that had been important to our family, of houses and streets and lakes and cemeteries, were all ending with me. The customs we had followed and the festivals we had celebrated—all was lost. As I mourned my father's relentless loss of memory and feared the day when he would no longer remember me, I saw how crucially human identity depends on memory, and I realized that I too was a sufferer of memory loss.

I often helped my father eat, giving him instructions on what to do with a fork or a sandwich. If I'd been able, I would have recited the

Swedish prayer before each meal. Childhood memories are the last to be lost by an Alzheimer's victim, so perhaps the Swedish prayer would have offered my father some comfort, some orientation amidst the constant bewilderment. But I couldn't recite the prayer. My grandfather's picture stared mutely from the wall. I sat mutely, unable to find the comforting words that in some form had graced Swedish dinner tables for centuries.

When my grandfather was in his eighties, my uncle tried to prevent the Swedish prayer from being lost. He set up a tape recorder and had my grandfather recite the Swedish prayer into it. When my grandfather was taken to the hospital to die in 1964, he refused to lie down on the stretcher but rode sitting up, reading a book, refusing to let go of the power of words. In 1964 young people all over the world couldn't get enough of four lads from Liverpool who had given a lively British style to the music white Americans had learned from African Americans. My twelve-year-old cousin Marilyn wanted to record the Beatles off the radio, so she set up the tape recorder. The next time my uncle tried to listen to the Swedish prayer, he was shocked to discover that the tape held only the Beatles. The Swedish prayer was gone forever.

I regret listing the Beatles as a force of cultural obliteration, for I enjoyed them as much as anyone. In 1966, when I was ten years old, my father took me to see the Beatles at the new riverfront stadium in St. Louis right next to the new Gateway Arch. Notice that I said *see* the Beatles and not *hear*. You couldn't hear a word they sang above the screams of tens of thousands of kids. At the time I thought this was a bit of a gyp, but, considering how the Beatles drowned out our Swedish prayer, I suppose it was only fair that they knew what it felt like to be drowned out. Apparently, the Beatles were quite tired of being drowned out, for a few days later they gave their final public concert.

Looming above the stadium was the arch, a ghostly silver glow in the night. The previous year, the president of the United States had dedicated the arch to Thomas Jefferson and his Louisiana Purchase. The arch symbolized the role of St. Louis as the gateway to the West. Through St. Louis millions of immigrants had funneled, moving ever more irreversibly away from their European birthplaces. Anywhere but in America it might have been unacceptable that a monument to an important national theme should be designed by an architect born in another country, but it was only appropriate that the monument to the

great American migration was designed by an immigrant. Eero Saarinen was born in Finland and at age twelve moved to Michigan with his
father, a prominent architect. Eero Saarinen's design for a monument
to the Louisiana Purchase was selected over many more traditional
proposals, such as classical temples and statue-laden pediments. Both
visually and as an engineering feat, Saarinen's arch was breathtakingly
original.

Most visitors to the arch see it as a gateway, but I see something
more. I grew up in a house that had some Scandinavian furniture. To
Scandinavian designers, nothing is as beautiful as the pure, natural geometry of wood. An Italian furniture maker might feel compelled to
carve the wood into ornaments, and an Englishman might need to
cover the wood with patterned cloth. But Scandinavians, who are everywhere surrounded by forests, are delighted to invite the forest indoors to embrace them with its strong graceful curves. To me, the
Gateway Arch is unmistakably a piece of Scandinavian furniture, even
though it's made of stainless steel. Many of Saarinen's other buildings
display the same respect for organic geometry. In fact, one of his buildings, a chapel on a college campus, is only two blocks away from where
I was born in Columbia, Missouri, and it too is an exercise in geometry
and natural materials. Saarinen might have been tempted to build the
arch out of wood if it had been possible. His affinity for Scandinavian
furniture is evident in the furniture he designed, which helped define
the organic design style of the 1960s.

The Gateway Arch immediately became one of the world's most
recognizable pieces of architecture, as grand and inevitable as the pyramids, the Parthenon, and the Eiffel Tower. Of twentieth-century architectural works, only the Sydney Opera House has inspired comparable
fascination. Interestingly, it was Saarinen, serving on the committee
considering over 200 designs for a Sydney opera house, who convinced
the committee to select the design of a fellow Scandinavian architect,
the Dane Jørn Utzon. The arch and the opera house, though entirely
different in purpose, are very similar in inspiration, both soaring tributes to pure natural geometry.

If the Gateway Arch symbolizes the dispersal of Americans from
their roots, St. Louis also provides the symbol of our reuniting with our
roots, and this symbol too is the work of a Scandinavian American. In
1926 a daring young pilot who had been flying a mail route between

St. Louis and Chicago approached some St. Louis businessmen with the idea of building a plane that could fly from New York to Paris. He convinced them that he had both the right plane design and the ability to fly it. The businessmen were eager to promote St. Louis as a national aviation center, and thus the *Spirit of Saint Louis* was born. The pilot, Charles Lindbergh, came from a family with a history of daring. His grandfather August had been a member of the Swedish Parliament, where he was an outspoken liberal reformer. Desiring a quieter life, August and his family immigrated to Minnesota. August's son became an equally outspoken member of the U.S. Congress in 1906, leading the Progressive attack on oligarchs and opposing U.S. entry into World War I. While Congressman Lindbergh was delivering campaign speeches, his son and driver, Charles, seemed more interested in tinkering with their car's engine.

Charles Lindbergh's landing in Paris in 1927 was more than just a triumph of courage and technology. It was the bridging of two worlds that had seemed separate. Even if Americans cheered Lindbergh out of an ingrained worship of pioneering heroes, it was hard not to notice that he had pioneered in the wrong direction, back to the homelands from which Americans supposedly had severed all loyalties. Perhaps some of the cheering was for roots that were not so forgotten after all. At the least, the *Spirit of Saint Louis* started an era in which millions of Americans could easily go looking for their roots. Ironically, Lindbergh didn't seem to learn the meaning of his own flight, as he followed his father's precedent and opposed U.S. entry into World War II on the grounds that America was a world apart.

In the summer of 1932, a dusty Model A Ford pulled up in front of the Lindbergh family home in Little Falls, Minnesota, and from the car stepped my grandparents, my father, then fourteen years old, and his two brothers. Charles Lindbergh had recently donated his boyhood home to the state of Minnesota, which opened it as a museum. My grandparents had driven a thousand miles north from Oklahoma on the first leg of a trip into Canada, west to Yellowstone and Seattle, south to the Olympic Games in Los Angeles, then east on Route 66 to the Grand Canyon and back to Oklahoma. At this time there were few paved highways or motels. The Model A Ford lacked a fuel pump, so if it met a hill too steep, the gravity-fed engine would be higher than the gas tank and conk out, so the driver had to turn it around and back up the hill. Flat tires were frequent, sometimes twice a day. The Lagos usually camped on the edges of towns, unfolding the kitchen my grandfather had rigged on the side of the car.

They drove through California during the dust bowl flight of Okies to California, and their Oklahoma license plate invited the mistreatment John Steinbeck later wrote about in *The Grapes of Wrath*. Yet my grandfather was simply a teacher on summer vacation, starting a family tradition of long road trips, a tradition my father would continue with me. My grandfather led similarly long trips to the East Coast, the Rockies, and Mexico, where my father, a strong swimmer, swam across Acapulco Bay, oblivious to boaters frantically signaling to him about the presence of sharks. As a civil engineer, my grandfather took special interest in engineering feats like bridges and dams. But few bridges won as much space in his travel journal as his description of the rooms and grounds of the Lindbergh home. I am sure that some of my grandfather's interest came from the fact that both he and Lindbergh were sons of Swedish immigrants. I'm sure he was proud to show his sons what a little Swedish engineering know-how and Viking courage could accomplish. On their trip to the East Coast, my grandfather showed his sons the remnants of New Sweden on the Delaware River, Sweden's unsuccessful 1638 attempt to found an American colony.

I told my father about his childhood trips all over America, but after awhile he showed no more memory of them. My fight against forgetting was a relentless retreat. The only way I could feel victorious against forgetting was by regaining memories for myself, memories I had never had. And so I headed for Sweden.

I have to confess that I arrived in Sweden feeling not much different from the average tourist in a foreign land. I felt little sense of personal identification with it. My Swedish background felt remote, nearly as abstract as knowing that humans evolved from fish. I hadn't made any plans to visit Gränna, partly because the relatives my father had met there had died, and he was under the impression we had no more family there. I supposed I might get around to visiting Gränna if I finished with the attractions of Stockholm. When I inquired about the bus to Gränna and found that it was sold out, this seemed decisive. Yet something must have been stirring in me on my long walks through the streets and history museums of Stockholm, for it became important for me to visit Gränna. I was getting a feel for what it meant to be Swedish, and this identity teased me like an elusive memory, like something I should know. When I went to the car rental and they gave me a Saab instead of an American car, it seemed right.

I was delighted to see the Gränna sign at the edge of town, though for now I was identifying less with the town than with my father and his arrival there two decades before. But the town charmed me and invited me to identify with it. It is located on Sweden's second largest lake and has a marina busy with sailboats. A ruined castle built by the family of Danish astronomer Tycho Brahe stands on an island in the lake. On the forested bluff behind town is a historical park where old buildings have been assembled. The town itself is one of the best-preserved examples of traditional Swedish timber architecture, with red tile roofs. I soon discovered that I could mention Gränna to any Swede, and he or she would recognize the name, for it is the source of a candy famous throughout Sweden. Busloads of schoolchildren come to watch the candy being made by hand in the candy shops on the main street. They also come to see the Andrée Museum, which depicts the famous attempt of a Gränna native to reach the North Pole by hot air balloon. The clerk in the museum told me how lucky I was to have such a charming town to call home.

It actually did start to feel like home when I spotted, amid the candy shops and cafes, the clothing store with my name over the door. I was pleased to see it was still there. Hesitantly, I stepped inside. I introduced myself to the man behind the counter. He explained that he was the new owner but was not a relative of mine. He had bought the store after the death of the Lago owner and kept the name because it was a local institution. He revealed that I did indeed still have relatives in the area; the couple my father had met who had died childless were only one branch of the family. In fact, I had a relative downstairs right now. The owner took me downstairs to the tailor shop and introduced me to Leonard Lago, who looked a lot like my father. Leonard had been tailoring here for sixty-five years, since the age of twelve. Because he didn't speak English and I didn't speak Swedish, the owner tried to translate for us. Leonard said he remembered my father's visit. I asked him about our family in Gränna. With our language barrier, it was an awkward conversation. Given the unexpectedness and shortness of my visit, I didn't have a chance to meet any more family, but since I hadn't expected to meet anyone, I was pleased enough. I bought a sweater and promised to come back by the time it wore out.

Wandering through the town cemetery and finding many Lago graves made Gränna feel even more like home. I realized that if not for the decisions of my great-grandparents, this might have been my hometown. The strangers buried here might have been my best friends for whom I would offer an old Swedish prayer. My never-questioned American identity now seemed like a science fiction parallel universe story. I could see the Swedish version of myself walking these streets, the only reality he had ever known, and reading about the exotic world of America.

Identifying with Sweden was made easier by the fact that I admired it as a society. If I had come from a country that was despotic, warlike, illiterate, and impoverished, I might be less willing to admit it. But I admired Swedish values, which the country practiced abroad as an advocate of world peace and human rights and at home by caring for both people and the environment. Sweden was also sophisticated scientifically, technologically, and culturally. As I set about exploring my ethnic inheritance, I realized it was no coincidence that my father and I shared many values with Sweden. I recognized that many qualities I had taken to be just my father's personality, such as quietness, a love of learning, an aversion to conflict and cruelty, were part of his Swedish inheritance. Without knowing it, I had been very Swedish all along.

My visit to Sweden convinced me that my Swedish roots should matter to me, but I wasn't sure exactly what they should mean. Fortunately, I had a good opportunity to pursue this question further. To support my writing habit, I had a day job a few months a year traveling to colleges in the Midwest, including the areas most heavily settled by Scandinavians. There were plenty of museums and historical sites and festivals dedicated to remembering Scandinavia. Thus far I had taken little interest in them. Now I would make them my school for exploring my roots. Ironically, my travels had always been dedicated to reconnecting with origins, for I promoted student travel and study in Europe, but I hadn't done for myself what I was doing for others. Fortunately, when I sold enough student trips to Europe, my company rewarded me with a free round-trip ticket to Europe. I began traveling to Scandinavia every year. Some trips were for city and cultural enjoyments, and some were for camping in the mountains. With each trip I got a better understanding of Scandinavia, and I saw how Sweden was part of a larger Scandinavian identity. Each trip also increased my interest in exploring Scandinavian America. After I had stayed in Lund, Sweden, I was curious to see Lund, Wisconsin. After I had seen a Norwegian fjord, it was more meaningful to see where immigrants from the surrounding area had settled in Minnesota. After I had seen living traditions in Denmark, it was fun to recognize them in Iowa. While I was curious about the folk traditions such as music, food, dance, costume, and crafts through which many Scandinavian Americans stayed in touch with their roots, I was more interested in identifying how core Scandinavian values and spirit had been transplanted to America, how they had influenced our society.

My wanderings in Scandinavian America became my way of fighting back against memory loss. At first, my visit to a Swedish American town was something I could share with my father. As my adventures meant less and less to him, it became more important for me to fight back against forgetting, to grasp something out of the past we both shared. My wanderings continued our family tradition of traveling that had brought my father to Charles Lindbergh's door and perhaps even brought my great-grandparents to America to begin with. Through my fight against forgetting, I would trace the uniquely American saga of our national forgetting and remembering.

Nightingale Echoes

W*hen my* great-grandmother stepped onto the shores of America in 1868, did she hear the nightingale singing?

She arrived in the busy port of New York City, so perhaps amidst all the ships' bells and rumbling carts she didn't hear the nightingale. She would have had a better chance of hearing it when she stepped inside the immigrants' receiving hall, but then perhaps she was distracted by the commotion of hundreds of immigrants speaking dozens of languages and by the important yet incomprehensible questions of the American clerks. It's unlikely that any of the non-Swedish immigrants even thought to listen for the nightingale. But there may have been one or two among the Swedes in every shipload who paused, looked up at the great ceiling, heard a distant song, and felt more at home already.

Before Ellis Island opened in 1891, immigrants landed on the southern tip of Manhattan, which was called the Battery because, starting with the Dutch in the seventeenth century, it was fortified to keep immigrants away. The Dutch wanted to keep the English away. Then the English wanted to keep the French and Spanish away. After the English decided not to be English anymore, the Battery went back to keeping the English away. In 1811 the Americans built a huge circular castlelike fort there, just in time for the War of 1812 and more unwanted English arrivals. A decade later Americans must have finally felt safe from immigrants, for the fort was given to the city of New York, remodeled into an entertainment hall, and renamed Castle Garden. For thirty years it served as the Carnegie Hall and Madison Square Garden of its era. In 1855 Castle Garden was turned into a welcome center for immigrants. With the acquisition of California a few years previously, Americans had finally realized what a huge continent they possessed, and they decided they could use a lot of immigrants to fill it. When Castle Garden opened its doors to immigrants, the population of the United States was about 27 million. Another 7.5 million would arrive through Castle Garden and later another 20 million through Ellis Island. After Ellis Island opened, Castle Garden returned to entertaining people, becoming the New York City Aquarium.

Five years before Castle Garden was turned into an immigration center, it hosted an event that became the start of one of the strangest chapters in American cultural history. It was the start of a mania that swept the nation, a mania that would not be matched until over a century later, when the Beatles arrived in New York City for their own first concert in America. This event was the first American concert of the most acclaimed singer of her time, Jenny Lind, the Swedish Nightingale. Jenny Lind toured America for over a year, giving nearly one hundred concerts, being seen by hundreds of thousands of people. Since Scandinavian immigration had barely begun by 1850, Jenny Lind would have been the first Scandinavian most Americans ever saw, and as such she would shape how Americans perceived and received Scandinavian immigrants.

Jenny Lind's extraordinary welcome in America may have encouraged Scandinavians to try America for themselves. Before 1850 only a few thousand Swedes had immigrated, most notably to the Bishop Hill colony in Illinois, founded in 1846. In the three years after Jenny Lind's tour, ten thousand Swedes immigrated. After those three years, Swedish immigration dropped to more modest levels, as low as two hundred a year, until it was reignited by the Homestead Act of 1862. The only other obvious stimulus for this sudden surge in immigration was the California gold rush, but few of the Swedes were heading for it.

In calling Jenny Lind's tour strange, I am not referring to the fact that practical-minded frontier cities like St. Louis and Nashville went crazy over a European opera star. The strangeness arises mainly from the person who masterminded Jenny Lind's tour: P. T. Barnum.

Before P. T. Barnum started his famous traveling circus, he was famous (or infamous) for his museum in New York City, just up the street from the Battery. When Barnum was on his best behavior, he exhibited genuine freaks of nature such as midgets, giants, bearded ladies, and Siamese twins. But he found it even more profitable to concoct hoaxes such as mermaids, monkeymen, or the 161-year-old slave woman who had attended the birth of George Washington. The press branded Barnum the Prince of Humbug, but the crowds kept coming. There was, indeed, a sucker born every minute.

Yet at age forty, Barnum found that fame and wealth weren't enough. He was tired of New York society looking down on him as a con man. He yearned for social respectability. One morning he read a newspaper story about the Jenny Lind mania sweeping Europe, and he saw his chance. He would become the impresario of the greatest high-culture event in American history. He would bring Jenny Lind to New York. He dispatched a respectable English musician to Europe to make Lind an offer. She refused. She was already tired of the commercial cynicism behind the pretty curtains of the music world, and Barnum's reputation was hardly reassuring. But Barnum was desperate, and he made her an unbelievable offer, an advance of $150,000, the equivalent of many millions of dollars today. And that was only the start. She would receive a generous share of the profits and have complete control over her schedule and repertoire. To make good this offer, Barnum would have to mortgage his museum and mansion, sell off more real estate, empty his bank account, and borrow a lot more. Jenny Lind decided that this was her chance to retire from opera touring and fulfill her dream of endowing a music school for poor children in Sweden. Ironically, it was to escape from the commercial hustle that Jenny Lind placed herself in the hands of the ultimate hustler.

To prepare America for Jenny Lind, Barnum launched the biggest public relations blitz America had ever seen. Hundreds of newspaper articles appeared praising Lind's angelic voice, spirit, and beauty. In truth, Lind was rather plain looking. When she tried to go to Matthew Brady's photography studio across the street from Barnum's museum, Barnum tried to stop her, not wanting to discredit his publicity drawings. As for her voice, Barnum hadn't even heard it when he signed her contract. No one today has heard it, for she lived before the age of recording. All that has come down to us is her extraordinary reputation. If this reputation was solely the work of P. T. Barnum, we would have every reason to suspect it. Yet Barnum signed her on the basis of a reputation that was already extraordinary, one that included the highest praise from Felix Mendelssohn, Robert Schumann, and Giacomo Meyerbeer. Queen Victoria had become Jenny Lind's adoring subject, showering her with gifts, begging her to continue her stage career. Hans Christian Andersen had fallen deeply in love with Lind and wrote his fables "The Nightingale" and "The Ugly Duckling" in her honor.

Barnum's reputation as a manipulator of public enthusiasm was also well deserved. When Jenny Lind's steamboat sailed into New York harbor, forty thousand eager people packed the wharves, streets, roofs, and windows to welcome her. Dozens of small boats swarmed around her ship. Banners hailed her. Barnum had salted the crowd with his agents to stimulate the excitement, but they proved unnecessary. When Jenny Lind appeared on the gangplank, hysteria broke out. When she got into her carriage, the crowd threw two hundred bouquets into her window, nearly burying her. A crowd of twenty thousand surrounded her hotel. That night, three hundred firemen carrying torches paraded past Lind on her balcony, and two hundred singers serenaded her with "Yankee Doodle." Merchants competed to present her with the finest gifts. Jenny Lind merchandise appeared all over town. A lady could wear a Jenny Lind bonnet, Jenny Lind gloves, and Jenny Lind earrings, and if she couldn't afford to buy a Jenny Lind dress, she could make one for herself on her Jenny Lind sewing machine. A gentleman could smoke a Jenny Lind cigar while stacking his Jenny Lind poker chips or riding in his Jenny Lind buggy. Kids could chew Jenny Lind candy while playing with their Jenny Lind dolls or casting their Jenny Lind fishing flies.

Barnum's most profitable promotional gimmick was to hold an auction for concert tickets. He had selected Castle Garden for a concert hall because it held ten thousand people, and he had scheduled six concerts there, but the demand for tickets still far exceeded the supply. Barnum had the nerve to charge admission just to get into the auction for tickets. The first ticket was bought for $225 by a hat maker named John Genin whose shop not coincidentally was next door to Barnum's museum. Genin's ticket purchase received nationwide publicity, prompting everyone to check their hats to see if they could brag about wearing a Genin. Such publicity was irresistible to businessmen, who were soon bidding outrageous amounts just to get their names in the newspapers. In Providence, a businessman paid $650 for a ticket he didn't bother to use. In Boston, an obscure singer paid $625 for a ticket because he hoped having one would boost his career. No socially fashionable person could afford to be without a Jenny Lind ticket.

After all the hype and hysteria, it was time for Jenny Lind to actually sing. She walked onto the Castle Garden stage wearing a simple white dress and little makeup and jewelry. Barnum's publicity had at least been true in portraying Lind as a natural, unaffected girl with a heart of gold. She was deeply sympathetic to the unfortunate and gave much of her earnings to charity. In her contract with Barnum she insisted on the right to do as many charity concerts as she wished. The entire earnings from her premiere New York concert, $10,000, ten times what she would have made for a concert in Europe, would be given to charity. Barnum must have been appalled at giving away such profits, but this turned out to be another public relations bonanza, convincing America of Lind's saintliness. Cities would start begging Barnum to be added to the tour.

As soon as Lind began singing, the audience was convinced that her voice was no Barnum hoax, but perhaps it *was* a freak of nature. She always included a few Swedish songs in her concerts. As her Swedish words soared uncomprehended through the hall, she could not have imagined that over the next four decades half a million Swedes would stand in this hall, their simple clothes a stark contrast with the bejeweled elegance of this night's crowd. The Swedes would stand here exhausted from their long journey, confused about what to do, worried about their fate, missing their homeland, yet hopeful. They would hold in their hands or in one trunk all their possessions. They would hold newborn babies who would become American legislators or hold the unsteady hand of a parent who would soon lie disconnected from his or her ancestral cemetery. They would be fishermen and lumberjacks and farmers and miners and craftsmen and servants from all over Sweden. They would be fleeing a past or seeking a future. They would hold beloved memories of places and people they would never see again. Some of them would hold memories of Jenny Lind, perhaps from before she became an international star and made Sweden proud. Some of them would remember reading all about Lind's premiere American concert at Castle Garden, and now they would look up and hear her voice again, hear her Swedish songs, and they would see her standing there in her long white dress, her arm stretched high. Before there was a Statue of Liberty, Swedes had their own harbor goddess to welcome them to America.

Jenny Lind cast a spell like a goddess. When she had performed in London, Parliament had to be adjourned because too many members sneaked out to see her. In America too the powerful flocked to pay homage. In Washington, D.C., the president called at her hotel, followed by senators and generals. Secretary of State Daniel Webster became a helpless Lindhead, seeing her in several cities. Reporters watched in amazement as the seventy-year-old Webster's normally sour face filled with childlike enchantment and as he rose at the end of the concert and bowed grandly to her. I don't know if there was any important diplomatic business pending between Sweden and the United States at that moment, but if I had been the Swedish ambassador, I would have recognized an opportune moment for presenting the secretary of state with a trade treaty favorable to Sweden. Cultural leaders too were enthralled. Longfellow went to eight of her concerts and declared: "She sings like the morning star: clear, liquid, heavenly sounds." [1]

Actually, Lind was only one of two goddesses Sweden sent to America in 1850. The other was the internationally famous author Fredrika Bremer. Bremer's novels of Swedish family life had won her a reputation as the Swedish Jane Austen. Walt Whitman declared her to be his favorite author. A feminist, Bremer portrayed the discomforts of women in traditional roles. A liberal, Bremer hoped America was the answer to Europe's ills. Like Alexis de Tocqueville, she traveled extensively in America and reflected on the strengths, flaws, and prospects of the young republic. When she reached Minnesota, she declared that with its lakes, forests, and Nordic climate it would become a new Scandinavia. The American travel book she published in 1853 greatly impressed Swedes with the promise of America. Bremer herself greatly impressed Americans. After James Russell Lowell hosted her for three weeks in Boston, he declared, "I do not *like* her, I *love* her."[2] Nathaniel Hawthorne agreed. John Greenleaf Whittier wrote an ode for her, beginning "Seeress of the misty Norland, / Daughter of the Vikings bold." Ralph Waldo Emerson invited her to Concord; later she would translate his works into Swedish. The president invited her to the White House twice. Washington Irving, after meeting both Bremer and Lind, seemed convinced that Swedish women were all unearthly. Iowa's governor Stephen Hempstead named a county after Bremer; today Bremer

County, Iowa, still has a town named Frederika. Poor Jenny Lind never got an American county named for her, only a few towns.

Jenny Lind and Fredrika Bremer left Americans with a remarkable, positive image of Swedes. This image must have played some role in Scandinavian immigrants being accepted into American society so readily, much more readily than most other ethnic groups. Undoubtedly, the primary reason for this acceptance was that as northern European Protestants, Scandinavians fit the Anglo mold better than did other groups. In the 1840s the influx of Irish Catholics stirred up an ugly debate about American identity and whether immigration should be restricted against undesirables. Scandinavians may have seemed like reinforcements to the Anglo majority. Of course, as peasants who couldn't understand English, Scandinavians suffered their share of scorn as oafs. But at least the Anglos soon decided that Scandinavians were honest, hard-working oafs who would be loyal to the republic. For the hundreds of thousands of Americans who had seen Jenny Lind, the sight of Swedish immigrants must have evoked associations not usually evoked by peasants. Many Americans must have overlooked the peasant clothes and looked for the nobility within. It became commonplace for Americans to refer to Swedes as "Lindmen."

It's hard to sort out the impact of Lind and Bremer from other factors, but one clue is the special reception Americans gave to Swedish women, who became highly desired as servants in wealthier homes. I should actually say Scandinavian women, but Americans often failed to make distinctions, annoying the Norwegians and Danes by calling them all Swedes. It was almost a status symbol to have a Scandinavian servant. But again, there were ethnic traits behind this. Scandinavian women were obsessively tidy and punctual, they seldom drank or stole, they treated children well, and they didn't bring alien gods into the house. Scandinavian women also gained from being servants, for they were fully exposed to American ways and could turn their own children into instant Americans.

Perhaps it was also an echo of Jenny Lind that Swedish and Swedish American women received a special welcome on American stages. When Hollywood went looking for its first stars, it came up with Greta Garbo and Gloria Swanson, then Ingrid Bergman, Myrna Loy, Susan Hayward, Ann-Margret, and Candice Bergen, not to mention Liv Ullmann, who was actually Norwegian but was often taken for a Swede due to her association with Ingmar Bergman. Then again, maybe Americans just liked blondes. No Swedish male has won similar stardom. Garbo and Ingrid Bergman did fit the Jenny Lind mold of the natural, modest woman who didn't require makeup, jewelry, or fancy dresses to cast a spell. The operatic stage too has welcomed a long line of Scandinavians. In 1870 America hailed the Swede Christina Nilsson as "the new Jenny Lind," and her three triumphant American tours set off new fashion trends. In the twentieth century, few singers earned the acclaim of Birgit Nilsson, Kirsten Flagstad, Jussi Björling, and Nicolai Gedda.

Nearly a century after Jenny Lind gave Americans the image of the Swedish woman as saint, this image won an Oscar for best actress for the 1947 movie *The Farmer's Daughter*. This movie was a project of producer David O. Selznick, who had imported Ingrid Bergman to America. Selznick wanted Bergman to star in *The Farmer's Daughter*, and then he tried Sonja Henie, the Norwegian Olympic gold medal skater turned Hollywood star, and then he turned to Loretta Young, who wasn't a Swede, but who was soon talking like one. Selznick hired the voice coach who had helped Ingrid Bergman lose her Swedish accent to give Young a Swedish accent. Young played a character much like Jenny Lind, a modest, natural, good-hearted girl who encounters the bombast and cynicism of American society and conquers it. We meet the farmer's daughter, Katie Holstrom, as she is leaving the farm for the city to study nursing at the Swedish Hospital. (In fact, there are three cities with prominent Swedish Hospitals—Seattle, Denver, and Chicago.) In an effort to be thrifty and save on bus fare, Katie accepts a ride from a hustler, who soon deprives her of her savings. Katie is forced to go to work as a servant, and, while working in the home of a U.S. congressman, she encounters the P. T. Barnum–like world of American politics. After speaking up for honesty and humanity and good social services, Katie is drafted to be a candidate for Congress. Her opponents represent racial bigotry and xenophobia and, it seems, the Republican Congress that President Harry Truman was then lambasting for not supporting his social programs. The final scene shows the newly elected Katie walking into the Capitol.

In the same year that Loretta Young was winning the best actress Oscar for her saintly Swede, a Norwegian American actress, Celeste Holm, won for best supporting actress in another film denouncing bigotry, *Gentleman's Agreement*, in which a cynical American society leaves it to Holm to deliver an uncompromising appeal for human dignity. The next year, Irene Dunne received a best actress nomination for playing a saintly Norwegian in *I Remember Mama*. Also in 1948, Ingrid Bergman was nominated for best actress for her role as a real saint in *Joan of Arc*. This was three years after Bergman had received another best actress nomination for her role as a Swedish-born nun in *The Bells of St. Mary*, in which she not only saves a convent school from being condemned and turned into a parking lot by a cynical American real estate developer but convinces him to donate a new building to the nuns. In 1949 Celeste Holm was nominated for best supporting actress for playing a nun in *Come to the Stable*, in which she convinces a cynical mobster to donate land for a children's hospital. All of these saintly images should put to rest the suspicion that Americans only liked Scandinavian actresses because they were attractive blondes. The next year, the 100th anniversary of Jenny Lind's visit was celebrated quite appropriately by two Scandinavian American actresses, Gloria Swanson and Celeste Holm, being nominated for Oscars for two movies that depicted the bombast of American show business, *Sunset Boulevard* and *All about Eve*.

After Jenny Lind's Castle Garden debut, she conquered the rest of America, sometimes setting off riots. Along the way she rendezvoused with her friend Fredrika Bremer and treated her to a private concert of Swedish songs. Bremer told Lind of the nationwide Lindmania she had seen.

Lindmania surely represented something more than just a love of music. One clue about Lindmania is how it was a point of pride for frontier towns to erect a stately opera house (they were called opera houses even though opera was a small part of what went on in them). Aside from answering the need for entertainment, opera houses answered an upstart town's craving for respect. The crowds cheering for Jenny Lind were also cheering for their own boost in status not just locally but for America as a whole. America had an inferiority complex in relation to Europe, and now it was being blessed by Europe's biggest star. It seems that P. T. Barnum's personal craving for respectability happened to match a national craving.

Jenny Lind did her best to be patient with Barnum's promotions, but increasingly she felt like one of his freak shows. It probably didn't help that he insisted she preside over a Broadway parade of elephants and human freaks. She resented his using her to extort a fortune from ordinary citizens. Like Garbo, Lind found the Great American Fame Machine to be bizarre and frightening, and she arranged for her escape. Two thirds of the way through her tour, she broke off her contract with Barnum, and after doing another forty concerts under her own management, she sailed for Europe and a quieter life, never to return. But she must have had some fond memories of America, for she had herself buried in a quilt made for her by American children.

America would remember Jenny Lind long after she died, even if the memory grew vague, even if the crowds couldn't explain why they were so ready to adore Garbo or Birgit Nilsson.

At the risk of being branded as a celebrity chaser but knowing I could hide in the distinguished company of Lindheads like Daniel Webster and Henry Wadsworth Longfellow, I decided I had to visit one of the towns named for Jenny Lind to investigate the persistence of memory. I wondered what kind of place and people would commit to identifying themselves with Jenny Lind forever. I wondered how the citizens of Jenny Lind remembered her, if at all.

There were two Jenny Linds still on the map, one in California and one in Arkansas. California once had two towns named Jenny Lind, but one of them had faded away. If there were more Jenny Linds, they have disappeared with thousands of other frontier towns, or perhaps their residents forgot the meaning of Jenny Lind and changed the town's name. California once had a Jenny Lind Creek, now called Big Arroyo. Perhaps it was once a nightingale of a creek and is now a monument to American carelessness about erosion. Jenny Lind Creek ran past the Jenny Lind mine. Both California towns named Jenny Lind were in gold rush country, which was booming at the time of Lind's tour. There was also a Jenny Lind mine in Colorado, though it wasn't started until 1882, three decades after her tour. There may have been some Swedish miners behind the Colorado mine name, for at about the same time, in the same area, two other new mines were called Stockholm mine and Swedenberg mine. By 1890 there were some 10,000 Swedes in Colorado. Fewer Swedes made their way to the California gold fields, but they could have been behind the Jenny Linds there too. Yet it seems it wasn't Swedes but just Lindmania that named San Francisco's Jenny Lind Theater in 1850.

It was much less likely that Swedes were behind the naming of Jenny Lind, Arkansas, for very few Swedes settled in Arkansas or anywhere else in the South. It was true that a hamlet in Arkansas had been named Sweden, but this seems to have been one of those quirky stories behind a lot of American town names. A plantation owner, not Swedish, asked the postal service to establish a local post office, and they agreed, but they rejected his proposed name of Lynn Wood because there was already a similar name nearby. Reportedly, the plantation owner retorted: "Well, then, just call it Sweden. That is a short name, and the negroes on the place won't misuse it."[3]

Curiously, Jenny Lind, Arkansas, was also a mining town. Did miners in 1850 simply have a thing about opera stars? I couldn't imagine miners today naming a town Luciano Pavarotti. Maybe it was a macho thing, a geographical pinup of the leading female celebrity. Or perhaps Jenny's nightingale nickname caught the tenderness or superstitions of miners whose lives were guarded by a small caged bird singing sweetly all day in the dark, grueling, dangerous mines, where silence meant that the air was poison and the miners must flee. According to folklore, it was canaries that served as mine alarms, but considering the fondness of nightingales for singing in the dark, we can suppose that some miners had carried nightingales.

My chance to visit a Jenny Lind came in Arkansas.

Jenny Lind, Arkansas, was located on the fringe of the Ozarks, a few miles from the Arkansas River. It was named at the height of Lindmania, in the spring of 1851. It must have been fading away by 1879, for its post office closed then, only to reopen in 1889. Around 1900 a coal-mining company opened a new mine a mile north of town and built a new town there, to which the post office was moved. The old town became known as Old Jenny Lind, which is how it appears on the map today. When the coal mine gave out, the new Jenny Lind faded away.

I wasn't expecting to find much of a town, as Old Jenny Lind wasn't big enough to earn a listing in the index of my road atlas, which seemed to go down to towns of about 300. As I drove into town I didn't notice any highway sign announcing the town. But I did see other signs: Jenny Lind Fire Station, Jenny Lind Furniture, Jenny Lind Tire. I followed Old Jenny Lind Loop Road through a residential area.

The town did not look very prosperous. There were some attractive homes but more old trailers. There was plenty of rusty junk sitting in the yards, something you seldom saw in the tidy Scandinavian towns in Minnesota. I did glance at the names on the mailboxes to see if there were any Swedish names, but I didn't see any. I passed the Jenny Lind Masonic Lodge and Jenny Lind Christian Day Care, owned and operated by Rose Garden Full Gospel Church. The loop road looped back to the highway. I stopped at one of the two gas stations in town and bought a snack just to have an excuse to speak with a resident.

"Was this town named after the famous singer?" I asked. The clerk looked at me blankly. I added, "There was a famous opera star named Jenny Lind back in the 1800s."

The clerk answered blankly, "I have no idea."

This was pretty much the same answer I had received at a gas station in Uppsala, Minnesota, when I asked if it was a Swedish town and at a gas station in Norway, Iowa, when I asked if it was a Norwegian town. I realize that convenience stores are not the best place to conduct historical research, but I theorize that they are a good place to gauge the state of public memory. I didn't blame the clerk in Uppsala, Minnesota, for not knowing she lived in the namesake of the religious capital of the Viking Age, but I was disappointed with the clerk in Norway, Iowa, who had been given a stronger clue.

A town like Old Jenny Lind, with no public library or chamber of commerce, offered few opportunities for talking with locals about their history. You couldn't really just knock on people's doors and ask them how they felt about Jenny. I drove across the street to the other gas station. Several dump trucks full of ore were parked outside. It seemed there was a mine still operating nearby. Inside the store, the truck drivers sat talking at several tables. This seemed to be the local gathering spot. I tried to come up with a subtle way of interrupting truck driver conversation about football to ask about a nineteenth-century Swedish opera singer. I suppose if I had considered this problem longer I might have come up with something like "Hey, did you know that Knute Rockne was a Scandinavian name?" And they would have answered, "And so was Jenny Lind. Man, what a loss that we'll never hear her join the Three Tenors singing the toreador song at halftime at the Super Bowl." But I lost my nerve.

However, I did see proof that the spirit of 1851 was still alive in Old Jenny Lind. I don't know about Lindmania, but the spirit of P. T. Barnum was still going strong. A tabloid barked headlines: "Scientists Discover Mermaids and Monkey-men!" "300-Year-Old Woman Recalls Birth of George Washington!"

As I was leaving, the clerk said with an unreserved warmth you don't always encounter in Scandinavian towns in Minnesota, "You have a *great* day now!"

I had passed a dump truck on the Old Jenny Lind Loop Road, so I retraced the road until I came to Gate 9 Road, a likely sounding name for a mine entrance. Sure enough, I soon came to a sign saying Jenny Lind Quarry and another saying Jenny Lind Asphalt Plant. It was a big quarry, perhaps big enough to have stayed busy since 1851.

The road continued in the right direction to have been the road to the new Jenny Lind, so I followed it, but I found nothing reminiscent of a town. I did notice a road named Booth Road, and it occurred to me that if the founders of Jenny Lind had simply been starstruck, they might have named a road for the most famous male actor of that time, Edwin Booth, or perhaps for his little brother, actor John Wilkes Booth.

I've found that sometimes the best library of local history, the best place to get a feel for people's lives, is the town cemetery. So I drove back to the old iron gate that read Jenny Lind Cemetery and drove beneath it. There was plenty of grass on the cemetery road. The cemetery was adjacent to an old church that was now the Jenny Lind Community Center. There was a bulletin board with a location list of all the names in the cemetery, compiled just the previous year by a cemetery association, which proved that someone was trying to keep memory alive. But the glass cover on the bulletin board was leaking, and the rain had washed out half the list, just as it had washed some of those same names off their tombstones.

I strolled among the tombstones. Again, I didn't notice any Swedish names. I watched for the name Jenny, born in 1851. I'm sure that many girls in America were given the name Jenny around 1850. I didn't see any Jennys, but perhaps I did unknowingly see the grave of the person responsible for naming the town Jenny Lind. Someone here may have been inspired by seeing Jenny Lind in concert. She had given two concerts near Arkansas, in Memphis and Natchez. Jenny's songs may have filled with joy one of the skulls now lying empty and deaf here. Was it Sarah A. Goforth, born in 1822? Was it John Walden, who died in May 1851, the month the town was named? Was it Jasper Donahoo, born in South Carolina, whose epitaph, "Safely Anchored in the Harbor of Eternal Rest," suggested a sailor, who would have had chances to see Jenny Lind in many ports? I wouldn't know, for the greatest fame and excitement of one generation can leave no more trace than a blank tombstone.

In 1851 tens of thousands of Americans had bought their Jenny Lind merchandise in an attempt to wrap themselves in her aura. Poor frontier women who had saved their pennies for years made one desperate grasp at elegance by buying a Jenny Lind dress. It would follow, then, that at death thousands of American women were buried wearing their Jenny Lind dresses, Jenny Lind gloves, and Jenny Lind shoes. Perhaps these memories too were buried here.

I guess it was true that I too was a fan of Jenny Lind. In coming to this town I was trying to keep her memory from being lost and acknowledging whatever she did to ease the way of my ancestors into a new land. I was even willing to acknowledge a debt to P. T. Barnum. Of course, Scandinavian Americans prefer to attribute their success as Americans to their solid characters and worthy accomplishments. Historians are disinclined to grant popular culture any power over history, preferring the actions of rulers and historical trends. Yet I suspect that P. T. Barnum was a better psychologist than most historians, and he proved that even American rulers would bow like servants to a singer. I don't know if my great-grandmother Gustava, who was a servant in Sweden and probably expected to be a servant in America too, looked up in Castle Garden and heard the echo of a nightingale and felt comfort and hope. But as I stood in the Jenny Lind Cemetery, amid all the lost memories, amid a pause in the rain, I could hear a distant and beautiful song.

3

Tippecanoe and the *Titanic* Too

P. *T. Barnum* wasn't the only American promoter to make a profit off a Swede. My great-grandparents came to settle where they did because of the hustling of another promoter. Their story was not unusual, except that they were hustled by one of the most eminent families in America.

Immigrants from every nation found dishonesty in their American dreams. It started back home, with folklore about America that was often too optimistic; there really were people who expected to find streets paved with gold. Steamship companies trying to sell tickets to America were happy to endorse the exaggerations. American railroad or mining companies, seeking cheap foreign labor, seldom mentioned low wages and hard conditions. Relatives who had already emigrated wrote back home to those who had discouraged them from going, and they tried to justify themselves by mentioning the good and not the bad. When immigrants arrived in America, bewildered, they might be delighted to be approached by one of their own countrymen, who offered to help them, perhaps to exchange money or buy a railway ticket, only to swindle them. And then there was the question of where to settle. Some immigrants were following the trail of relatives, but many had no real idea of where to go. At the dock they were met by agents passing out flyers and making promises. The future of millions of American families was decided by advertising slogans and ridiculous bragging.

Back home in Sweden, as in many countries, the fate of naive emigrants gave rise to a rival folklore about America. A serious movement sprang up to discourage emigration, and it portrayed America as a land of swindlers where even honest people were swallowed up by rabid materialism. It was not entirely a coincidence that the first American to whom the Swedish Academy awarded the Nobel Prize for literature was Sinclair Lewis, who denounced the destructive materialism of small-town Minnesota, that Swedish promised land.

Of course, from a sociological viewpoint the boosterism denounced by Sinclair Lewis could be considered an adaptive function in a frontier society. Confidence was the name of the game, even if it led to confidence games. For people to leave Europe at all they had to believe in their destiny. For pioneers to cross the prairies and the mountains they had to believe in the West. For pioneers to build the infrastructure of civilization they had to believe that someone was going to follow them. Frontier towns had to convince potential settlers that they were not just one of a thousand destinations but a destiny. The fate of many new towns was decided by whether they attracted enough settlers or attracted a railway station, a county seat, or a college. Often enough, towns succeeded or failed entirely by their ability to brag about themselves and their future. Unfortunately, Scandinavians were socialized to be modest and honest, so they were especially unprepared to deal with a society that made a virtue of bragging.

It was because of bragging that my great-grandparents came to settle in Tippecanoe County, Indiana.

If the name Tippecanoe sounds familiar to you, it may be because your high school history textbook mentioned the 1811 Battle of Tippecanoe, in which Gen. William Henry Harrison defeated Tecumseh near the Tippecanoe River, making a large region safe for white settlers. But your recognition of this name may owe more to the power of advertising in American life. When William Henry Harrison ran for president in 1840, he seeded future skyscrapers on Madison Avenue by launching the first great modern advertising campaign, blanketing the nation with his slogan "Tippecanoe and Tyler Too." This slogan reminded voters that Harrison was a military hero, a strategy that had worked well enough for George Washington and Andrew Jackson. Aside from that, it was a pretty meaningless ditty, unless you were fond of his running mate, John Tyler. But Americans were less jaded by advertising slogans then, and this slogan swept the nation in songs and banners, making such an impact that it is still widely recognized today. All subsequent presidential campaigns would center less on philosophical discussions and more on advertising slogans. As with most slogans, "Tippecanoe and Tyler Too" delivered less than it promised, for Harrison caught pneumonia on the ride to his inaugural and died a month later.

But my great-grandparents didn't settle in Tippecanoe County because of the famous battle or slogan. They came at the behest of an American dynasty, though a dynasty that fell into disgrace because of Sweden, at the very same time P. T. Barnum was rising from disgrace because of Sweden.

The Ellsworth dynasty began not long after the *Mayflower*, and it reached its high point when President Washington appointed Oliver Ellsworth the third chief justice of the United States Supreme Court. The Ellsworths missed a bit of distinction when Oliver joined the Continental Congress too late to sign the Declaration of Independence, but he made up for it as a delegate to the Constitutional Convention. It was Oliver who settled a paralyzing conflict over how to allocate representation between the Senate and the House. Oliver then served in the first Senate, as the leader of the Federalists under President Washington. He authored the Judiciary Act of 1789, creating the present federal judicial system of district and circuit courts. As chief justice, he presided over the first case deciding the constitutionality of an act of Congress. When Napoleon started interfering with American shipping, Oliver became a diplomat and went to Paris to negotiate a treaty.

Oliver's son Henry Leavitt Ellsworth also became a congressman. But there is a danger in being well connected. Henry had the chance to acquire from the government large tracts of land on the frontier, which in the 1830s was Indiana. Soon he was a land agent in Tippecanoe County. When the president appointed him commissioner of patents and he returned to Washington, D.C., he left his son, Henry William Ellsworth, in charge of the land business.

Henry William Ellsworth started off following the family tradition of studying law at Yale, but a few years later he was living in Indiana and writing a book called *The American Swine Breeder: A Practical Treatise on the Selection, Rearing, and Fattening of Swine*. I intend no slight against swine breeders, but considering the Ellsworth role in writing the U.S. Constitution, I think the Ellsworth dynasty was showing signs of decline. Henry William also wrote a book promoting the rich opportunities for settlers along the Tippecanoe and Wabash Rivers: *Valley of the Upper Wabash, Indiana, with Hints of Its Agricultural Advantages, etc.* I don't know if he mentioned that he was the major land salesman there.

Henry William Ellsworth continued the family tradition of taking part in politics. In 1844 he campaigned for Polk for president and served as a presidential elector. Polk was the ultimate champion of Manifest Destiny, campaigning for the annexation of Texas, California, the Southwest, and the Pacific Northwest. President Polk rewarded Ellsworth by appointing him the chargé d'affaires to Sweden.

Ellsworth believed in the Manifest Destiny of Tippecanoe County. When he arrived in Sweden in 1845, there were no Swedes living in or near Tippecanoe County. By 1855, there were 500 Swedes living there. I don't know for sure, but I wouldn't be surprised if many of them were living on land once owned by Henry William Ellsworth. Since in 1855 there were only about 15,000 Swedes in America, the Tippecanoe settlement represented a significant portion of the total.

Ellsworth arrived in Sweden at a prime moment for encouraging emigration. The Swedish newspapers were full of interest in America, and the Bishop Hill colony was only a year away. There were few Americans in Sweden to ask for advice, and surely a man as prominent and trustworthy as Ellsworth was the best source for finding out where to find land with agricultural advantages. Among other things that Ellsworth didn't tell the Swedes was that the best land in Indiana was already taken and that what remained was a lot more expensive than land farther west.

For some reason, Swedes in the Gränna area were especially responsive to the call of the Tippecanoe River. The connection may have been the local magistrate, Carl Peter Moberg, who had traveled to America in his youth before returning to Gränna in 1844. Moberg remained enthusiastic about America and shared his stories with his neighbors. Perhaps Moberg and Ellsworth became acquainted, either through their official duties, their shared interest in the law, or just because Ellsworth came to Gränna on vacation. In any case, when Gränna residents began setting off for America, they headed for the Tippecanoe area. Moberg himself, with family and friends, re-emigrated in 1850 and settled in Tippecanoe County. His example prompted many more to follow.

Apparently, Swedes weren't deterred from following Ellsworth's advice by the revelation that he was a crook. In 1849 newspapers in America and Sweden accused Ellsworth of plotting to smuggle British goods into Sweden. There was enough evidence for the secretary of state to ask for Ellsworth's resignation. Ellsworth proclaimed his innocence and used his family connections to appeal to the President. For months the scandal went unresolved, filling the newspapers with accusations and denials. The press pointed out the irony that the first case Ellsworth's grandfather had heard before the Supreme Court was about smuggling. Finally, the secretary of state angrily demanded that Ellsworth step down. Ellsworth returned to Tippecanoe County to practice law and sell land. The Ellsworth name never recovered from the scandal, but Ellsworth held onto the trust of prominent clients such as Samuel Morse, the inventor of the telegraph and a close friend of Ellsworth's father; Morse had retained Ellsworth to protect his patent rights.

But the Swedes arriving in Tippecanoe County were soon disillusioned to find that the best land was already occupied and that they couldn't afford the rest. In 1855 the young local minister, Eric Norelius, organized an exodus to Minnesota. Norelius blamed the unhealthily hot Indiana climate for his falling ill, and he sought a more sensible climate where winter lasted its natural six months. Norelius would play a large role in establishing Minnesota as the main destination for further Swedish immigration, and he became one of the most prominent leaders of Swedish America. Many Tippecanoe Swedes helped Norelius found the Minnesota communities of Vasa and Vista. Vista was the name of the judicial and ecclesiastical district that included Gränna. I have walked through the cemetery of the Minnesota Vista Lutheran Church and found several graves that read "Born in Gränna." Better yet, I've met some living Vistans. Ron Johnson, whose wife, Janet, traces her roots to Gränna, shared with me his extensive research on the Vista/Tippecanoe County connection. While having dinner with the Johnsons, I was struck by the notion that my ancestors and Janet's ancestors may have sat and chatted at a table in Gränna long ago, and now we were sitting and chatting as if no long, strange journey had intervened.

After Minnesota and other areas became the focus of a greatly increased Swedish immigration, the Tippecanoe community would hardly be noticed in histories of Swedish America. On a map, the only clue is the town of Monitor, named after the Civil War ironclad warship, designed by the Swedish immigrant John Ericsson. Yet the call of the Tippecanoe would linger in Sweden. Twenty years after Ellsworth left Sweden, my great-grandparents arrived in the town of Battleground, the site of the Battle of Tippecanoe. When my father went there as a child to visit his grandmother Gustava, he had fun pulling musket balls out of the trees. Having a pioneer address called Battleground serves to temper any temptation I might have to portray Scandinavian pioneering as a wholly heroic deed, for Battleground is an unmistakable reminder that this continent was the home of someone else who didn't willingly give it to us.

I don't know if the land my great-grandparents bought once belonged to Ellsworth. Since my great-grandfather was a tailor, he wasn't concerned about acquiring farmland, and in fact he needed an established community. Many of the Tippecanoe Swedes who ignored Norelius's exodus were also nonfarmers. Most of my great-grandmother's brothers and sisters settled nearby, and today I have numerous cousins in the area.

It seems that the call of Tippecanoe still lingered in Sweden in 1912, the year a twenty-seven year old named August Andersson set off for America. He was to spend a quiet life as a gardener in the town of Culver, dying there in 1951, a few miles from the Tippecanoe River, about fifty miles upstream from my great-grandparents' house. I haven't been able to determine if Andersson came there because he had relatives already there or because of some flickering rumor that northwestern Indiana was a good place for Swedes. All I really know is that to reach the Tippecanoe River, he boarded a ship called the HMS *Titanic.*

Andersson was a radical socialist journalist who had become notorious for attacking the Swedish establishment, calling the king "the king of thieves." Rapid industrialization in Sweden had led to high political tension, most notably a general strike in 1909. For Swedish reformers, including Charles Lindbergh's grandfather, America had always beckoned as a refuge, either to escape persecution at home or to find a young republic more open to change. Andersson gave up on Sweden a bit too soon, for Swedish reformers were on the verge of many successes at integrating industrial capitalism with egalitarian values. To evade both Swedish and American authorities who might prevent his migration, Andersson acquired forged papers identifying him as August Wennerström, a name he borrowed from his political friend Ivar Vennerström, who, after the reformers triumphed, became Sweden's minister of defense.

The maiden voyage of the *Titanic* was an ironic way for a radical socialist to escape from rich capitalists. The White Star Line had launched not just a ship but a publicity campaign that assured that the maiden voyage would be the high-society event of the decade. The ship was packed with the lords of Wall Street and Madison Avenue, the owners of America's greatest banks, corporations, retailers, and, yes, advertising agencies. They were the masters of slogans for selling anything to Americans. The *Titanic* had been sold as "the unsinkable ship."

It was normal for Scandinavians to immigrate to America on British ships. Most frequently, Scandinavians started off with a short voyage to the east coast of England, then crossed by train to Liverpool and sailed from there. There were 254 Scandinavians on the *Titanic*, half of them Swedish. Most of them were emigrants traveling third class.

August Andersson was in bed in his third-class cabin when the word spread that something was wrong and that passengers should get up. Some third-class passengers stood up and found that the floor was wet. Andersson and his fellow Swedes left their cabins and went to the third-class lounge. Deciding that there was nothing else to do, they started playing the piano and dancing. After a while some Italians came in and started crying out to Mother Mary. Andersson had little sympathy for people who gave up on human effort and trusted their fate to God. As a Scandinavian conditioned to a natural world that could be overpowering, he was especially unsympathetic to people who surrendered to the forces of nature. "They acted like they were crazy," Andersson later said of the Italians, "jumping and calling on their Madonna. We made a circle about them and started a ring dance all around them."[1]

Andersson's socialist sensibilities were outraged by the caste dynamics he observed throughout the sinking of the *Titanic*. The British seamen treated first-class passengers as more worthy of saving than the lives in third class. Almost all of the first-class women and children and a third of the men were given places in lifeboats, while a majority of third-class women and children drowned. Andersson was especially contemptuous of British indifference to the Irish and of Irish long-trained submission to the British. Some Irish blindly followed orders to just sit in third-class lounges and wait, not even investigating the situation for themselves.

Andersson figured out his way around the barriers containing the third-class section and reached the boat deck, where lifeboats were being loaded. He went back down and led two Swedish women to a lifeboat and made sure they were admitted. He stood there smoking a cigar as the boat was lowered. He was too awestruck by the whole scene to feel any fear. "It was more like we were part of an audience in a wonderful, dramatic play."[2]

Returning to third class, Andersson was appalled at the passivity of the underclass: "Hundreds were in a circle with a preacher in the middle, praying, crying, asking God and Mary to help them. They lay there still crying till the water was over their heads. They just prayed and yelled, never lifting a hand to help themselves. They had lost their own willpower and expected God to do all the work for them."[3]

Andersson led other Swedes to the boat deck. By now it was obvious there weren't enough lifeboats. The Swedish inventor of the lifeboat hoist mechanism, Axel Welin, had drawn up plans for enough lifeboats for every *Titanic* passenger, but he had been overruled by the British, who wanted plenty of deck space for promenading.

As the *Titanic* tilted alarmingly, people lost their grip and slid into the water. Andersson was holding hands with two Swedes, Mr. and Mrs. Edvard Lindell, when they lost their footing and slid together down the deck and into the water, almost into a collapsible canvas lifeboat that was floating empty and swamped, bumping against the forward funnel. They climbed aboard.

From only fifty feet away, Andersson watched in horror as the *Titanic*, with a thousand desperate people clinging to its stern, tilted ever higher and then slid under the waves.

Andersson was now right in the middle of a nightmare: "Close around us in a two-hundred-foot circle lay a thousand souls, crying, praying, yelling, and doing their best to save their own lives. . . . They swam to us, hanging all around our canvas boat, and we all turned over. For how long a time I was away from the boat, I don't know."[4] Andersson blanked out in the frigid water, and when he recovered his senses, he found he was floating on a raft of corpses. He swam back to the lifeboat, which had remained afloat only because of its cork railing, and climbed back in. Edvard Lindell also regained the boat, but not Mrs. Lindell. Looking around, Andersson saw her and grasped her hand, but he lacked the strength to pull her in. After half an hour he lost his grip and watched her disappear. He turned in despair to Mr. Lindell, only to find that he had frozen to death. Andersson himself was totally numb below the waterline. Every so often, one of the lifeboat occupants "gave up hope and died" and was eased overboard to lighten the boat.

The yelling in the dark gradually faded into silence. The lords of Wall Street and Madison Avenue found that all their mastery of advertising slogans won them no influence over nature. But even the poorest Scandinavian peasant knows something about boats and very cold water. In fact, the Scandinavians survived the *Titanic* in a noticeably higher percentage than the rest of the third-class passengers.

Andersson's lifeboat became a legend of its own. His rescuers, convinced that the lifeboat would quickly sink, set it adrift with three frozen bodies still aboard, one of them in expensive evening clothes. A month later and 200 miles away, it was discovered, still afloat, by the *Titanic*'s sister ship *Olympic*.

And all the time the *Titanic* was sinking, the wireless telegraph operator clicked out pleas for help, using Morse code, using equipment invented by Samuel Morse, earning profits for the Morse patents, patents so effectively protected by one Henry William Ellsworth of Tippecanoe County.

After his *Titanic* ordeal, was Andersson ever able to sit in a rowboat on the Tippecanoe River or even stroll alongside the river without being gripped by dread? In his occupation as a gardener, he found a way to spend every day gripping the solid earth.

Yet the call of Tippecanoe did end up drowning someone. When my father took me to Battleground as a kid, and we were crossing the bridge over the Wabash River, he told me that my great-grandfather had a cousin who had drowned in the Wabash. I believe the cousin's name was Adolf Lagerstam. In Sweden it had been Adolf Carlson, but upon coming to America he had sought more distinction by renaming himself after a Swedish noble family that had died out. He doesn't seem to have shared August Andersson's democratic impulses. I don't remember anything about how, after Lagerstam had safely crossed the Atlantic, he came to drown in the Wabash River.

One time, in a most unlikely place, I came upon the wake of the *Titanic*.

Well before I reached Stanton, Iowa, I saw its landmark, a giant Swedish coffeepot. Actually, it was the city water tower atop the highest hill in town. In the 1970s it was given a spout, a handle, and a lid and painted with Swedish flower designs. Stanton advertises it as "The World's Largest Coffee Pot."

Stanton was the central town of one of Iowa's three Swedish regions, all mostly rural. Stanton had only seven hundred inhabitants. The first region, settled in 1845, was actually the first enduring Swedish settlement in America, preceding Bishop Hill by one year. The second region produced the first Swedish American first lady, Mamie Eisenhower, whose maternal grandparents were immigrants named Carlson. Her birthplace in Boone, Iowa, has many Swedish heirlooms.

The third region, around Stanton, was called the Halland settlement after its founder, the Reverend Bengt Magus Halland. Halland envisioned his settlement as a religious stronghold where Swedish farmers could continue their traditional ways uncorrupted by city life or other evils such as Methodism. He energetically recruited nondrinking, God-fearing Swedes, meaning Lutherans only, and took great pains to help settlers succeed. There is no doubt of his devotion to his mission, which included the founding of an orphanage in Stanton. Then again, there is no doubt that he made a small fortune selling railroad land to settlers, for he was also a land agent for the Burlington Northern Railroad.

Railroads played a major role in settling the frontier, for Congress granted them huge tracts of land to sell and thus finance their expansion. Neither East Coast investors nor nonexistent western industries were going to pay for laying track through empty prairies and mountains. The railroads competed fiercely to recruit settlers, and they found that their strongest allies were local boosters. Sometimes the boosters were religious groups. Since it was in the interest of the railroads that the settlers succeed and not abandon their land, the railroads in the Northern Plains often preferred Scandinavian settlers. Both in Europe and on the New York docks, Burlington Northern agents distributed flyers in Swedish or Norwegian or Danish. The agents avoided immigrants from the Mediterranean, including the French and Italians, who were spoiled by pleasant climates. The railroad was happy to tell Swedes about the wonderful Swedish towns rising in Iowa. Reverend

Halland preferred recruiting from the established Swedish Lutheran congregations in the Midwest, where his name was known and trusted. In 1870 alone, Halland earned over $3,000 in commissions from the railroad.

I do not bring this matter up to indict Reverend Halland in the same docket as P. T. Barnum and Henry William Ellsworth but more to point out that boosterism was so integral to frontier America that everyone ended up playing the game. The reverend and the railroad didn't always share the same goals, as when the railroad required him to sell land to Swedes who were non-Lutherans. The railroad even prohibited him from naming the town Halmstad, after the capital of his home province, and instead named it Stanton, after Lincoln's secretary of war. But the railroad and the reverend needed one another, and they both mastered the game of advertising.

Stanton, Iowa, is equally far away from Madison Avenue and Hollywood, yet advertising reigns like a Greek temple over the town. The Swedish coffeepot was in fact a tribute to the American culture of advertising. It was created to honor the town's most famous child, actress Virginia Christine, who appeared in movies as significant as *Judgment at Nuremberg, High Noon,* and *Guess Who's Coming to Dinner?* but who only became famous when the Folger's Coffee Company selected her to play the role of Mrs. Olson in its commercials.

I drove past all the white houses for which Stanton is called "the Little White City." I drove past Virginia Christine Street. I parked beneath the Swedish coffeepot, which could hold 640,000 cups of coffee. As I stared up at it, I considered the phenomenon of Mrs. Olson. She must have been very good at selling coffee, for Folger's kept her on the air for many years. I wondered if Mrs. Olson's Swedish accent was the key to her success. Hollywood had already decided that Swedish women were coffee experts, for in *The Farmer's Daughter,* the first thing that Katie Holstrom did upon going to work at the congressman's house was to replace the butler's notoriously bad coffee with her own delicious brew. Mrs. Olson fit perfectly into the Jenny Lind image of Swedish women as natural, strong, and wholesome. As far as I could recall, Mrs. Olson was modest and kindly too. Surely a coffee company would like its product to be perceived as natural and wholesome and hospitable. Folger's couldn't have associated more wholesomeness with itself unless Mamie Eisenhower herself was promoting it. Folger's claimed that mountain-grown coffee was the richest kind, and those nature-loving Swedes surely had to be experts on that issue.

I felt the ghost of P. T. Barnum looming above me, but I wasn't so sure that he stood here in conquest of rural Iowa. Perhaps it had worked out the other way around. Perhaps it was the natural and modest character of Scandinavians that had won out over the braggarts of Madison Avenue. Madison Avenue could have chosen a sports star or dancing showgirls to jazz up its coffee. Instead, it had reached for something more genuine and in doing so had paid tribute to Swedes who had hidden in rural Iowa to escape the insincerities of the city.

Starting right at the foot of the water tower was that other thing you often find on the highest hill in town, the pioneer cemetery. I strolled among the graves, which included Reverend Halland, who died in 1902. There was the usual mixture of Swedish names: Anderson, Johnson, Carlson, Olson. Then there were a few less common Swedish names. For instance, there was Ernst Danbom, who died April 15, 1912, drowned on the HMS *Titanic*.

I stared at the marker, incredulous. Drowned on the *Titanic*. How many thousands of cemeteries would you have to search through for how many years before you randomly stumbled upon a victim of the *Titanic*?

A few blocks away at the Swedish Heritage Center, a surprisingly good museum in an old brick schoolhouse, I asked the host for the story. He told me that when Danbom's wife became pregnant, Ernst took her back to Sweden to give birth among family. Then the couple and their new baby and several other family members who were immigrating to Stanton boarded the *Titanic* for the journey home. They had all drowned. Ernst Danbom's frozen body was found and brought home for burial. His wife and baby were never found.

There was incongruity enough in finding a *Titanic* victim's grave on the Iowa prairie, but to stand there and stare up at a giant Swedish coffeepot was asking too much of reality. I stood there, baffled. I tried to relate the two incongruities. The sinking of the *Titanic* had been widely interpreted as a punishment for human arrogance. Perhaps I was receiving a message here, a denial of my imagining that the modest and natural Swedes of Stanton, Iowa, had conquered an arrogant culture. Clearly Ernst Danbom had been crushed by this arrogance. Perhaps Mrs. Olson was really a victim too, her Swedish accent exploited to earn fortunes for Madison Avenue.

There was the story about Senator William Alden Smith, who conducted the Senate investigation into the *Titanic* disaster and who had only one day left to finish his report and prepare a Senate speech blaming the disaster on human arrogance. He needed to cross the street to the Treasury Department, but the street was filled with a parade. Too impatient to wait, he tried to dart through the marching band, only to be forced to march to its beat to avoid being trampled. When he slipped away from the band, he found himself trapped between the elephants and horses and was swept farther down the street. The parade was a promotional event for Barnum and Bailey's World-Defying Circus.

Was kindly Mrs. Olson too, like Senator Smith and Jenny Lind, merely being swept along by a bombastic parade?

I wasn't sure what it all meant. The incongruities were too great. But then perhaps my confusion was the truest summary of a nation that was itself confused, a culture where Lutheran preachers against mammon were also railroad land agents, where the grandsons of founding fathers were humbugs, and where P. T. Barnum and Jenny Lind contended, like a wrestling devil and angel, for the soul of America.

All I was sure of was that it was a strange journey indeed when Swedes, content to live for centuries obeying the rules of winter, would entrust their lives to those who thought themselves above the rules of ice, when Swedes came to lie in the Iowa prairie alongside Native American arrowheads beneath a giant Swedish coffeepot.

4

Down the Mythissippi River
and the Saga Fe Trail

ying jetlag-awake at 3 A.M. in the Hotel Finn in downtown Helsinki turned out to be a productive time for contemplating the national mythology of America and how Scandinavians fit into it. I do not normally pursue such dissertations at 3 A.M., and I only did so this time in wondering about a much simpler question: why did Mark Twain use a Scandinavian name for the hero of his American epic, *Huckleberry Finn*? It would turn out that this question was questionable, but like many a scientific experiment with a flawed premise, it yielded interesting results.

It had been a rainy evening, so I had spent it browsing in bookshops and in Stockmann's, a huge department store that combined three eras of architecture and an even greater mixture of cultures, as I learned by overhearing Russian shoppers and Finnish clerks talking in English about French perfume and Swiss chocolate. I find bookstores a good indicator of national personality. In Paris bookshops, for instance, you can worry about the abnormal French interest in Edgar Allan Poe. In contrast to French bookshops, where it was a breach of national pride to offer books in English, the Finnish bookshops offered large selections of English titles. Though Scandinavians are the highest per capita book buyers in the world, they realize that their small domestic markets can't support the translation of every foreign title into their languages and that English is the key to participating in the modern world. The

Finns are especially unarrogant about their language. While Swedes, Norwegians, and Danes can understand one another fairly well, the Finnish language has very different roots, as do the Finnish people. The Finns don't expect outsiders to learn their difficult language, and for most of their history they themselves were discouraged from using it. From Viking times until 1809, Finland was part of Sweden, and Swedish was the official language, Finnish being left for peasants. When the Russians seized Finland in 1809, the Finns began groping for their own identity, and the redemption of their language became an important cause. Two books played a crucial role in elevating Finnish into a respected language and in encouraging the national identity so that in 1917 the Finns were inspired to rebel and finally become an independent nation. The first book was the *Kalevala*, an assemblage of ancient Finnish folklore, and the second was *Seven Brothers*, the first modern novel written in Finnish. I bought English translations of both books and headed back to my hotel.

When I woke up in the middle of the night, I picked up the *Kalevala*. When the *Kalevala* was published in 1835, it astonished the literary world as much as the discovery of a herd of living dinosaurs would have astonished the scientific world. At a time when the Greek and Roman classics were still the core of an education, the literati revered ancient epics but assumed that the Homeric oral recitation tradition was long dead. Then the Finnish scholar Elias Lönnrot announced that many Homers had been hiding in the wilderness of eastern Finland for centuries, passing down elaborate songs of pagan myths and heroes. Literacy had never arrived in this wilderness, and the Russian Orthodox Church hadn't roused itself to stamp out ancient pagan traditions there. Lönnrot spent years recording these songs and arranging them into a traditional epic form. The Finns were delighted to suddenly have their own *Iliad*, and the rest of the world looked upon the Finns in a new way.

When Henry Wadsworth Longfellow read the *Kalevala*, he had a revelation. Longfellow was inclined to write epic poetry, but in a nation only a few decades old there was a shortage of epic material. He did what he could with Paul Revere and Miles Standish. The *Kalevala* convinced him he could write an American epic if only he drew upon the ancient pagan traditions in the American wilderness. Using the *Kalevala's* distinctive meter, he wrote *The Song of Hiawatha*. Americans who had never heard of the *Kalevala* became aware of it through a loud, unpleasant controversy in which critics accused Longfellow of plagiarizing whole episodes from the *Kalevala* and dressing them up in Native American clothing. Longfellow admitted the similarities but insisted that they only reflected the worldwide similarities of pagan customs and that he had drawn upon American anthropological texts. Other critics scolded Longfellow for romanticizing heathens who were savagely resisting the destiny of the American nation.

As for the destiny of the Finnish nation, the *Kalevala* served it well, inspiring Sibelius to compose a national music and Gallen-Kallela to paint a national art.

Sixty years after the publication of *The Song of Hiawatha*, Finnish paganism set off another echo. Igor Stravinsky was born in one of the Finnish-speaking provinces where Lönnrot collected songs, though on the Russian side of the border. The vigorous paganism that came out in the *Kalevala* also burst out in *The Rite of Spring*.

As I read, I found that the *Kalevala* began with the creation of the world out of chaos and continued with the struggles of shamanistic heroes to master the powerful forces of nature and to master one another. It seemed to me that the *Kalevala* shared something with the other Scandinavian epic, the Icelandic sagas, which set both of them apart from other European epics. The Scandinavian epics were preoccupied with the powers of nature, a nature that was far mightier than humans. Even when the Scandinavian epics focused on two heroes in conflict, the heroes were surrounded by nature, and they might try to enlist nature in their cause. This preoccupation with nature reflects the everyday experience of Scandinavians throughout their history. Even today, in a more urban society, while not all Scandinavians have to worry about volcanoes, mountains, forests, or the sea, all are still overwhelmed by winter. In nations where nature is less formidable, human survival and sanity are determined less by nature and more by the workings of society, and, accordingly, their national myths are more concerned with social order or relations between societies. England's King Arthur legends, France's *Song of Roland*, Greece's *Iliad*, and Rome's *Aeneid* are concerned with leadership and conflict within their societies and with warfare against other societies.

In this respect, at least, Longfellow was justified in transporting the *Kalevala* to America, for the American national experience has been defined first of all by our confrontation with a whole continent of wilderness.

I picked up *Seven Brothers* by Aleksis Kivi and read the translator's introduction. He compared the novel to *Huckleberry Finn*, at least for the content of its story. He could also have made the point that *Huckleberry Finn* too has been granted the status of a founding work of a nation's literature. Though there had been many American novelists before Twain, they usually imitated European subjects and styles. Twain, like Whitman in poetry, made it okay to use a distinctly American voice to explore our distinct national experience.

It was odd, but I had never before thought about Huck's last name. I had never associated it with Finland or imagined Huck as a Scandinavian. But now, at 3 A.M. in the Hotel Finn, it all seemed clear that Twain had a purpose in making Huck a Finn.

Perhaps I was already thinking about Huck before I picked up *Seven Brothers*. Earlier that day I had stood gazing up at the huge arch that was the commanding feature of the Helsinki train station, an Art Deco precocious design by Eliel Saarinen. It was Eliel's son, Eero, who designed St. Louis's Gateway Arch. Eero used soaring arched roofs in many of his buildings, and now I thought I saw why. As I wandered around Helsinki the next few days, seeking out more of Eliel's buildings, I saw that he too liked arches. As I looked at this arch I thought of the arch by the Mississippi River, with its cobblestone wharf and row of paddlewheel tour boats and restaurants. It's hard for me to visit the arch without imagining Mark Twain at the helm of a paddle wheeler or Huck on his raft.

If the Gateway Arch, like Hiawatha, had been transported from Finland, then why not Huck's last name? Wasn't Huck supposed to have a Viking spirit, bravely setting off on unknown, dangerous waters? What better way to invoke a hardy wilderness soul than to call him a Finn?

Twain didn't set out to write an epic, but he soon entangled himself in the two great themes of American life: our confrontation with the wilderness and the tension between freedom and social order. A raft trip down a great river offered the scope for an epic, but it was Twain's grappling with the dilemmas of freedom that flushed T. S. Eliot out of his disguise as an English gentleman and made him admit that he was born and raised in St. Louis, just downstream from Twain's Hannibal, and that he had a lasting fondness for Huck and an admiration for

Twain, who "wrote a much greater book than he could have known he was writing." Twain became so entangled with the conflict of freedom and social order that he set the unfinished book aside for years, unsure how to finish it. Most critics would agree that he never did come up with a satisfying ending, but this seems only an appropriate reflection of our national inability to resolve this issue.

A national mythology cannot be artificially created by a writer. It exists first as the shared experience and values and dreams and conflicts of a people, and if a writer is a good lightning rod, he or she absorbs this energy, perhaps unconsciously, and finds a literary form that expresses it for all. It was only because the Scandinavian epics expressed the soul of life in a northern wilderness that they were recited on winter nights through the centuries.

I once rode with a busload of Mark Twain scholars to Hannibal as part of a conference celebrating the centennial of the publication of *Huckleberry Finn*. Some of the scholars had never been to Hannibal before, and they were surprised to find that any writer could spawn a lively tourist industry, drawing a third of a million visitors a year to Hannibal, offering them Twain museums, festivals, plays, riverboat rides, bookshops, and souvenir shops. It's a safe guess that these visitors are not attracted by Twain the bitter, atheistic social critic. But I doubt that it's just a case of nostalgia for a Tom Sawyer childhood either. I think it's a case of nostalgia for our national childhood, an exercise in national mythology. Twain, especially in his roles as riverboat pilot and western prospector, represents a time when there was a clearer connection between our national myth and our personal lives. In Twain's time the frontier was still a real, westward-moving boundary, a treasure chest open to anyone with initiative. Today, the American Dream involves a maze of university degrees, corporate politics, and urban stress.

In our national mythology, America was a promised land set aside for a chosen people who would choose themselves. America wasn't a Garden of Eden but a biblical wilderness that would test our worthiness and reward the worthy with wealth and happiness. The wilderness was also a haven from the repressive societies of Europe. To cross the ocean and inhabit this wilderness demanded courage, strength, and independence. Even if you started out deficient in those qualities, the wilderness would develop them for you.

It was this mythology that drew tens of millions of emigrants from Europe. Some nations contributed to this migration far more than others. After Ireland, the nations that sent the largest percentage of their populations to America were Norway and Sweden. Between 1850 and 1910, 2 million Norwegians and Swedes emigrated, over a quarter of the countries' total population. Though other nations had much larger populations to draw upon, Sweden and Norway still rank seventh and eighth in the total numbers they sent to America. (Sweden ranks above Norway in total numbers of emigrants yet behind it in percentage, since Norway had a smaller population to begin with.)

Historians have explained immigration to America as a result of famine, poverty, or persecution. Certainly for Ireland, the potato famine, added to a history of British persecution, is a convincing explanation. But these factors don't seem sufficient explanations for why a highly disproportionate number of Scandinavians emigrated. Political and religious persecution in Scandinavia was less severe than in most of Europe. It's true that in the late 1860s a crop failure struck Scandinavia, resulting in the first huge surge of emigration, including my great-grandparents. But for the next fifty years, even in good harvests, emigration levels often exceeded those hungry years. It's true that a growing population and a nongrowing supply of farmland limited the opportunities for Scandinavians, but there were other nations with the same problem, and their peoples resigned themselves to poverty and stayed home.

As the tales of the *Kalevala* and Huck Finn mingled in my mind, it occurred to me that perhaps it wasn't just in my mind that the myths of Scandinavia and America merged. Perhaps the American national myth had fit the psychology of Scandinavians especially well. The idea of confronting a tough wilderness was more familiar to Scandinavians than it was to a London slum dweller or a Polish farmer. Their own mythology assured Scandinavians that they were ready for such a challenge. Perhaps this is why Scandinavians responded more readily than other peoples to the American challenge.

One aspect of the American myth may have been especially attractive to Scandinavians. In Scandinavia, nature was a force far stronger than humans. The best humans could do was to obey nature's rules. There was little conception of humans totally subduing nature and actually making it give them great wealth and freedom. Yet this was the conception of nature that Americans were proclaiming. In America, nature was a temporary obstacle to the superior power of humans. This wasn't because American nature was flimsy. On the contrary, the forests were endless, the rivers were massive, the mountains were enormous, the wildlife (including Indians) was ferocious. But this couldn't stop a free people and their clever machines. Whereas a London slum dweller or a French farmhand might be intimidated by the mere idea of any kind of wilderness at all, Scandinavians were being offered a wilderness less resistant and more rewarding than the one they had already proven they could match.

In his book *A Nation of Immigrants*, President Kennedy said: "Physically hardy, conditioned by the rigors of life at home to withstand the hardships of the frontier, the Scandinavians made ideal pioneers."[1] In further comments Kennedy was especially generous about the Scandinavian contribution to America. He even gave the Scandinavians their own section, along with the Irish and the Germans, whereas everyone else got dumped into the section "Other Immigrant Groups." But then, Kennedy's ghostwriter was named Ted Sorensen, a Nebraska Dane. Kennedy once sent Sorensen a postcard from Copenhagen saying it was such a beautiful city he couldn't understand why anyone would leave it.

So what better name for a robust wilderness hero than Finn?

When I got back to America and did some checking, I turned up a flaw in my Huck theory. In a letter, Twain reported that in working on Huck one of the memories he stirred up was of Hannibal's town drunk, Jimmy Finn. In the novel, Twain made Huck's father the town drunk. I checked out the name Finn and found that it is quite Irish, deriving from a folklore hero, Finn McCool. I had checked the Helsinki phone book for the name Finn and found not one. If history was a clue, then in the Hannibal of Twain's youth he was much more likely to have met Irish than Finns.

This seemed a perfect case of what Twain called "a beautiful theory spoiled by one ugly fact." Actually, maybe it was one of those Huxleys who said this, but since sooner or later Twain gets credit for every pithy saying, I see no reason to deprive him of this one. Twain would be the last person to let a mere fact stand in the way of a good story. Even if the name Finn had an Irish origin, Twain was very aware of the symbolism of names, starting with his own penname. It's still possible that Twain realized that his readers might associate the name Finn with Finland and that this fit his purposes.

I did discover that another of Twain's novels had a Scandinavian inspiration. In the preface to *Tom Sawyer, Detective*, the sequel to the original *Tom Sawyer*, Twain acknowledged that he borrowed the idea from a noted Swedish criminal trial. In 1899 Twain spent a long summer in Sweden in pursuit of treatment for his daughter's epilepsy. He had given up on American physicians and turned to a Swedish physician named Kellgren, who had developed a form of osteopathic medicine and opened a sanitarium. It was ironic that Twain went all the way to Sweden to find an osteopath, for the world's first osteopathic hospital was in a Missouri town near his own Hannibal. Twain's daughter and wife learned Swedish dances, Twain took Kellgren's treatments for himself, and he became a partisan of all things Swedish. Twain may have helped shape America's image of Sweden as a place of healthy living, an image evident in American advertising today, in claims that some health product was invented by Swedish scientists. In a letter, Twain even insisted that Swedish sunsets were far superior: "Venice? land, what a poor interest that is! This is the place to be. I have seen about 60 sunsets here; & a good 40 of them were away & beyond anything that I have ever imagined before for dainty & exquisite & marvelous beauty & infinite change & variety. America? Italy? The Tropics? They have no notion of what a sunset ought to be."[2]

If Scandinavians were tempted by the American conception of wilderness as tamable and as obtainable wealth, then what about the American conception of wilderness as freedom?

The uniquely American equating of wilderness with freedom has complex roots both in our national experience and in intellectual history. For the religious and political refugees fleeing persecution in Europe, the American wilderness meant they were safely far from their persecutors and unrestricted by any existing authority. On a more personal level, the wilderness meant that anyone with a restless or exploring spirit could always move on. Two intellectual traditions contributed to our attitudes toward society, freedom, and wilderness. The Enlightenment held that humans are rational beings, stifled by autocratic rule, trustworthy to organize and conduct society in a rational way. Romanticism held that humans in a state of nature are moral and happy and that it is organized society that corrupts and oppresses us. For both traditions, the American wilderness beckoned, though for one it was a realm for engineering a more perfect society and for the other it was a realm for escaping from society. If there was a wide national agreement that wilderness represented freedom, there has been a lasting confusion, visible in our literature, politics, and popular culture, over exactly what this means.

For Huck Finn, the wilderness means escaping from society. He is escaping from an abusive, alcoholic father. His companion, Jim, is escaping from slavery. The society they encounter on their voyage is pathetic with cruelty and stupidity. At the end of the voyage, Huck decides that he has to escape civilization by heading west.

The West is the setting for what, more than any other literary effort, became our most recognized national mythology, the Western. While psychologists tend to dismiss the Western as an enclave of immature male behavior, from a sociohistorical perspective the Western deserves more credit for dealing with the primary issue of American history, the tension between freedom and social order. The typical Western hero is trapped between the two contradictory American visions of the wilderness, the romantic vision of wilderness as liberation from society and the Enlightenment vision of wilderness as a platform for building a new and good society.

In his personal attributes, the Western hero is clearly a romantic hero. He lives on the land, a land of immense grandeur and wildness. He sleeps under the stars, far from towns and their restrictions. When he does go into town, it's not to go to church to learn about moral restrictions, it's to go to the saloon. He's a loner and lives by a code of self-reliance. In a world where survival depends not on manners or ideals, he is a master of force, the force to control wild animals, cattle, Indians, and outlaws.

If Huck Finn did find his way west, he easily could have become a Western hero, riding into the mountain sunset, away from town.

Yet it is not the hero's romantic inclinations that make him a hero. It is the fact that he always ends up defending social order. He saves the town from villains who are really not much different from himself, rough asocial men who live by the rule of force. Sometimes, the hero himself has been an outlaw in his secret past. In saving the town, the hero proves that after all his temptations by romantic escape, it is social order that matters most. The American Western has addressed this tension thousands of times, inventing new situations to test new characters but always delivering the same answer, that the American wilderness means freedom *with* social order.

Was there anything in the experience of Scandinavians that inclined them to see wilderness as freedom in any form? Since I have been relying on literature as an indicator of national experience, perhaps I can look for an answer in the pages of *Seven Brothers*.

The reason the translator of *Seven Brothers* compares it to *Huckleberry Finn* is because, like Huck, the brothers rebel against the demands of society and flee into the wilderness. They have little patience for the efforts of the sexton to teach them how to read or for the requirements of working their family farm. They envision a life of complete freedom living off the land. Yet their efforts to live in the wilderness are repeatedly thwarted by the harshness of the land and by their own foolishness. They can't always find enough game to eat. In one of their rowdy fights, they accidentally burn down their own cabin and are left standing nearly naked in the winter night. In pursuing a bear into a bull pasture, they are surrounded atop a boulder by angry bulls and have to shoot the bulls to escape, infuriating the herd owner. To repay him, the brothers agree to clear forests and plant grain, but they also build a distillery and use the grain to make alcohol, leading to more drunken wildness. A brawl with another family leaves them convinced that their only escape from the law is to join the army, disappear to a distant outpost, and die heroically. But when the sheriff shows them some unexpected mercy, it's their turning point. They realize that their wild life in the wilderness is unsustainable. They teach themselves how to read. They return to their family farm and turn it into a model farm. They become kind and wise and responsible. They become husbands and fathers and community leaders.

For the brothers, the wilderness succeeds neither as an escape from society nor as a better society. It serves rather as an education about their own wild impulses and the value of civilization. Society isn't an evil to avoid but a community essential to human well-being. The more severe the wilderness, the more essential is human cooperation.

If the evidence of one novel is to be trusted, we could say that while Scandinavians were more ready than other peoples to take on the American wilderness, it wasn't with the escapist motives of Huck Finn.

But is there any better evidence for a truly Scandinavian attitude toward the value of human society?

I think that the attitude of *Seven Brothers* is evident throughout twentieth-century Scandinavian history, whose main project was the building of an all-embracing social welfare system, serving every basic human need from childbirth to education to healthcare to retirement. The attitude underlying this system is that society is a nurturing, cooperative, egalitarian, family-like unit. What most impressed the rest of the world was that Scandinavians pursued community without smothering individual freedom. The Scandinavian "middle way" became a model for other nations that weren't satisfied with the choice between the totalitarian collectivism of Russia and the Darwinian capitalism of America. Historians have debated the origins of the Scandinavian welfare state, and it has even been suggested that America deserves indirect credit for it, as the Swedish government, desperate to stop the exodus of its citizens to America, felt compelled to guarantee them a better life at home. I find it more plausible to believe that modern Scandinavian society isn't any sudden, arbitrary departure from centuries of peasant society but is a natural outgrowth of long-rooted values that encourage a strong sense of community. The most obvious source for these values is the northern climate and landscape, which created an extra demand for mutual help. I generally distrust environmental determinism, which seeks to explain every cultural trait by a material cause, but if any environment on Earth is going to leave its imprint on human culture, it's the Scandinavian environment. It seems quite plausible to connect a demanding environment with the Scandinavian spirit of social cooperation.

To give you an American parallel example of what I mean, in America it was the Rocky Mountain states that first gave women the right to vote, for in the West family survival didn't allow women to be helpless damsels, and men learned to respect women for their strength. Scandinavian nations were the first in the world to give women the right to vote and to fully welcome them into political and economic life, and this reflects a similar environmental incentive for strong women and for male respect for women. You can go down the list of Scandinavian traits and find similar environmental molds. For instance, Scandinavians are noted for their aversion to anger and conflict. It doesn't take much imagination to see why people trapped indoors together for many months of the year can't afford to allow conflicts to get out of control. You can't afford to get too angry at your neighbor either, for someday you'll need his or her help. To more openly argumentative cultures, the Scandinavian aversion to conflict seems odd if not neurotic, but within Scandinavian society this has promoted healthy methods of peace making, and it has served Scandinavians well in their role as international peacemaker. In a world divided between an angry Soviet Union and an angry United States, the world was again grateful that Scandinavians stood in the middle dispensing Nobel Peace Prizes for peaceful resolution of conflicts and supplying the United Nations with its first two secretaries-general.

On my flight from London to Helsinki I had an interesting conversation about Scandinavian values and society. I sat next to a Swede named Berth Jönsson who had traveled to America hundreds of times as a business consultant. As a manager at Volvo in the 1960s, he had been instrumental in one of Sweden's most famous social experiments. Faced with assembly line workers who hated the mindless repetition of their jobs, Volvo reorganized the whole production system into teams that would finish a whole vehicle, giving them a social bond, an intellectual challenge, and a creative achievement. The rest of the business world scoffed at this latest example of Swedish high-minded foolishness, which placed worker satisfaction above productivity. But by the time Volvo had become the world's second largest truck maker, American automakers were regularly touring the Volvo plant and copying its ideas.

When I expressed my skepticism that American corporations would be willing to take business lessons from Sweden, Jönsson cited an impressive list of corporations and university business schools that had consulted him. Still, he admitted that American corporations were generally so obsessed with immediate profits that they not only created unhappy workers, they couldn't even recognize their own long-term self-interests.

When I asked Jönsson if the Volvo experiment represented distinctly Scandinavian values, he said definitely. He agreed that Scandinavians had a stronger sense of community than Americans and suggested that we could trace these values all the way back to the Viking Age. We knew enough about the Vikings to recognize the same emphasis on cooperation, the same taking care of one's tribe, that characterizes Scandinavia today. I expressed my skepticism about this, and Jönsson admitted that the Vikings may not have been so considerate toward outsiders, but he insisted that the roots of modern Scandinavia went that deep.

I had to admit that my image of the Vikings was dictated by their old enemy, the British. American history textbooks are often written from a British point of view. American history starts with Jamestown, and Viking history starts when shiploads of barbarians showed up in Britain in A.D. 793 and looted a monastery. It's as if the Vikings had no existence apart from raiding Britain. In London the previous evening, I had seen a BBC news story about a meeting of a national association of societies for historic reenactments. The association had decided to expel the Viking reenactors because they were too violent, reenacting torture, rape, and mutilation. The BBC interviewed a guy dressed in Viking costume who protested their expulsion, claiming that they were just trying to be historically accurate.

I was more willing to allow a Volvo executive to speak for the Vikings. Jönsson's version of the Vikings was borne out by at least one thing I knew about Viking history. A thousand years ago, while Europe was ruled by feudal monarchies, the Icelandic Vikings established a democratic congress, the Althing, which met annually in a volcanic amphitheater called Thingvellir. The chieftains of all the Viking clans were presided over by a law speaker. The most famous of all the law speakers was Snorri Sturluson (1178–1241), the compiler of the *Prose Edda*. The Althing was meant to make laws, settle disputes between clans, and prevent the rise of any one autocratic ruler. Frequently enough, a clan that lost a decision resorted to their swords anyway, but the Althing managed to last for centuries. And while the rest of Europe practiced feudalism in the Middle Ages, Scandinavian farmers remained free men.

One can't get too carried away in trying to portray the Scandinavians as natural democrats. One need only look at the nineteenth century, which makes quite a contrast with the twentieth century. Long after the American Revolution ignited democratic fever in Europe, Scandinavian countries remained sluggish monarchies with serious class stratification.

Yet this raises another possibility. If it's true that Scandinavians were inclined toward democratic values and that their own governments were failing to represent those values, this would only add to the attractiveness of the young democracy across the sea. Such a match between Scandinavian values and American values is another way to explain why Scandinavians emigrated more readily than other peoples. America was not only a wilderness where Scandinavians could expect to survive, it was a democratic wilderness where they could expect to build the right kind of society.

This suggests another way in which Huck Finn had the right name. In Huck's protection of Jim against slave hunters, in his revulsion against a feudalistic southern society, Huck was being a good Scandinavian.

Scandinavians were also the only people for whom the idea of sailing west to find new lands was long part of their history, enshrined in their legends. The Icelandic sagas told of the Vikings boldly sailing into the unknown Atlantic and settling Iceland, Greenland, and then Vinland, which could only be America. The sagas didn't promise success; in fact, they seemed to guarantee hardships. When Erik the Red sailed from Iceland to settle Greenland, only half of his twenty-five ships arrived. Vinland was later discovered only when a ship was blown off course by a storm. The attempt to settle Vinland failed, yet the sagas offered Scandinavians a unique sense of America as their place of destiny. The sagas also upheld the promise of freedom: many Vikings settled in Iceland to escape from a tyrannical king in Norway.

That Scandinavians have remained deeply fascinated by the idea of sailing west and settling the American wilderness is evident in two modern sagas on this theme, one by the Norwegian Ole Rölvaag and one by the Swede Vilhelm Moberg. In length alone, each well over a thousand pages, Rölvaag's trilogy of novels and Moberg's quartet could be called epics, but it's their literary skill and psychological insight that make them the most masterful portrayals of the epic European immigration to America and settling of the frontier. Both works seem like the completion of a first chapter written in Iceland a thousand years ago.

Unlike the frontier heroes of American folklore, including real ones like Daniel Boone and Davy Crockett, who seem to belong nowhere else, the heroes of Rölvaag and Moberg are deeply rooted in the land and traditions of their birth, they leave their home with great ambivalence, they remain haunted by it, and they are never quite sure how to make America a true home. This reflects the experience of both authors, who remained Scandinavians at heart yet who were drawn irresistibly to America. Rölvaag emigrated when he was twenty years old, in 1896, helped by his uncle in South Dakota. Moberg, born two decades after Rölvaag, planned to emigrate as a teenager but never quite made it. Rölvaag couldn't get Norway out of his mind and became a professor of Norwegian at the very Norwegian St. Olaf College in Minnesota. Moberg couldn't get America out of his mind and finally moved there to research and write his novels. Ironically, while both authors set their stories on the Great Plains, both found the plains insufferably bleak. Rölvaag couldn't forget the fjords and mountains of his youth. Moberg finished his research in Minnesota and fled to Carmel, California, to do his writing. Both authors were also troubled by the social landscape of small-town Great Plains Scandinavian America, which had little community life outside the church and the tavern and whose values were too American, focused on money rather than culture.

Both epics belong to the Scandinavian epic tradition in which wilderness is the central reality. Neither epic follows the American Western tradition in which a villain offers an easy contrast between good and evil and an easy resolution. The wilderness may be a villain in that it can kill, but it is also the source of hope and home. The wilderness is a huge, immortal force against which humans can progress only slowly and with great struggle, and they can never wholly conquer it, only borrow it between winter's taxation. The heroes arrive in Minnesota woods or on Dakota prairies that bear little trace of human habitation and begin years of work to build homes and farms. They endure bleak winters, hunger, illness, injuries, and crop-destroying attacks of grasshoppers, hail, drought, freezes, and wildfire. Most importantly, they struggle with their own minds, with loneliness, depression, and existential doubt, with uprootedness from the past and uncertainty about the future. Rölvaag's heroine, Beret, slowly loses her mind until in her religious fervor she sends her husband out into a blizzard, and he dies. Yet finally the pioneers succeed in making the wilderness a home. Moberg's heroine, Kristina, has the deathbed satisfaction of tasting the first ripe apple grown from seeds from her Swedish home.

Moberg's epic, *The Emigrants*, includes a subplot reminiscent of *Seven Brothers*. In this case there are two brothers, and their contrast teaches a lesson about the American visions of freedom and society.

The older brother, Karl Oskar, dreams of painstakingly building a farm where his wife, Kristina, can raise a family. His impetuous younger brother, Robert, who has been ill-treated by a master in Sweden and who imagines America to be a place of no masters and complete freedom, soon tires of toiling for his brother and dreams of instant wealth in the California goldfields. He takes a steamboat down the Mississippi River to St. Louis (no doubt stopping in Hannibal along the way and at the precise historical moment to pass Huck Finn on his raft) and heads west as a mule driver for a Spaniard. Robert never makes it to California, but he comes into a small fortune when the Spaniard dies of yellow fever. Robert loiters in a raw frontier town, but finally, swindled out of his money and terminally ill, he returns to his brother's now-prospering farm to die.

Both epics are centered on the struggle to tame the land, but Moberg is also interested in the foreground story, while Rölvaag is more interested in the aftermath. Moberg devotes his entire first novel to life in Sweden, the decision to leave, the leaving of family and home, and the hard voyage to America. Rölvaag begins *Giants in the Earth* with his Norwegians already trekking across the prairie. Moberg seems proud that his Swedes have become Americans. The elderly Karl Oskar feels only amused wonder that his children have married Irish or Norwegians. At his death, his children are incapable of writing in Swedish to Karl Oskar's sister in Sweden, and they have to ask an elder to help them. Rölvaag thoroughly explores the experience of the second generation facing assimilation into American society. When Beret's son marries an Irish Catholic, it causes bitter conflict. Rölvaag regards the loss of Norwegian language, religion, and traditions as a betrayal and impoverishment; the melting pot means dissolution into a bland, unhealthy society.

Scandinavians' continuing fascination with the American frontier and their part in settling it is measured by the report that Moberg's emigrant novels are the most widely read novels in Sweden today. In the 1970s the prominent Swedish director Jan Troell made them into two films, *The Emigrants* and *The New Land*, starring Liv Ullmann and Max von Sydow, and, quite appropriately for a story starring a Karl Oskar, *The Emigrants* became one of the few foreign-language films ever nominated for an Oscar for best picture, and Ullmann was nominated for an Oscar for best actress. Swedes can pursue their fascination with the American West at High Chaparral, a western theme park named af-ter the 1960s American TV show that starred an actor named Leif Erickson. Now that most Swedish and Norwegian families have cous-ins in America, there is a more personal connection to America. Yet be-neath the personal interest lies a need to understand why a quarter of their people would desert their own country, and there's a mythic fas-cination at the idea of turning a whole continent of wilderness into wealth, freedom, and a more perfect society.

The Moberg novels aren't nearly as well known in America as in Sweden. I didn't discover them until my first visit to Sweden. I needed something to read in the evening after I was too tired to wander any more museums or streets. The Moberg story seemed like a good way to continue my explorations. I noticed that Moberg and his characters were from Småland, the same province as my ancestors, so this prom-ised to be my own story. I was soon engrossed in the struggles of Karl Oskar and Kristina to survive on their small, rocky farm in Småland. Moberg was a gifted storyteller, combining honesty about human na-ture with tender compassion for his characters, and he had a keen eye for incident and symbolism. Most importantly for me, he was com-mitted to a historically accurate examination of the Swedish exodus to America.

On my last day in Stockholm I returned to the bookstore to buy the other three Moberg novels to take home with me. In a curious way, my progress through the novels began paralleling my own experiences. As I was packing my bag that evening, Karl Oskar and Kristina were pack-ing their emigrant trunk. As I was sitting in the airport awaiting my plane, Karl Oskar and Kristina were in a wagon heading for their ship. As I flew the Atlantic, Karl Oskar and Kristina were crossing it too; I could look down and see their schooner full of misery and hope. At least their grueling experience made my ten hours of being stuffed into a Boeing 747 seat seem easy. By the time I landed, the emigrants were gathering excitedly on deck to see America on the horizon. I even landed in Chicago, which was the gateway west for most Swedish emi-grants, including Karl Oskar and Kristina.

My reading pace then slackened off for a while, but this meant that I was in the appropriate chapter when I continued my exploration of my roots that autumn. I revisited Battleground, Indiana, for the first time since I was a kid. I got lucky and met the author of a history tour guide of the town who was also a schoolteacher and whose pupil lived in my great-grandfather's house. He told me that when he was researching his book, he interviewed a 104-year-old woman across the street from the Lago house who still remembered the Swedish tailor who didn't speak any English. He took me to the house and gained me entrance. The house had been remodeled over the course of a century, but there remained corners that looked a century old and helped me imagine my great-grandparents' presence here. Genetically, I had been present here too. I felt that I should recognize the house, yet it all remained a strange planet to my reincarnated eyes. Next to the house was a cottage where Gustava's mother had lived out her final years.

I also visited the cemetery where my great-great-grandmother, my great-grandfather, and his son who had died at age fifteen were buried. By now I had wandered into a half-dozen Swedish pioneer cemeteries. I had felt a bit guilty at using cemeteries for historical tourism, yet now I saw tombstones that bore my own name, and it was startling. I felt the way I had felt in Gränna, seeing my name attached to strangers in an unfamiliar place. Yet here the mist of the unknown past parted and yielded a story I knew. Here the history books turned into my personal story. Here was the person responsible for my calling this continent home. The strange American earth he had reached and now become was the only earth I had ever known. Mere remembering wasn't a strong substitute for knowing people personally, but afterward I felt more rooted in this particular earth and in these lives.

By now I was reading the third Moberg novel, *The Settlers*. Over lunch in a local cafe I read of Karl Oskar and Kristina building their house and farm and burying his brother in the new cemetery. Now the story seemed more real.

A few weeks later I was in Minnesota and decided to spend the weekend exploring the Lake Chisago area, where Moberg had set his novels. I was almost done with the final novel. To my surprise, the local highways bore signs designating this the Vilhelm Moberg Historic Route. In its town square, Lindstrom held a statue of Karl Oskar and Kristina. It portrayed the moment they were leaving home, with Karl Oskar gazing determinedly ahead and Kristina looking over her shoulder with uncertainty and longing. Every year, Lindstrom held a Karl Oskar and Kristina Festival.

Near Lake Chisago I found the site Moberg had imagined as his characters' home. In Center City I stopped at the Swedish Pioneer Cemetery. As I walked among the headstones, many listing birthplaces in Sweden, I felt that this was where I was supposed to finish the Moberg story. I returned to my car and got *Last Letter Home* and sat in the grass. Kristina was long dead, and now Karl Oscar was old and ailing. I watched him die and be buried in the pioneer cemetery beside his wife. His children asked an elderly neighbor to write a last letter to Sweden.

The year after my Moberg adventure, Moberg's epic became a hit musical in Sweden. It was written by two men who were already Sweden's most successful composers but in a very different idiom, as members of the rock band ABBA. After ABBA disbanded, Benny Andersson had immersed himself in Swedish folk music. It was from this tradition as well as Broadway and classical music that he and Björn Ulvaeus had drawn *Kristina från Duvemåla*. It stirred such interest in Sweden that there was a yearlong waiting list for tickets.

The next year I heard that there would be one special performance of *Kristina* in America at Orchestra Hall in Minneapolis, starring the Swedish cast. I was lucky to get a ticket, as they sold out fast. Rumor had it that Swedes who were too impatient to wait a year were flying to Minneapolis to see *Kristina* here. I never heard if this rumor was true, but the woman sitting next to me had flown from New York City just to see *Kristina*, and previously she had flown to Sweden just to see it.

It was magical to see the characters who had told me my family history step off the page and into bodies and voices. The music succeeded in expressing the spirit of the books. Though it was sung in Swedish and I couldn't understand a word of it, the personalities, moods, and story came through, offering more honest humanity than most Broadway musicals. One of the best songs was straight out of a Bergman movie: an ailing Kristina angrily confronts God, demanding to know why he inflicts suffering on her and the rest of creation. Kristina's brave spirit came through in brighter ways too.

After joining in the enthusiastic applause, I stepped out into the cold downtown Minneapolis night. Unlike the usual experience of stepping out of a theater and its enfolding story back into a forgotten world of parking lots and traffic, I did not feel I had suddenly left the world of Karl Oskar and Kristina. The Minneapolis skyline seemed like the continuation of their story. This was the world they had built.

I drove among the skyscrapers, toward my hotel just across the Mississippi River. As I crossed the bridge over the waterfalls that had founded the city, I saw the mills and grain elevators where the wheat from Kristina's farm started its passage down the two-thousand-mile-long throat of the nation. As far north as I was, I was not too far away to smell the French donuts in New Orleans and hear the jazz from Beale Street in Memphis. Even here, it was hard to see the Mississippi River without seeing Huck Finn on his raft, traveling at night for the sake of human freedom, turning a mere river into the mythology that is as necessary as bread if people and nations are to live.

• • •

On the other side of Minnesota, in Moorhead, on the banks of another river, the Red, sits an impressive symbol of the adventurous Scandinavian spirit transplanted to America.

Underneath a soaring sail-shaped white dome sits a seventy-six-foot-long Viking ship. In design it is Norwegian, but its timber is American, and the hands that built it and sailed it back to Norway in 1982 were American. The *Hjemkomst* was modeled after the Gokstad ship unearthed in Norway in 1880 and now residing in Oslo's Viking Ship Museum, just around the corner from the *Kon Tiki* museum, which houses the rafts of a modern Viking, Thor Heyerdahl. Like Heyerdahl, who set out to prove that ancient peoples had the ability to cross oceans, Robert Asp was called crazy when he set out to build a Viking ship and sail it from Duluth through the Great Lakes, down the Hudson River, through New York City, and across the Atlantic. Asp was a Moorhead high school counselor, but even if he had been a professional shipbuilder and sailor, building a Viking ship, for which there are no blueprints and instruction manuals, required figuring out everything.

Asp was inspired by his Viking heritage. He searched out the right trees, some of them from near the town of Oslo, Minnesota, some of them Norway pines. He had them milled in the town of Viking, Minnesota. He turned an abandoned potato warehouse into a shipyard. He labored for years, against the advancing tide of leukemia. When the ship was ready, one of the walls of the warehouse had to be removed to get the ship out. Before the ship could sail, Asp died, but his children were among the crew.

Many ships full of Scandinavians have sailed past the Statue of Liberty. It is not out of the question that the original Vikings wandered as far south as New York harbor. They couldn't have imagined that a giant Greco-Roman goddess would one day preside over the harbor, welcoming steamships full of their descendants. Yet they would have understood their descendants' motives, for they too had been willing to trade their homeland to take chances on unfamiliar lands. When the Asp ship sailed past the Statue of Liberty, with dozens of cameras framing its dragon head against the skyscrapers, it framed a thousand years of history and undiminished boldness.

The *Hjemkomst* took five weeks to reach Norway. It survived storms that threatened to capsize it. Its design proved correct, and the prairie kids proved to be worthy sailors. When they sailed into Bergen harbor they were welcomed by a huge flotilla and a crowd who didn't need to be told the meaning of the ship's name: Homecoming.

Outside the *Hjemkomst* museum is another American-made Norwegian landmark, a full-scale reproduction of a stave church. Nine hundred stave churches were built in Norway at the end of the Viking era and the start of the Christian era. The churches retained the Viking ship habit of posting a dragon head at either end to scare off evil spirits. Their wooden shingles are reminiscent of reptile scales. Like Viking ships, stave churches are masterpieces of wood construction. The builder of this seventy-foot-tall church, Guy Paulson, ended up in awe of the Norwegians' skills, which weren't aided by modern tools. Like Robert Asp, Paulson wanted to honor his Norwegian heritage, and his wild dream was matched by skill and determination. That he succeeded in replicating the Hopperstad *stavkirke* from the town of Vik, Norway, was attested by a Minnesota farmer named Per Hopperstad, who grew up two hundred feet from the original *stavkirke* and who at age ten had climbed to its top.

To me, the combination of two quintessential and magnificent Scandinavian structures makes the Moorhead site the most impressive monument in Scandinavian America. Of course, people going there in search of their identity might end up having an identity crisis instead, as the two structures represent contradictory eras of Scandinavian history. I'm not sure that either the church-pillaging Vikings or the Crusade-era Christians would approve of being associated with one another. Yet Americans have long been ready to borrow from its true context anything that can serve as a symbol of our own unique identities, and for Scandinavian Americans, the Vikings have served as an irresistible symbol of pioneering boldness. Symbols of the Vikings, not of stave churches, are found throughout Scandinavian America, even in Lutheran churches. Even the most ardent Christians among Scandinavian Americans seem to have little problem adopting Viking symbolism, for it is understood to represent the spirit that turned Scandinavians into Americans and helped turn the northern prairie into a contributing part of a great nation. Scandinavian Americans have often been more enthusiastic about Viking symbolism than are modern Scandinavians, for whom the Vikings' roughness sets a bad example for a peaceable modern society. But then, America has a higher tolerance for roughness than does modern Scandinavia. Perhaps such roughness was an unavoidable part of pioneering, and in this, too, the Viking symbolism reassured us about our character and destiny.

In the spring of 1997, the Red River overflowed its banks, flooding the twin cities of Moorhead and Fargo on either side. The water steadily rose around the Viking ship until it was almost surrounded. The Red River is a rare American river that flows north, into Canada and Hudson Bay. I can imagine the Viking ship waiting eagerly for the river to lift it and send it northward, where it belongs. Yet the ship remained parked on the prairie. It was an absurd place for a vessel that had mastered the seas, yet it was also a perfect place for it. The Viking ship proved that the spirit of the ancient sagas was still alive and belonged in America.

5

Leaving Gothenburg

As *I drove* into Gothenburg, Nebraska, a quiet town of three thousand people on the Platte River and the Oregon Trail, I thought of my arrival in Gothenburg, Sweden, Sweden's second-largest city and primary port, with half a million people.

I had arrived in the original Gothenburg by train, and I walked out of the train station onto a large plaza busy with people. In my tourist guide I had studied the lodging choices within walking distance, and I liked a hotel in the form of an old sailing ship docked in the harbor. I didn't know that this was the very dock from which my great-grandparents had sailed for America. If I had known this, then when I set out for the ship, lugging my suitcase and soon realizing that I had misjudged the scale of the map and had a tiringly long distance to go, I might have invoked my great-grandparents' far more tiring journey as an encouragement to keep going. Certainly, I would have found it meaningful to dream on the spot where their hesitant American dream had turned into huge white sails certain with wind.

Yet instead of my dreaming an emigrant's sea-rocked dreams, I ended up decorating my night with the other extreme of nineteenth-century Swedish society. I noticed another hotel that had an appealing historic theme. It was the former palace of one of Sweden's richest families, the Fürstenburgs. The Fürstenburgs had amassed a famous art collection, including Swedish masters like Carl Larsson and Anders Zorn, that later became the core of the Gothenburg art museum. The palace had been a social center for Sweden's elite. Today, hotel rooms are more expensive than on the ship, but then it was a lot closer. I got a corner room looking back on the plaza. As I stood there gazing out, I thought of how easily I had crossed into a world barred to my ancestors. I imagined the thousands of weary emigrants who had walked past this palace, heading from the train station to the docks or cheap inns, hauling trunks that held a life's possessions, looking at the silhouettes in the palace windows, hearing the music of balls, seeing the guard at the door as symbolic of everything that had been closed to them in Sweden, hoping that America was an open gateway.

The next day I explored the city. It was one of the first pleasant days of spring, and the Swedes were out en masse. The parks were crowded; the sidewalk cafes had waiting lines; the sidewalks were a parade of baby carriages. Everywhere were smiles at winter's ending, just as the Scandinavian landmass itself had lifted when the burden of Ice Age glaciers melted away.

I strolled along the elegant boulevards, canals, and parks and explored the museums and shops. I went on a boat tour of the canals and harbor, and we went right past the dock from which most Swedish emigrants had embarked for America, but the tour guide didn't even mention this. At the end of the tour I asked the guide if there was any emigration landmark here, and she said, Oh yes, we had passed the building where the emigrants had been processed, the old tollhouse. She gave me directions to it, and I set off, no longer just a tourist but someone making a homecoming.

The old tollhouse looked as if it had been here in 1868, but there was no indication that it had served as a reverse Ellis Island. You would think that the building would make a powerful museum for Swedish Americans, but perhaps its invisibility represented the ambivalence of Swedes about their countrymen who had deserted their country. Most Swedes will proudly tell you that their own relatives who emigrated were unusually brave and smart and hardy, contributing great things to the world's leading nation; but when emigration is discussed in more general historical terms, one can hear echoes of the anti-emigration campaign that portrayed emigrants as moral weaklings who were betraying their homeland, families, and church to chase after foolish dreams of worldly wealth. An exodus museum in the most visible part of Sweden's busiest harbor might feel like a symbol of national failure.

Swedes prefer that their country be represented by today's exodus of freighters loaded with Volvos.

As I entered the tollhouse, I felt the presence of my great-grand-parents. I could only guess how the building had appeared 128 years ago. Today it was an art school, filled with art and bohemians. But I could imagine my great-grandparents walking over these very tiles, handing their papers to a clerk at a desk. It was harder for me to imag-ine their feelings as they walked out the back door and saw the great ship waiting and stepped off of Swedish soil for the final time, stepped into the unknown. Their steps had created a parallel universe, deciding that I would belong to another continent. My returning steps had trig-gered a time warp in which I could feel my own presence here long ago.

I climbed the stairs to the second floor and studied the old fixtures, the peeling paint, the doors, the ceilings as if I would recognize some-thing. I went out the harborside door and thought it appropriate that a grand old sailing ship was docked there. Then I recognized from the name on the ship that this was the hotel where I could have slept last night. I regretted having missed the boat.

The tollhouse had two wings, one of which was a maritime store. I wandered through the aisles of boating and fishing supplies, again as if I was supposed to recognize something. Then I left and walked slowly along the harbor. I watched the sailboats and motorboats cruising along, their Swedish flags flying. I watched the giant freighters heading for America. Then I stopped and headed back to the maritime store. There was something that every maritime store was supposed to sell. I wan-dered through the aisles again until I found it, in many sizes. I selected a foot-long Swedish flag. Better than any sea-rocked dreams, it would symbolize my passage through here 128 years ago and once again.

Having thus enjoyed the original Gothenburg, I had to investigate the American version.

It was a dangerous thing for Americans to name their pioneer vil-lages after the great cities of Europe. It was okay if you named a village after your similarly humble native village; this was probably a good cure for homesickness. It was okay if you named villages after Euro-pean kings or heroes, for then it was understood as a way of honoring someone or of claiming glory for your mediocre little town. But to name your town London or Paris was to invite comparisons that were almost always unfavorable to American towns. Only rarely did a New

York outclass its namesake. Thus it was not entirely my fault that my first reaction to Gothenburg, Nebraska, was to see what it wasn't.

The most obvious thing missing was the ocean. For a harbor town, this Gothenburg was badly misplaced, unless you recalled the poetic name for the American prairie, "the sea of grass." The Platte River wasn't much of a substitute for an ocean, for it was too shallow and braided to be navigable for much more than a rowboat. That was why pioneers had quit the riverboats back in St. Joseph, Missouri, and set off on the Oregon Trail. The towns that sprang up along the trail, which followed the Platte River through Nebraska, learned not to plant themselves too close to the river, for while it offered reliable irrigation, it offered too much irrigation during spring floods. The Union Pacific Railroad and Interstate 80 later followed the route of the Oregon Trail.

Gothenburg didn't seem to be benefiting much from being on one of the major east-west interstates. Where other towns had a forest of franchise signs at their interstate exits, Gothenburg had only three fast food restaurants. The rest of the businesses in town were homegrown, serving a local farming and ranching economy. The downtown was pleasant yet had its share of empty storefronts. The most striking sight downtown was a kinetic, multicolored mural of a Pony Express rider.

I drove up the tree-shaded main street and looked at some of the houses listed on the historic guide sent to me by the chamber of commerce. Some had been built by successful Swedish immigrants, like Gus Dahlquist the clothing store owner, Ernest Calling the real estate agent, and John Dahl the builder. Only one of the houses showed any hint of Swedish architecture.

The only real sign of Sweden I saw in town was a Swedish flag in the city park, in front of the Pony Express station. The log cabin station was one of the few original Pony Express stations still standing.

The log cabin calibrated just how far away I was from the other Gothenburg, with its Parisian boulevards, its Dutch canals, its grand architecture and statues, its streets full of Volvos, its museums full of masterpieces, its cafes full of elegant food and people. The contrast could be amusing or it could raise doubts about the judgment of the emigrants. If the emigrants had stayed home, then a pickup-driving grain elevator clerk might be a Volvo-driving office tower executive. But even if you recalled that most emigrants were farm kids seeking, and certainly finding, better land than they could find at home, the contrast between the two Gothenburgs could tempt you to make fun of the baby Gothenburg.

Yet as someone who had proudly obtained a Swedish flag from an old travelers' station in old Gothenburg, the Swedish flag flying outside the Pony Express station would not allow me to be condescending.

The flag posed a riddle. The flag was incongruous here, not at all belonging with the Pony Express station. The incongruity arose not just from the contrast between Sweden and the American West. It arose, I think, from the Pony Express station being not even a real place but a figment of mythology.

The American West is a real place with a real history, and it is also a mythology. Every nation has a mythology that codifies its national experience, values, and goals. America's mythology has been generated by a people engaged in settling a vast wild continent. We needed heroes and moral lessons to encourage us to take the risks and endure the hardships of pioneering. Long after the pioneering was over and America had become a suburban nation, we continued trying to live by our pioneer mythology, given new life by Hollywood. We enthralled ourselves with images of wagon trains heading into the sunset mountains and of good triumphing over evil in dirt street shoot-outs. We didn't seem to notice that our national mythology had become dysfunctional. For an industrial nation to be guided by a myth of heroic conquest of unlimited nature was to bring ruin on our land. For the world's superpower to be guided by a myth of utter disregard for nonwhite peoples was to bring anger and failure upon ourselves. For an urban nation to be guided by the myth of the gun was to fill our streets with violence and assassination. Yet national mythologies are powerful and slow to change, especially when they have brought great success.

The mythology of the American West selected its symbols from real history but without much regard for the real importance of things. Historically irrelevant people and events were magnified into greatness. The shoot-out at the OK Corral was a grubby backwater feud that was transformed into a titanic battle between good and evil. The Pony Express also took on a greater life as a symbol than it ever had as history.

The Pony Express was started in 1860 and shut down only sixteen months later, rendered obsolete by the completion of the intercontinental telegraph. If the founders of the Pony Express had had a bit more foresight, they could have saved themselves from losing a fortune. The telegraph contributed far more to tying together the growing nation than did the Pony Express, but you don't see statues to heroic telegraph operators, or movies depicting their skill and exhausting vigils, or tourists spending their summer vacations retracing the route of the telegraph wires.

Perhaps the Pony Express captured our national imagination because it was such a bold symbol of triumph over the wilderness. Pony Express riders started by taming wild mustangs and then endured frequent attacks by wild Indians, survived wild weather, and passed through rugged landscapes, risking their lives for the sake of national greatness. Telegraph operators only sat in their chairs in cozy rooms in town.

The citizens of Gothenburg, Nebraska, were experts on the mythological power of the Pony Express. Their station was their main lure for getting travelers off the interstate to spend money in town. Gothenburg had promoted itself far and wide as "the Pony Express Capital of Nebraska." Originally, the station had been outside of town, but in 1931 the city moved it into the city park and turned it into a museum and gift shop. Out front, a horse and carriage offered rides. It was common for Gothenburg to be visited by pilgrims retracing the whole route of the Pony Express.

For anyone coming to the Pony Express station to find American mythology, the Swedish flag might seem out of place. But I had come here to find some sort of Swedish town, some reflection of old Gothenburg, and for me it was the flag that belonged here and the Pony Express station that was out of place. Clearly, something was wrong with my reaction. I needed to come to terms with an American myth flying a Swedish flag. The mythological experts of Gothenburg seemed to think the flag belonged.

Of course, I shouldn't have been surprised to find that Gothenburg, Nebraska, was a thoroughly American town and even a capital of American mythology. Scandinavian Americans had enlisted in that mythology as enthusiastically as anyone else. Scandinavians had arrived a bit too late to be trailblazers or to personally shoot many Indians, but they were certainly true believers in the national destiny of settling the frontier. In fact, there was no better town in which to be reminded of this, for Gothenburg was the home of the greatest of all Scandinavian American frontiersmen, Febold Feboldson. If Febold's name doesn't ring a bell, you surely have heard of his close friend, Paul Bunyan. Febold never became as famous as Paul Bunyan, for Febold's exploits weren't recorded until the 1920s and then only in the Gothenburg newspaper. But his feats aroused such admiration that the University of Nebraska Press devoted a book to him: *Febold Feboldson: Tall Tales from the Great Plains*. The term "tall tales," of course, refers to Febold's unusual height. Since I can't recount all of Febold's amazing adventures, I'll select a few.

The summer Febold arrived in Nebraska from Sweden, it was so hot that the mountains that had covered Nebraska all melted into a great plain. Since there were no trees for building houses, Febold walked all the way to California to get some redwood trees. As he dragged the redwoods back to Nebraska, he failed to notice that they were scraping out canyons and disintegrating into the red dust you find in the West today. By the time he reached Nebraska, the redwoods were worthless stumps, so he built a sod house instead.

During Febold's first winter in Nebraska, blizzards covered the whole Midwest with ten feet of snow. Feeling right at home, the Swede built a huge snowplow and lassoed a herd of buffalo to pull it, but the buffalo stampeded and dragged Febold and the plow all the way to the Missouri River before they tired out. The resulting furrow became the Platte River.

When spring floods on the Platte River allowed sharks to swim up from the Gulf of Mexico, Febold caught some baby sea horses and fed them hair tonic until they were big enough for him to ride. Then he mounted a sea horse and galloped down the river, lassoing enough sharks to eat all spring.

Drought too was a chronic problem, but Febold outsmarted it by ordering green-tinted glasses from the Sears catalog and placing them on his cows, who then went on happily grazing on the dry brown grass. When the drought got really bad, Febold got out his guns and shot holes in the clouds until they rained.

When Febold first arrived in Nebraska, tornadoes were a constant threat, but after Febold had lassoed them enough times, they were so afraid of him they stayed in Kansas.

It was Febold whom the U.S. government hired to establish a straight boundary line between Kansas and Nebraska after Paul Bunyan had produced a hopelessly crooked line. Febold bred bumblebees as big as eagles, hooked up his plow to one, and traced a perfect beeline.

Febold was so tough that the rumor spread that every rattlesnake that ever bit him had died, but this wasn't true. Once when Febold was attacked by a whole nest of rattlesnakes, he was sure he was a goner, but fortunately the mosquitoes were so thick that summer that they sucked all the poison out of him, falling in piles around him. It was true that Febold had a pet rattlesnake named Arabella, who crawled into his bed every morning and rattled to wake him up.

How could I have doubted, in Febold Feboldson's own town, that Swedes could be heroes of American mythology?

Another legendary character lived in Gothenburg, but he was a bit more real. Rumor has it that his pioneer exploits inspired the legends of Febold Feboldson. He was Olof Bergstrom, the founder of Gothenburg, who had lived in Gothenburg, Sweden. Bergstrom emigrated in 1881, worked for the Union Pacific Railroad, and then became a railroad land agent. Bergstrom was also a Baptist preacher. In 1882 he returned to Sweden and preached about the promised land in America, and a few hundred Swedes followed him back to Nebraska, expecting to find a miniature Gothenburg only to find no town at all. So they built one. Bergstrom made several more recruiting trips to Sweden. On one trip he introduced the temperance-minded Good Templar Order into Sweden. On another trip he saw a talented opera singer and decided he would make her the next Jenny Lind and make a fortune for himself. He started by marrying her. But Mrs. Bergstrom's opera tour of America fell far short of Jenny Lind's. She would settle for entertaining the folks of Gothenburg. One night during a party at the Bergstrom home, a guest was shot and killed, and Bergstrom was charged with murder. At the trial the accounts of what happened varied considerably, perhaps because everyone at the party was drunk. He was found not guilty. Bergstrom lived the American Dream by becoming a millionaire, only to lose all his money in speculations. The temperance crusader ended up as an alcoholic in a shabby hotel in Tennessee.

In another town in Nebraska, I had once come upon another odd juxtaposition of Sweden and the Wild West. That time I had been looking for the West and found Sweden by accident. I was heading for the town of Bancroft, home of a museum dedicated to John Neihardt, author of *Black Elk Speaks* and other evocations of Native American life and the frontier experience. A sign announced that I was about to pass through the town of Oakland, but suddenly I was in Sweden. There were Dala horses everywhere, painted on store windows and hanging from lampposts. The Dala horse, typically made of wood and painted with floral designs, is the quintessential piece of Swedish folk art, often used as a flag of Swedish identity. There were other Swedish motifs and murals painted on the buildings. I stopped and confirmed that this was a Swedish town, dating from the 1860s. Lately, townsfolk had set out to revitalize their Swedish heritage, decorating the town and holding a regular Swedish festival. But it seemed to me that they had gotten a bit carried away, holding a Swedish Basketball Classic and a Swedish Golf Tournament. It looked like they were trying to challenge Stromsburg for the title of "Swedish Capital of Nebraska."

In one of the Oakland shops I saw an attractive piece of folk art I'd never seen before. It was a round wooden plaque painted with a brightly colored Dala horse posed in a landscape, just like a real horse. The clerk told me that the artist, Grace Schrock, lived here and had a lot more art at home if I wanted to call her up. So I did. When I told Grace I lived in Arizona, she warmed right up to me. She spent her winters in Arizona.

When she opened the door I saw that her living room was indeed a gallery of her work but not quite what I expected. John Wayne smiled at me. Cowboys rode horses through rugged landscapes or frontier streets. Wild mustangs bucked in corrals. There were some Dala horse plaques and paintings on one wall. As I looked them over I paid new attention to the background landscapes. There were sharp mountains, purple at sunset. I asked Grace if she had ever been to Sweden, and she said no. It sure looked to me like her Dala horses were posed in front of Arizona mountains, the same mountains in her cowboy paintings. I bought a Dala horse plaque and hung it on my wall in Arizona, beside my window showing Arizona's highest mountain.

A few weeks before I visited Gothenburg, Nebraska, I had seen another intrusion of Sweden upon the Wild West. I was standing in front of the original 1890s trading post in downtown Flagstaff, Arizona, watching our local Fourth of July parade. The parade included all the usual Americana but with a more western accent. There were cowboys on horses, Native Americans in powwow garb, and a horse-drawn carriage carrying a couple dressed in nineteenth-century fashions. The couple, Richard and Sherry, who had Norwegian and Danish roots, could often be seen in their frontier costumes leading walking tours of downtown Flagstaff. One time when I knew they had just returned from Europe, I couldn't resist asking them if they weren't embarrassed to return from thousand-year-old cities to brag about a town where the oldest building was barely a century old. They said not at all, because their tourists came from those thousand-year-old cities, and they were fascinated by the American West. Soon after Richard and Sherry's carriage went by, I was surprised to see a Swedish flag coming around the corner and then a whole flock of people in Swedish folk costumes carrying Swedish folk instruments. It turned out they were from old Gothenburg. They were on a performance tour of the American West, and the Flagstaff Fourth of July parade just happened to fit into their schedule. They spent the afternoon at the concert in the city park, trying to keep their wool costumes out of the sun and fascinating the crowd with Swedish folk music and dances. I mingled with them and told them I had been to Gothenburg and found it fascinating. I asked them how they liked the West, and they answered they had been here before and were always fascinated by it, its abundance of open space, its mix of cultures, its pioneer history, its vigorous young society. I asked them if they knew there was a town in Nebraska called Gothenburg, and they answered yes, they had been there on last year's tour, and they found it fascinating.

Now that I was standing in Gothenburg, I wished I'd asked the Swedes more specifically what was so fascinating about it. If not for the Swedish connection, which was almost invisible anyway, I would have dismissed Gothenburg as just one more of hundreds of sagging prairie towns trying to milk some glory and tourist dollars from a pioneer past.

It was time for me to meet the Swedish connection. The chamber of commerce had sent me the name of the unofficial town ambassador to those looking for Swedish American history, Marilyn Carlson. I had written to Marilyn and she had said, Sure, stop on by. So I did.

I required a lot less attention than the busload of forty-four Swedes Marilyn had hosted a few weeks ago. The Swedes were touring Swedish America. The local Swedes had stashed Swedes in every free room of their houses. Few of the hosts spoke much Swedish, and many of the Swedes didn't speak much English. It had been Midsummer Day, so something special was called for. The hosts threw a picnic in the park, and the Swedes sang for them.

Marilyn told me that the local Swedes were never allowed to forget their heritage, for they were reminded of it by a steady stream of Swedes and Swedish Americans attracted by the name of the town. Few local Swedes had actually been to Sweden, but they had numerous friends there after hosting them in town. Some local Swedes had heard more about the corners of Sweden than they knew about Nebraska. The Nebraska towns of Stromsburg and Oakland had to work harder to attract Swedish-minded tourists. But Marilyn admitted there was another reason why those towns were decorated with Swedish motifs and Gothenburg wasn't. Gothenburg had a German majority that was unwilling to see Gothenburg decorated or promoted as a Swedish town. They wanted it to be "the Pony Express Capital of Nebraska." The only Swedish symbolism the Germans would allow was the Swedish flag in front of the Pony Express station. Thus, she said regretfully, Gothenburg couldn't even compete with Stromsburg and Oakland to be "the Swedish Capital of Nebraska." But the Swedes who came to town didn't seem to mind. Most of them were far more interested in the Pony Express station than in the same old Swedish folk art they could see at home.

The Nebraska Board of Tourism seemed to have a good focus on what would attract Swedes. It had run an advertisement in Swedish magazines, showing a lasso-gripping cowboy on a horse. The headline said, "No. Seriously. There are cattle, cowboys, and rodeos in Gothenburg." The text read:

> You may enjoy the Scandinavium, the trolleys, and the Avenyn, but an ocean and a continent away sits Gothenburg, Nebraska, USA. The only other Gothenburg in the world besides Sweden.
>
> It's a place where hats are still tipped and doors are still opened, a place where there are more cattle than people. You'll not only find cowboy boots and cowboy hats but cowboys as well.
>
> Visit an actual Pony Express station. Enjoy a ride in a horse-drawn carriage. Browse through the Sod House Museum featuring a barn, sod house, windmills and life-sized barbed wire sculptures. Catch an authentic rodeo.
>
> All of this under the big open sky on the sprawling plains of Nebraska. You'll see the history of the Old West in the buildings and artifacts, but most importantly, you'll see it in the people.

You'll notice that the Nebraska Board of Tourism takes it for granted that Swedes are so familiar with the Old West that they require no definitions of terms such as Pony Express and sod house and barbed wire. You'll also notice the assumption that Swedes will come to Nebraska for a cowboy Gothenburg, not Dala horses hung from lampposts.

Marilyn admitted that Swedish folk traditions were fading away in town. There used to be a Swedish restaurant here, but it was gone. The Swedish folk dancing group had pretty much fizzled out. But I wasn't one to equate ethnic memory with folk traditions.

After I had looked through some of Marilyn's books of local history, she drove me out to the pioneer church and cemetery north of town. I would like the record to show, before I get a reputation for lurking in cemeteries, that I am not the only person who finds cemeteries a good place to make history come alive.

When the cemetery was started a century ago it was only prairie grass, but now it was thoroughly shaded by a grove of tall thick trees. The surnames on the tombstones were Swedish, but as those born in Sweden were followed by those born in America, the first names became more American. The prairie hadn't given up on its old home: tall grass obscured some of the names. Marilyn started tugging grass away from one of the tombstones. She explained that it was the tombstone of her immigrant father. I saw the name Nelson appear. Then Oscar. Then Carl. Carl Oscar Nelson! The hero of Vilhelm Moberg's epic. The quintessential Swedish pioneer. With legends coming alive around me, I wouldn't have been entirely surprised to see the grave of Febold Feboldson.

Next Marilyn drove me to a cemetery with only three graves. They were the children of Anna and Peter Berg, and they had died between 1885 and 1889. The oldest had been only two years old. Anna's father, Benjamin Palm, who was Gothenburg's first blacksmith, sent to Sweden for some Swedish steel, which he fashioned into crosses decorated with scrollwork, stars, and hearts and inscribed with the children's names. I remembered coming upon one area in Sweden where iron crosses had become an elaborate art form. A whole cemetery was filled with ornate iron crosses with dangling iron leaves that fluttered in the wind, making the strangest music.

The three graves were protected by a chain-link fence that, curiously, had a mailbox attached in front. The mailbox really did contain letters to the dead. It contained a visitor register in which people had written testimonials. Visitors from all over the world had found this spot, most of them just from noticing a brochure at the Pony Express station. There were many Swedes listed but plenty of other Europeans as well as Americans from California to New Jersey. I read over the comments, and they were honest and touching. People spoke of the lonely brave lives of the pioneers, of the symbolism of Swedish crosses on the American prairie. One man from Arkansas wrote: "I came to see the great prairie, and this is the spot I will always remember."

I looked around. It was indeed a classic prairie scene. We were on a knoll amidst rolling hills of pastures and wheat fields beneath an enormous sky. The broad horizons easily turned metaphorical. It was the unlimited social and economic horizons of America that had drawn immigrants here. They had gladly left the grand architecture of Gothenburg for the sod houses of Nebraska because the palaces of Gothenburg were closed to them. They were drawn to America because it didn't have the social hierarchy represented by palaces. They were drawn by the dream that anyone could earn his own palace, even if it was only a lonely frame house on a plot of rich topsoil. They were drawn to America precisely because America didn't have any history, the kind of history that defined people for life before they were born. This astonishing lack of history is what still draws Swedes and the rest of the world to the American West today, as tourists, to see a vigorous young society that invented itself out of a few constitutional rules and sheer bold effort. It was time for me to admit it. It was the mythology of the American frontier that had drawn my own great-grandparents here. I couldn't honor their migration with a Swedish flag alone. The most important thing to remember about the dock in Gothenburg was that they had boarded a schooner and left forever. In Gothenburg I had literally missed the boat, missed my chance to honor my ancestors, by being seduced by European history and high society. But perhaps I could still catch a prairie schooner.

This is not to say I could ever accept the frontier myth as a religion, an ordained history and moral guide, complete with John Wayne and Wyatt Earp as saints. At a frontier shrine in a nearby Nebraska town there was a good summary of this credo. A Norwegian orphan named Harold Warp had made a fortune in plastics in Chicago and used his money to build a pioneer village, including the original stone land office where in 1876 his father bought his homestead. Behind the pioneer village are warehouses packed with Americana, from antique tractors and cars to thousands of styles of salt and pepper shakers. In the middle of the pioneer village is a plaque that reads:

The cowards never started
The weak died on the way
Only the strong survived
They were the pioneers

There is a lot of historical truth to this, but it is a pretty poor philosophy on which to build a complex technological society. If the frontier myth embodies our noblest promises, it also contains values that can result only in an immature and neurotic and heartless society. At its worst, the frontier myth rests upon genocide. It sanctions greed, violence, destruction of our land and wildlife, and disregard for one another.

But at least I was ready to accept the Pony Express station and its Swedish flag, accept them as symbols that really did fit together. Only together could they symbolize my ancestors leaving Gothenburg for America.

It was time for me to leave Gothenburg. It was almost sunset, the archetypal time to head west, over the rolling prairies, into the golden mountains, into the endless horizon. But once again I had blown it. Once again I was out of sync with the myth of the West. I was heading east.

But as I passed the Pony Express station, my mythological imagination did not fail me. I saw that someone was right on time to ride off into the sunset. Someone in a cowboy hat was emerging from the Pony Express station with his mail pouch full of urgent messages. He was, of course, Febold Feboldson. He tossed his mail pouch over his horse and secured it. The horse could not be any ordinary horse. It was, of course, a Dala horse, bright red, painted with floral designs, made from redwood trees, huge and strong enough to carry Febold Feboldson. Febold placed his mighty foot in the stirrup and swung into the saddle. The Dala horse neighed proudly. Febold pointed westward and, with a great pounding of hooves and stirring of dust, off they rode, into the sunset, into the rolling prairie, into the golden mountains, into the endless horizon, ever westward.

I t *was* a good day for listening.

Burntside Lake was beautifully calm, not just on its surface but also in its quiet. Even two weeks ago the lake would have been busy with boats, filling both the water and the air with waves. Though Burntside Lake was on the edge of one of America's great wildernesses, the Boundary Waters in northeastern Minnesota, it was also close enough to Duluth and Minneapolis that there were many summer homes and cottages alongside it. But now it was late October, and the city folks had closed up their lake homes for the winter. Today I wouldn't see a single boat on the lake or even at dock.

The mirrorlike calm of the lake was perfect for reflection. With every stroke of my kayak paddle I saw the blade in duplicate, once in the air and again in the water, moving toward one another until they merged and then separated again. I also saw my kayak and myself reflected in the water. It was a perfect invitation for reflection of the mental kind, especially about how we humans meshed with nature or separated ourselves from it. The lake had been the site of a great deal of reflection on this subject, for it was the site of Listening Point, a granite peninsula on which Sigurd Olson had his cabin. My goal for the day was to visit his cabin. Olson had a house in the town of Ely not far away, but it was to Listening Point that he came to do much of his nature writing and to rest from his nationwide campaigning for conservation. Through both his writing and his public activism, Olson was one of America's foremost environmentalists at a time when environmental problems were reaching the crisis point, yet the environmental way of thinking remained outside the mainstream.

The 1960s was the turning point for American environmentalism. At the start of the decade, nature lovers were still regarded as eccentrics. It was one thing for Teddy Roosevelt to advocate wilderness as a school for pioneer virtues where boys could learn the shooting and riding skills that might still come in handy in U.S. foreign policy. It was something else to advocate wilderness for its own sake. Even when a scientist like Rachel Carson published *Silent Spring* in 1962, she was savagely attacked as a hysterical crackpot. Yet by 1970 politicians were scrambling to enlist as environmentalists.

This triumph of American environmentalism was presided over by a trio of Scandinavian Americans: Sigurd Olson, Wallace Stegner, and Roger Tory Peterson. There were other important environmentalists in the 1960s, yet I think it's fair to say that none of them had established the rapport with the public that Olson, Stegner, and Peterson did. David Brower, for instance, was much less recognizable as a person than as his public mask, the Sierra Club. Olson, Stegner, and Peterson won wide influence because they were writers. Each reached a different public. Olson reached outdoor adventure lovers, who wanted to hear about canoeing and camping trips and wildlife encounters. Stegner reached the literary crowd, who were ready to analyze the values of American society. Peterson reached suburbia, where he was the Trojan horse of environmentalism, or perhaps I should say the Trojan bird, his field guides offering housewives a bit of entertainment out their backyard windows yet turning them into city council crusaders. The three writers then became the public voices of key environmental organizations, Olson for the Wilderness Society, Stegner for the Sierra Club, and Peterson for the Audubon Society. I would like to suggest that not only did Scandinavian Americans play a crucial role in the breakthrough of American environmentalism but that they were inspired by a deep Scandinavian cultural tradition of love and humility toward nature.

Humility toward nature is not an attitude that has come naturally for Americans. We have seen nature as an economic resource and seen ourselves as the appointed conquerors of nature. Yet for Scandinavians, humility comes with the territory. It's difficult to imagine oneself to be the master of nature when one spends half the year buried by winter, when one's fishing boat is regularly tossed by North Sea storms, when one lives on a thin strip of farmland beneath a fjord cliff, or next to a smoking Icelandic volcano. You could well be master of an axe or a miner's pick, but there remains plenty of reminders that a person is a small thing beside a forest or a mountain.

That humility toward nature is deeply rooted in Scandinavian history and psychology is evident in the cosmology of the Viking sagas. I have already pointed out that the sagas were more preoccupied with nature than the national epics of other peoples. Yet the quality of nature in the sagas is different too. In the Judeo-Christian cosmology, God creates nature as a mere stage for the human drama and later discards it when it has served his purposes. In the sagas, nature is the predominant power to which are subordinate not just humans but the gods themselves. The gods emerge out of natural forces and will later be consumed by them. Right from the start the world is doomed to be destroyed by nature, as personified by the giants. All of the gods and all of the Viking heroes from Valhalla will do battle against the giants, but they have known all along that they will lose. There are other mythologies with apocalyptic visions, but it is quite extraordinary to kill off all of your gods and to burn down your heaven. The sagas are also unusual in the degree to which they see the universe as unstable, constantly threatened by chaos, and see humans as vulnerable. In the saga world, a human claim of mastery over nature would be an act of insanity or blasphemy. Though the Scandinavian people converted to Christianity, Saint Olav seems to have neglected to convert Scandinavian nature, for it continues behaving just as it did in saga days and having some of the same psychological effect.

Yet humility is only part of the Scandinavian attitude toward nature. In spite of nature's burdens or perhaps I should say *because* of nature's burdens, Scandinavians also feel a strong love for nature. When green fields and sunny days are not taken for granted, they are appreciated that much more. Spring arrives like a liberation from prison, the prison of houses and coats and darkness, and people flock to the parks, the seashore, the forests, the mountain trails. Since pagan days Scandinavians have celebrated spring and Midsummer Day more festively than most peoples. Old pagan rituals like the Maypole still survive. And perhaps in a diluted, merely emotional way, the pagan sense of identification with nature survives too.

This identification with nature is most literal in the Scandinavian custom of naming people after natural forces. In England you name yourself after your profession, such as Smith or Miller, thus publicly revealing your social class. In Scandinavia it's a strong tradition to name yourself after rivers or mountains or trees. The name Nordstrom, for instance, means "north stream." The name Lindbergh means "linden tree on a mountain." My own name, Lago, is Latin for "lake," my ancestors having lived on Sweden's second largest lake.

Identifying oneself with nature is an ancient religious impulse. Psychologists who have tried to define the psychology of religious belief have described it as an identification with the mysterious source of our lives, which requires both dependency and gratitude, fear and joy. Since Scandinavian nature imposes a greater dependency, perhaps it also elicits a greater gratitude when it upholds our lives. The pagan Scandinavians filled the natural world with spirits, such as trolls, that represented both threats and gifts. More modern Scandinavians have filled culture with a similar dichotomy of spirit. On the one hand, a Kierkegaard, a Bergman, a Munch, or even a Hamlet sees life as terrifyingly tenuous, just like in the sagas. Yet at the same time, Scandinavian poets, artists, and musicians have devoted much of their time to celebrating nature.

This unique Scandinavian experience of nature has set Scandinavians apart from the view of nature that came to dominate European culture under the romantic movement. The romantics, led by city intellectuals, tried to answer the scientific view of nature by seeing nature as a visible gospel, a manifestation of divinity, and they attributed to nature the most important attribute of the Christian God: perfection. A perfect nature originally included moral order, social harmony, and personal happiness. Everything that was wrong with civilization had occurred because humans had gotten away from nature. Human cruelty, greed, power seeking, poverty, fighting, and spiritual malaise were all products of human society. If only we could get back into harmony with nature, human life would be harmonious again.

One of the more curious developments of romanticism was how, in its search for noble savages who proved the superiority of the natural life over city life, it decided that the Vikings fit the role. The romantics rediscovered the Viking sagas and hailed them as pure poetry inspired by nature, far more vigorous and sublime than the polite and trite poetry of civilization. The romantics didn't seem to notice that nature in the sagas was hardly what they had in mind.

Scandinavian intellectuals watched with puzzlement as young artistic Europeans started worshiping the Vikings. Many Scandinavians found the whole thing ludicrous. Yet when the Napoleonic era struck some hard blows against Scandinavian identity, the Scandinavians finally decided to join in the Viking worship, which served national pride. Viking worship has continued going in and out of style in Scandinavia, with intellectuals sometimes joining in and sometimes denouncing the whole idea as an embarrassing joke. Yet Scandinavian intellectuals were more receptive to the artistic developments of romanticism, and they adopted romantic styles in painting, music, and poetry, often to express a love of nature. The focus on nature was one thing about romanticism that resonated with Scandinavians. Yet I doubt that many Scandinavians took to heart the romantic ideology that nature is perfect and benevolent. It's difficult to take this idea seriously when your daily experience tells you that nature is chaotic and often brutal. Romanticism has not prevented the saga's vision of human insignificance and fear before the universe from being expressed anew in Munch's scream or Bergman's darkly brooding modern Hamlets.

The concomitant plank of romantic ideology, that human society is inherently evil, is also alien to Scandinavians. For a people who are outmatched by nature, the human community is absolutely essential for survival, both physical and emotional. The Swiss psychologist Carl Jung theorized that attitudes toward human society are different when a society is in an overpowering environment. It sets a limit to human arrogance, not just toward nature but within society itself. The social imperative is for cooperation, for the day will come when neighbors who may not even like one another will need one another, perhaps just to do the larger tasks of farm life, perhaps in an emergency, or perhaps just for company against the depressing and isolating winter. Jung's theory is on display in Scandinavian society. For instance, much of Scandinavian child-rearing practices and social behavior can be interpreted as attempts to minimize social conflict and maximize cooperation and interpersonal respect. These old social values have led readily to the modern welfare state. Polls of national attitudes toward government have put Scandinavia at the top in seeing government as a positive thing, and, accordingly, surveys of corruption in government and business have placed Scandinavians at the bottom. Scandinavians have tried to offer their sense of human respect and community to the rest of the world by playing the role of international conciliator, a role best symbolized by the Nobel Peace Prize.

The influence of ideas on history is a problematic subject, but I'm going to venture to say that the foreignness to Scandinavians of the romantic ideology of nature and society has had important consequences. It was a German intellectual sitting in a London library who dreamed up a political movement to implement the romantic ideology. It was Russian and French and Asian intellectuals who became enthralled with the idea of curing humans of all corruption by returning them to a natural society. In Scandinavia, Marxism was relatively ignored.

I'll also suggest that the contrast between the romantic and the Scandinavian visions of nature and society has had consequences in the American environmental movement. American intellectuals have long taken their cues from London and Paris, and thus our thinking about nature has been heavily influenced by romanticism. Since American environmentalism has often spoken in the language of romanticism, a language foreign to the American mainstream, it long remained a hopeless outcast. That environmentalism finally triumphed under the leadership of Scandinavians is not entirely a coincidence. Wallace Stegner in particular waged a long battle against the influence of romanticism in American environmentalism, and he offered an alternative vision of nature and society, a rather Scandinavian vision, one that strongly honored the importance of human society. This was a language Americans were more ready to hear.

I'll come back to Stegner in a moment. It's time to find Listening Point.

I wasn't sure exactly where Listening Point was, for I had received only a vague description in Ely. But I thought I had come the right distance, and the spit of granite sticking out into the lake in front of me looked like the description in Olson's book *Listening Point*. At first I didn't see any cabin, for it was well hidden amidst the trees and huge granite boulders. Then I spotted it. I paddled up as close as the shoreline allowed. The cabin too looked like its description, an old Scandinavian pioneer log cabin. Olson had moved it here and rebuilt it after searching all over the area for just the right cabin. It seemed to be meaningful to Olson that it was a Scandinavian cabin.

I decided to wait until the end of my day on the lake to get out and look at the cabin. In Ely I had been told that the cabin was privately owned and not open to the public, but I decided that if no one was around, I would take a look. Now, to Americans this might be called trespassing, but you have to understand that this was a matter between two Swedes, and for Swedes it's not a question of trespassing, it's a matter of *Allemansrätten*, or "all man's right." This Swedish law, dating at least back to the Middle Ages, guarantees free passage or camping on private land. The root idea is that private property rights are not as important as public access to nature. Of course, this law assumes that passers will show a high degree of responsibility toward both the land and the privacy of the landowner. They are expected to ask permission to camp or pick berries, to camp out of sight of the house, and not to leave trash. Such a law would never work in a society where people don't respect the land or one another.

I could bring up many other examples of how Scandinavian respect for nature has shown up in law and public policy. For instance, Sweden was the first European nation to establish a national park system and has been the world pioneer in sustainable forestry. Denmark is leading the world in wind energy technology. And just so I won't be accused of romanticizing the Scandinavians, I could also bring up their mistakes, such as Sweden's major commitment to nuclear power. But back to Burntside Lake.

It occurred to me that Olson's cabin could serve as a good symbol of the difference between the Scandinavian and romantic visions of nature and society. You just had to compare it to that other famous cabin at Walden Pond.

Henry David Thoreau was the classic romantic, rejecting a corrupting society for a life close to nature. For him nature was a spiritual landscape, offering endless lessons in divine wisdom, moral living, and personal happiness. He insisted that the material sacrifices of living a simple life were better than the spiritual sacrifices of a life pursuing material success and social status. It is revealing that Thoreau became the patron saint of environmentalism, for he barely saw nature as ecosystem, and he had little to say about protecting nature from development. It was his rejection of American social values that made him a hero. Rejecting society has sometimes been the primary business of American environmentalists, and appreciating nature has been secondary.

Sigurd Olson's Scandinavian cabin was a lot farther out in the wilderness than was Thoreau's cabin. You would never guess from reading *Walden*, but Thoreau had plenty of neighbors in a highly civilized town, and he went home to his mother's house every day for lunch. Yet Sigurd Olson never put on any pretense of rejecting society. He did share Thoreau's belief that nature was a place for spiritual revelation, and he preached that nature was an essential balance for city life. Yet it was no secret that Olson's main house was in town, where he was dean of Ely Community College. Even his excursions into the wilderness were usually social, his canoeing trips bonding the participants not just to nature but to one another. The challenges of getting a canoe party through a rugged wilderness only emphasized the importance of human cooperation. This was not a quality Thoreau tested much while sitting alone beside Walden Pond most of the day. For Olson, human society was not inherently evil, although it could do evil when it imagined itself to be the only reality and violated nature. His goal was to find the right balance between nature and society.

Actually, Thoreau too was inspired by Scandinavia, but in a most peculiar way. Thoreau convinced himself that he was a Scandinavian.

In Thoreau's day the center of the Boston literary world was Henry Wadsworth Longfellow, who became a great student of Scandinavian literature, translated a lot of it, and spent a lot of time in Scandinavia. Longfellow's enthusiasm for Scandinavia influenced many of his Boston contemporaries, including Emerson, and no one seemed more inspired by it than Thoreau. As a student at Harvard, Thoreau attended Longfellow's lectures on Nordic literature. As Thoreau read the Viking sagas, he found a people who identified with nature as strongly as he did. It did not escape Thoreau's attention that the saga god most associated with nature was named Thor and that many saga characters were named Thorer. Even better, Leif Eriksson's brother, who accompanied him to America, was named Thorvald. Thoreau began to toy with these similarities to his own name, and it developed into something well beyond a playful fantasy.

It wasn't just the sagas that tempted Thoreau. The naturalist in him was a great admirer of the Swedish botanist Carolus Linnaeus and of Linnaeus's disciple, Peter Kalm, who traveled to America to study its natural history. The mystic in Thoreau was intrigued by the Swedish seer Emanuel Swedenborg. Thoreau found many things to admire about Scandinavia, such as the custom of taking surnames from nature. "Such a custom suggests," he wrote in his journals, "if it does not argue, an unabated vigor in the race, relating it to those primitive times when men did, indeed, acquire a name, as memorable and distinct as their characters."[1] Pointedly for someone whose name was French, Thoreau contrasted French feudalism with the Scandinavian history of free landowners, and he dismissed the French: "They are a nation of peasants."[2] Thoreau sprinkled his writings with references to the Northmen and Norse mythology. In *Walden*, for instance, he notes of spring: "Thaw with his gentle persuasion is more powerful than Thor with his hammer."[3]

In the privacy of his journals, Thoreau's identification with Scandinavia turned into the idea that he must be a descendant of the Vikings. He made extensive notes on the sagas, especially the twenty characters named Thorer, assessing his affinities with them and repeatedly declaring that he was a descendant of one or another Thorer. "Perhaps I am descended from that Northman named 'Thorer the Dog-footed,'" who was a powerful leader.[4] But Thoreau was more attracted to Thorer the Silent, a skald to King Olav II who matched his own poetic spirit. Thoreau explained away his French name by asserting that he was descended from the Vikings who had conquered Normandy and later England. He constructed a genealogy in which "it seems that from one branch of the family were descended the Kings of England, and from the other branch myself."[5] Thoreau was captivated by the idea that the Viking's Vinland was in fact Cape Cod. He filled pages with speculation about it, asserting that Thorvald Eriksson was the first European to see Cape Cod. On his own visit to Cape Cod, Thoreau saw for himself a mirage recorded in the sagas in which a whale carcass on a beach appeared to be a bleached log.

> Professor Rafn, of Copenhagen, thinks that the mirage which I noticed . . . had something to do with the name "Furdustrandas," i.e. Wonder Strands, given as I have said, in the old Icelandic account of Thorfinn's expedition to Vinland in the year 1007, to a part of the coast on which he landed. But these sands are more remarkable for their length than for their mirage, which is common to all deserts, and the reason for the name which the Northmen themselves give—"because it took a long time to sail by them"—

is sufficient and applicable to these shores. However, if you should sail all the way from Greenland to Buzzard's Bay along the coast, you would get sight of a good many beaches. But whether Thor-finn saw the mirage here or not, Thor-eau, one of the same family, did; and perchance it was because Leif the Lucky had in a previous voyage, taken Thor-er and his people off the rock in the middle of the sea, that Thor-eau was born to see it.[6]

"Thor-eau" was smitten by the romantic's vision of the Vikings as noble savages, yet however much he romanticized the Vikings, his yearning to be a Scandinavian was born from a clear recognition that they were a people who shared his own immersion in nature.

I'm going to leave Listening Point for the moment and return to discussing Sigurd Olson when I return at the end of my day exploring Burntside Lake. There is an issue that needs to be explored too before I can plausibly assert that Olson was acting out of Scandinavian values. He was, after all, the son of immigrants and grew up a long way from Sweden. It may be an obvious persistence of Old World habits when it's a case of a New York Jew knowing Hebrew or a Chicago Italian running a popular spaghetti restaurant, but when it comes to ideas and values, claiming such a persistence becomes more problematic. It will be easier to consider this issue through the case of Wallace Stegner, for he was an intensely autobiographical writer who carefully studied the origins of social values both within American history and within his personal history. Stegner was also a serious student of Scandinavian society, and he spent years considering whether his alienation from American society derived from his being a Scandinavian.

In the spring of 1954 Wallace Stegner arrived in Denmark for a six-month-long exploration of his Scandinavian roots, including a trip to Norway's Hardanger Fjord, where his ancestors had built a hotel, still owned by cousins. The novel he wrote about his Scandinavian visit, *The Spectator Bird*, would win the National Book Award. But Stegner didn't come to Scandinavia to write a novel. He came to write a sociological study contrasting the values of Scandinavia and frontier America. He was convinced that he would find significant differences in two values: responsibility to community, and respect for the land. In both areas, he expected that Scandinavia had much to teach America. He wanted to find a Scandinavian village he could compare to his boyhood town in the West. Though Stegner was born in Iowa, his father had moved him to a Canadian farm touching the Montana border.

Stegner chose Denmark instead of his own Norway because Denmark had an especially strong cooperative movement in agriculture and retailing. From America Stegner had studied the Scandinavian cooperative movement and liked its values. When he arrived in Copenhagen, the daughter of Niels Bohr helped him find a place to live and introduced him to prominent Danes. He arrived at the home of Karen Blixen (Isak Dinesen) just as she had dug up a Viking rune stone in her garden. After making inquiries, Stegner selected a Danish village for his study, but after spending two weeks there he realized that his project was unworkable. For one thing, he didn't speak Danish. For another, he wasn't a sociologist. But the most important reason is evident enough in *The Spectator Bird*: he realized that his personal needs for identity had tempted him into overidealizing Scandinavia. More than once he chided himself for expecting too much: "The cultural vitamin deficiency is not appeased by nibbling the clay and plaster of the old home. The cultural amputee is still trying to scratch the itch in the missing limb."[7] "I like the Scandinavians as much as anybody, and once went hunting my identity among them, but they didn't invent more than their share, and they are no monsters of goodness. Even now, when they have given up Viking raids and become the world's umpires and ombudsmen, they consort with evil like other folks, and confuse it with good like other folks. I didn't find what I was looking for in Denmark."[8] Stegner was looking for a bit too much perfection and a bit more belonging than an American could really find in a foreign land.

Stegner's project and high hopes originated in the schism of his youth. He identified strongly with his Norwegian mother, a gentle, caring woman who encouraged his love of learning. By contrast, Stegner blamed his childhood miseries on the American frontier values of his father, whose get-rich-quick schemes inflicted on his family many dislocations, both physical and emotional, ending with his suicide. Looking back with the perception of a novelist, Stegner would see his father as a tragic figure, the perfect man for a frontier that had already vanished, robotically trying to act out a national mythology that no longer worked. But in Wallace's youth, one cure for his rootlessness was to identify with Norway. Stegner's biographer, Jackson Benson, observed:

> Wanting to have a past to which he could be committed and having some desire, even as a child, for a sense of tribal continuity, he found himself

forced to turn to Norway, from which his maternal grandfather and grand-mother had emigrated. All throughout his childhood, he signed his books and most personal documents with the Norwegian name, Hardanger, that his grandfather had given up in coming to America. "It seems to me now an absurdity that I should have felt it necessary to go as far as the Hardanger Fjord for a sense of belonging," he wrote many years later.[9]

Stegner didn't stop admiring Scandinavia, but he did realize that he couldn't belong to a society thousands of miles away and that he had to find his identity on American soil.

Stegner's whole career as a writer of both fiction and nonfiction would focus on assessing the cost to a people of not knowing how to belong, either to the land or to one another. He repeatedly took aim at the myth of rugged individualism, the civic faith that national great-ness and personal happiness would arise through individuals pursuing their own success without regard for their community or the land. When America was a young frontier nation this civic faith may have been adaptive, and the vast wilderness may have been able to with-stand it, but when the frontier was gone, our national mythology be-came dysfunctional, destructive of families, society, and nature. While other novelists had explored the dysfunctions of the American Dream, Stegner was the first to concentrate on how the American Dream was malfunctioning in our relationship with the land. Stegner repeatedly advocated the values of respectfulness between individuals, coopera-tion in society, and conservation of nature. He might now be hesitant to admit it, but he was essentially urging America to be more like his Scandinavian ideal.

Stegner's sociological project in Denmark wasn't the first time he had caught himself idealizing something Scandinavian. A few years previously he had set out to write a novel about the Swedish-born hero of the American labor movement, Joseph Hillström, better known as Joe Hill. Joe Hill was an organizer for the IWW, the most radical of un-ions, and he was trying to organize Utah miners when he was arrested for killing a shopkeeper during a robbery. Labor sympathizers nation-wide protested that Hill had been framed, and indeed the legal pro-ceedings were so irregular that when he was convicted and sentenced to death even President Wilson appealed for clemency. When Hill was executed, he became a worldwide martyr. Massive memorial rallies were held in many nations, and Hill's ashes were divided, like medieval relics, among unions in every U.S. state. Stegner, who was fond of singing "The Ballad of Joe Hill" at parties, intended his novel as a study of a cruel, dysfunctional society. But as he researched it, interviewing people who had known Hill, Stegner was led to conclude that Hill was a cruel, dysfunctional man who was indeed guilty of a brutal murder. He ended up portraying Hill as just another example of rugged individualism leading to destruction and of sociopathic western outlaws being turned into heroes. While Stegner's books were routinely panned by conservatives for his debunking of American mythology, his Joe Hill novel was also denounced by liberals. Stegner had violated not only a liberal hero but the inclination of liberalism to see only innocent victims and a guilty society. Stegner believed in human respect, and he had no use for any ideology that cheapened this virtue.

Stegner started his teaching career at the Swedish Augustana College in Illinois, and he then became director of the creative writing program at Stanford, where he had a huge influence on several generations of writers. His own reputation as a novelist was secured in 1943 with *The Big Rock Candy Mountain*. Stegner said it was inspired by the Norwegian Knut Hamsun's peasant novel, *Growth of the Soil*. As a writing student at the University of Iowa, Stegner had two Scandinavian professors who prescribed a lot of Scandinavian fiction, and this "revived the latent Scandinavian in me. . . . I thought if an American could write a *Growth of the Soil*, I could."[10]

The title of Stegner's autobiographical novel refers to the fortune always awaiting over the next western horizon, the pursuit of which ruins a family. The fictional father is loyal to a frontier ethos that no longer functions in a postfrontier society, and he ends up as a bootlegger and a suicide. Stegner's real father too was a bootlegger, constantly moving his family from house to house to stay ahead of the law.

Stegner's alienation from the myth of rugged individualism was furthered by his spending his teenage years in Salt Lake City. While Stegner had no sympathy for Mormon doctrine or authoritarianism, he did come to admire the Mormons' emphasis on community instead of individualism. For the Mormons, pioneering was a community action with the goal not of striking it rich for lone heroes but of benefiting the community. Stegner was to write two histories of the Mormon pioneers, and he contended that one largely unacknowledged reason for their persecution was their violation of national mythology in favor of community values.

What set Stegner apart from other social critics was that his concept of community didn't stop at the city limits. Stegner believed that people had to identify not just with other people but with the land. Living apart from nature was just as unnatural as being a recluse from society. It was natural to feel an affinity with forests and wildlife, rivers and mountains. Stegner constantly repeated his basic message that for humans to be healthy, they had to belong to a community, and for a community to be healthy, it had to belong to the land.

What set Stegner apart from other conservationists was his sociological diagnosis of the origins of the problem. Stegner had a sharp focus on how Americans' unique history shaped our attitudes toward nature. This historical perspective may have been Stegner's most important contribution to the conservation movement. His landmark study of American attitudes toward the land was the book *Beyond the Hundredth Meridian*, published in 1954, the same year he headed for Scandinavia to find a better example of attitudes toward the land.

In *Beyond the Hundredth Meridian* Stegner examined our national attitudes to the land through the life of John Wesley Powell, who experienced both sides of our frontier mythology, becoming both a hero and a villain in it. When Powell led the first expedition down the Colorado River, he became a national hero. Yet as a public scientist, Powell found himself opposing the enormous power of the frontier myth. Having thoroughly explored the mountain West, Powell understood that the settlement practices that worked in the Midwest were hopeless in the low-rainfall, poor-soil West. Yet settlers continued flocking west of the hundredth meridian and meeting grueling defeat. Not only did national policy encourage them, but scientists more loyal to national mythology than to meteorology encouraged the belief that "rain follows the plow," that previously dry lands would suddenly bloom if only pioneers planted them. Powell opposed this folklore not just as a scientist but with a river runner's conviction that water obeys laws of its own and that humans have to obey them too or die. Powell's campaign to teach Americans to obey the limits of their land and water was a pioneering event of American environmentalism. Yet even a frontier hero couldn't overcome the power of frontier mythology, and it would take hundreds of thousands of grim homesteading failures to teach

Americans to obey the limits of their land and of their faith in national destiny. As a child of the High Plains, Stegner had personally known both the land and the people wrecked by this faith.

Stegner also made a large impact for conservation through a 1963 best-seller he helped ghostwrite for Secretary of the Interior Stewart Udall, *The Quiet Crisis*. Stegner's dozens of essays provided some of the rallying phrases of the environmental movement such as "the geography of hope."

The 1960s was a time of frustration for conservationists, for while conservation organizations were growing and winning battles on some specific policy decisions, the environmental way of thinking still remained alien to American society. It had been a century since Thoreau and later Muir proclaimed nature to be a divine testament, but for most Americans, who found their God in the Bible, the romantic vision remained unpersuasive. Next it was the scientists' turn to make the case. Aldo Leopold taught the general idea of ecology, and Rachel Carson made the more specific point that even if we didn't care about the mystical oneness of humans and nature, we couldn't escape from the biochemical oneness of humans and nature. Yet by Carson's death in 1964, even the scientific case hadn't tipped the scales. I think that what was lacking, what was the next essential phase of environmentalism, was a social vision, a sense of how nature and society should fit together. Millions of Americans read Rachel Carson but were left clueless about how to combine ecological realities and suburban realities. The romantic answer of rejecting society wasn't very helpful. It was at this moment that environmentalism found leaders who combined a strong respect for human society and a strong respect for nature.

In the 1960s Stegner watched a surprising development in his Stanford classroom. The children of affluent America, who should have been loyalists to the American Dream, were instead very angry at America. They were angry because America hadn't offered them sufficient spiritual, community, or personal values. This cultural anger started drawing young people to everything that seemed to oppose American society, whether the civil rights movement, Third World revolutionaries, bohemian lifestyles, or environmentalism. The 1960s counterculture was captivated by the romantic vision of nature, seeing nature as the cure for America's social ills, although this cure could take various forms, whether Native American spirituality, back-to-the-land communes, the Marxist version of communes, or just backpacking with a copy of Thoreau or Kerouac.

In his classroom by day and grading papers at night, Stegner was constantly confronted by the romantic vision of nature and society. Some of his students would soon become leading spokespersons for this vision, such as Edward Abbey and Ken Kesey. Stegner decided that this romanticism was a dangerous enemy of environmentalism, leading it astray and dooming it to defeat, and he set out to fight back. In his classroom, Stegner conducted a long running battle with Ken Kesey, who at the time was starting his influential affair with LSD and writing *One Flew over the Cuckoo's Nest*, a typical statement of society-as-sickness for which the cure is anarchy. Edward Abbey too was a self-proclaimed anarchist for whom nature often seemed to be a mere symbol of freedom and environmentalism a mere weapon for attacking society.

Stegner carried on his attack in two novels, *All the Little Live Things* in 1967 and *Angle of Repose* in 1971. The latter won the Pulitzer Prize, and in 1998 it was named by the Modern Library as one of the one hundred greatest English-language novels of the twentieth century. *Angle of Repose* takes place in parallel timelines, primarily in the pioneer West but also in the 1960s. Stegner conducts his usual critique of the rugged individualism of the pioneers and simultaneously critiques the youth culture of the 1960s. This might seem a strange combination, but it works because Stegner has decided that the counterculture is just the latest outbreak of a rootlessness at the core of American life. Just like the pioneers, the hippies are discarding history, family, home, and society for their own American Dream of freedom and paradise. Just like the gold rushers, the hippies are obsessed with quick self-gratification, if in less material ways. At least the wagon train pioneers had a sense of destination; the hippie ideal is the open road. As suburban kids, they barely know nature. Instead of feeling humility beside nature, they use it for spiritual self-aggrandizement; instead of feeling the importance of community beside nature, they see nature as freedom.

Countercultural romanticism did infuse a great deal of new energy into environmentalism and helped turn it into a mass movement that won attention in Washington. Yet in many respects, Stegner's fear that romanticism would mislead environmentalism has proved true. The romantic vision of nature and society has continued to thrive in academic formulations, New Age enthusiasms, and ecoterrorist rhetoric, alienating Middle America and providing conservatives with easy targets for ridiculing the whole idea of environmentalism.

Stegner put his talents at the service of the Sierra Club, serving on its board of directors and editing and helping to write the first of an influential series of books combining first-rate photography and writing on wilderness places and issues. This was a time when the Sierra Club was struggling for its own identity, still transforming itself from a California hiking club into the leading national voice of environmentalism, and Stegner left his imprint upon it.

Stegner was politically active out of a sense of duty; his heart was in his writing. But he did practice what he preached about the land. When he wasn't at Stanford, he spent much of his time at a cottage in Vermont. He found in Vermont the sense of community so lacking in California. His Vermont land had been overlogged by earlier settlers, so he and his son planted eight thousand trees. Decades later, when the trees were eighty feet tall, his son cut down some and built a house from them. The trees were Norway pines. It was a fitting symbol of a life and an outlook rooted in Norway. In the last analysis, it remains unclear how much of Stegner's Norwegian identity was inherited from his mother and how much he reconstructed on his own. But it's fair to say that even though his quest in Scandinavia convinced him that he was an American after all, his values weren't entirely a product of America.

I paddled around the lake for several hours, looping around its many granite islands. As I was rounding a curve of one island, I startled a large bird into flight. I glimpsed only the tip of a wing, and I assumed it was a heron. Since herons usually don't waste much energy fleeing a quiet little boat and only fly around the next corner, I continued around a couple of corners, expecting to see it, but I didn't. Then I glanced up. From a high pine branch a bald eagle was watching me. I stared back. It appeared that I had interrupted his lunch. Well, it was time for my lunch too, so I dug mine out of my boat. After a good while staring at me, the eagle flew off to a neighboring island, which appeared to include a nest. When he showed no inclination to entertain me by flying around, I picked up a magazine I had spotted on the sales counter when I rented my boat in Ely. It included an excerpt from a new book about the first man to do a solo boat trip through Grand Canyon, Buzz Holmstrom. I read it in between glances at the bald eagle.

At age twenty-eight, Holmstrom designed and built a unique boat and set off alone on a one-thousand-mile trip down the Colorado River. The next year he repeated this journey and became the first person to run every rapid instead of portaging many. These were not his first bold river adventures or his last. It wasn't just a physical adventure, for Holmstrom's journal reveals the soul of a poet in deep enthrallment with the river and the canyons as well as deep humility before them. Holmstrom is reminiscent of Charles Lindbergh in how he didn't seem to think twice about making such a trip alone and how he was genuinely surprised that other people found it so astonishing. Once again we face the question of whether you can attribute an American's values and achievements to a Scandinavian heritage. It's impossible to prove that Holmstrom was encouraged by a legacy of boat building, navigating rough waters, wilderness fortitude, and a taste for adventure that goes back to the Vikings. Yet it makes his otherwise highly peculiar aptitude seem far more natural. For a river runner, you can't have a more encouraging name than Holmstrom, which in Swedish means "home stream." Yes, perhaps it was all just a coincidence. But add to Holmstrom's case the case of Fletcher Anderson, a Colorado Swede who named his son Leif and whose solo kayak trip through Grand Canyon set a speed record. Add the case of the Swedish Quist family, who own one of the rafting companies in the Grand Canyon. For that matter, add the case of Wallace Stegner's strong identification with the original Grand Canyon boatman, John Wesley Powell. At some point, the circumstantial evidence forms an undeniable pattern. I once asked one of the Quists if it was his Viking spirit that drew him to run the Colorado River. He smiled and replied, "No, it's just my damn stupidity." It's definitely not a case of stupidity.

This discussion is quite relevant to Sigurd Olson. I found that Olson didn't leave the kind of autobiographical trail that Stegner did, and I was left with a lot of circumstantial evidence regarding his Scandinavian inspirations. Take, first of all, Olson's life as a wilderness boatman, which was central to his identity as a person, a writer, and a conservationist. Olson spent years exploring the Boundary Waters and remote canoe routes in Canada. In the summertime he worked as a professional canoe guide and was greatly respected for his abilities. Though his trips weren't as heroic as navigating the Grand Canyon, they were still wilderness treks, far from help and demanding great judgment, skill, and fortitude. His experiences on these treks provided much of the raw material for his writing, and it was to protect his beloved lake country that he became an activist.

Was it just another coincidence that another Swede was drawn to boat trekking in a beautiful wilderness? Consider that Olson's father was from Dalarna, a Swedish province with six thousand lakes and heavy forests, a lot like northern Minnesota. In Dalarna it's not speculation whether Viking boating traditions are still alive. All you need do is observe a wedding ceremony that includes rowing the couple across a lake in a church boat that looks and rows much like a Viking longship, if without dragon heads. If you are in Dalarna on Midsummer Day you will see a lot of church boats bringing hundreds of people to the festivities. A long tradition of boating skills doesn't die out the instant one immigrates to America, especially if one settles in a place that also depends on boats.

Though Olson was born in Chicago, his boyhood memories belong to Wisconsin's Door Peninsula. Today the Door Peninsula is a popular vacation spot, full of resorts and marinas, the Cape Cod of the Great Lakes. In Olson's boyhood the peninsula villages were more concerned with fishing. Olson's father wasn't a fisherman, but Olson grew up surrounded by boats and sailors, many of whom were Scandinavian. Today the Scandinavian influence in Door Peninsula is obvious in the number of lodges and restaurants that boast Scandinavian themes. The town where Olson lived, Sister Bay, is famous for Al Johnson's Swedish Restaurant, a timber building with a turf roof on which goats spend the day munching on the grass. A constant huddle of tourists watches and photographs the goats, and at the start and end of the day the goats are paraded from and to their barn, a changing of the guard that attracts even more tourists.

The Door Peninsula offered Olson an immersion in nature that shaped him for life. It was full of woods, cliffs, creeks, shores, and wildlife. His explorations were encouraged by his nature-loving grandmother. "To her," Olson wrote, "the playing of bridge was a hopeless and criminal waste of time, coffee parties and frittering around with society a deplorable loss of precious hours that could much better have been spent out of doors." She knew "there was something other folks did not understand about the sound and feel of running water, the smell of bursting buds."[11] At the end of a day of tramping and fishing,

Sigurd found a sympathetic listener in her. They spoke in Swedish, for he learned Swedish before English.

Yet one has to look hard in Olson's writings to find any acknowledgment of his Swedish roots as an inspiration. When it came to his canoe treks, he was more likely to acknowledge the French Canadian voyageurs. Olson may have deliberately avoided crediting human culture for determining our attitudes toward nature, for he became devoted to the idea that humans are biologically programmed to live in nature and feel rapport with nature. Olson was inspired by Carl Jung's idea of the collective unconscious, and he developed his own version of it as a justification for conservation, insisting throughout his writings that we have a deeply rooted psychological need for wilderness and that to deny this need is to be sick. In this belief, Olson was a contrast to Wallace Stegner, who emphasized the cultural and historical factors defining our rapport with nature. In his book *Runes of the North*, Olson mentions his Swedish roots only once, and then as vague evidence for his theory of racial memory. In considering his joy at cutting firewood, he suggests it is "a joy that came, I knew, not only from my own experience, but from that of generations of my forebears preparing for the cold and storms of northern Europe."[12] That Olson could suggest that even woodcutting was imprinted in us is a measure of his commitment to a biological way of thinking that not only fit his professional training as a biologist but seemed to him the only satisfactory explanation for his own deep enthrallment with nature.

Nevertheless, that Olson was drawing upon his Scandinavian roots is evident in the idea of runes in the book's title, in his using long quotes from *The Kalevala* at the book's beginning and end, and in the first sentence: "Like the ancient bard in the Finnish epic poem *Kalevala*, I have listened to the rapids of rivers, to the winds of summer and winter, and to the waves of many lakes."[13] When Russia invaded Finland in 1939, Olson showed his true Nordic pride in his journals: "All that is worthwhile now is keeping the Russian hordes from overrunning the beautiful civilizations of the north, Sweden, Finland, and Norway. They are the bulwark of civilization. All other activity, writing . . . of a man's love of the earth and the wilderness, seem[s] foolish when men are dying and women and children are being bombed. The only important thing at all is the maintenance of the kind of civilization that we think is worthwhile."[14] This might seem a surprising statement from a man who usually insisted that maintenance of wilderness was the most important thing, yet for Olson a "worthwhile" civilization included appreciation of wilderness, and by this definition the Scandinavian countries were quite worthwhile.

Olson's belief in the biological roots of our rapport with nature was only one expression of his biological way of thinking. One of his goals as a writer was to incorporate the ecological and evolutionary perspectives of modern biology into the tradition of literary nature writing. In this he was following the cue of Aldo Leopold. When Leopold and Olson came along, literary nature writing was dominated by romanticism, seeing nature in aesthetic terms, as if it was only a painting, or seeing it as a symbol of divinity. Nature had neither depth in time, evolutionary creativity, nor ecological dynamics. Leopold was one of the first biologists to study nature as ecosystem, and Olson nearly became his colleague. When Leopold became America's first professor of game management in 1933, he asked Olson to become his first doctoral student. But Olson was tired of academia and its propensity for seeing nature as mere scientific data; he was yearning to find the nature poet in himself. Though Olson declined to become a professional ecologist, he had already made a landmark study in ecology; his master's thesis was the world's first scientific study of wolves and their relationship with their prey. In his nature writing Olson pursued an ecological vision, not preaching about principles or disasters but quietly showing how nature fit together. Olson's nature was not the romantic's nature. His wolves were not a symbol of a nature that was friendly and cuddly. His wolves were predators struggling for survival in a tough environment. All of his stories took place in a landscape that had been bulldozed by Ice Age glaciers, which destroyed all the life in their path and which were only waiting to come again. In the granite of Listening Point itself Olson saw the tracks of the glaciers.

Nevertheless, Olson's landscape was deeply beautiful, its life amazing. The inhuman ruggedness of the North only made it more of a wonder that such a nature allowed humans to exist at all. In nature's depths we humans could discover the depths in ourselves, which we seldom heard amidst the city's traffic and superficial concerns. Olson remained ready to find God in nature, but his God was a saga god who would not or could not stop the ice from destroying life.

Olson felt contempt for a society that imagined itself to be the master of nature. His whole career as a conservationist was dedicated to teaching people to be humble before nature. He started by waging a fight opposing airplane flights into the Boundary Waters because they shattered the peace for canoeists, terrified the wildlife, and encouraged the building of upscale lodges in pristine areas. He felt that the Boundary Waters weren't for the human power of planes and motorboats but for nature's power, which humans could approach only with the humility of a canoe paddle. Olson started an alliance and a friendship with Minnesota's newly elected Scandinavian senator, Hubert Humphrey, who helped persuade President Truman to sign a ban on aircraft. Years later, Humphrey would introduce the Wilderness Act of 1964, a landmark environmental law that had Olson's fingerprints all over it.

Olson's victory in the Boundary Waters dispute won him national prominence and election as president of the National Parks Association. In the 1950s the national parks were under siege by loggers, miners, dam builders, and an unsympathetic Republican administration. Olson campaigned tirelessly to rally public support for the parks, and he helped win several major battles. As his books became national best-sellers, his stature rose further. In the 1960s he became president of the Wilderness Society. Like Wallace Stegner, Olson was perturbed by the countercultural energy flowing into environmentalism in the 1960s, and he scolded hippies who tried to turn him into a nature guru. Yet when Earth Day in 1970 marked the success of environmentalism, Olson was indeed one of its spiritual fathers.

I spent the afternoon crisscrossing Burntside Lake, investigating its coves and islands. At the houses I passed I never saw a person. This seemed a good omen for my plan to sneak up to Olson's cabin. Finally, I headed back to Listening Point. As I was rounding the point to land at a small beach, I spotted four people sitting there having a picnic. So much for my plan. I said hello and inquired if Listening Point was open to the public and then confessed the reason for my interest. It turned out to be my lucky day. One of the men said he was the caretaker of the cabin. He had come out to close it up for the winter. He would be glad to show me around. His name was Chuck Wick, and he had been Olson's friend and colleague, teaching biology at Ely Community College for a quarter of a century. He had bought Olson's house in town and now lived in it. He was also the head of a foundation that maintained Listening Point and hoped to use it for environmental retreats. The cabin was being kept just as Olson had left it on his death in 1982.

Chuck led me up to the cabin. It had tightly fitting logs. Chuck explained that Olson had expanded the windows to enjoy the lake view on three sides. The original Scandinavian builder had preferred small windows to minimize exposure to winter cold and wind. When Chuck opened the door, the first thing I noticed was an old canoe lodged in the rafters. This was the vehicle of many of the adventures Olson had written about. On the stone fireplace mantle and on the walls were canoe paddles. That these too had been on some of Olson's adventures was evident in the signatures on the paddles, written by the trip participants. One of the paddles was painted with the name "Sig." In his book *Listening Point*, Olson wrote about how he loved to carve his own canoe paddles, how in the grain of the wood he saw the journey of the tree, its wet years and hardships, that was to propel his own journeys.

The cabin wasn't very big, just one room, with a kitchen on one side and two beds on the other. There was a writing table and plenty of books. I glanced at the titles. A lot of natural history, of course. I saw a pair of skis, primitive by today's standards, with a cracked tip. Outside, Olson had built a sauna.

I asked Chuck if he knew anything about Olson's Swedish roots, and he answered that he did indeed. Chuck himself was Swedish, so this was another common element of their friendship. Chuck had been to Sweden many times, stayed in touch with family there, and was trying to set up a student exchange program between Ely and Scandinavian colleges. Chuck recalled the Christmas he had arranged a celebration on Saint Lucia Day, the Swedish tradition when a girl wears a crown of candles and a white dress. Olson was the first one invited, and he was so delighted that he called up his sons, as far away as Alaska, to tell them about it. In 1945 Olson had visited Sweden but not his ancestral home. He didn't seem to have much family feeling for Sweden. When I mentioned that Wallace Stegner's identification with Norway arose through personal sympathy with his mother, Chuck speculated that perhaps Olson's difficult relation with his father had short-circuited any identification with his family past. Later, I wrote to Olson's son Robert, and he offered a different theory as to why Olson wasn't much interested in Sweden as family history. Robert pointed out that his father was second generation, and second-generation Americans typically feel an imperative to hide their Old World ties and be fully accepted as Americans. Yet Robert agreed that his father was very Swedish in other ways: "There is no doubt that he was an avatar of the old Swedish naturalist tradition. The Swedes like his books, and I even have Swedish cousins who think he is more Swedish than American. This passionate love of nature and naturalness is certainly a distinct 'racial' trait, and he had it in spades. . . . He was indeed a throwback or avatar of the old Swedish tradition whether he knew it or not."[15]

In *Listening Point*, Olson admitted to one link with this tradition, saying that his favorite flower was the linnaea, which the Swedish naturalist Linnaeus named for himself because it was his own favorite flower. Olson liked it because it was a shy flower, growing only in the shadows, delicate yet filling the toughest northern wilderness with beauty. It was a perfect symbol of a nature that was simultaneously rugged, beautiful, and requiring protection.

Without recognizing it, I had been looking at another sign of Olson's affinity with Sweden. Above the front window, above his view of the lake, was a textile whose geometric patterns had looked southwestern to me. But Chuck said it was an old Swedish weaving that Olson had bought in Norway. It seemed to mean something to Olson to have his vision of nature framed by an old Swedish design.

I thanked Chuck for opening up the world of Sigurd Olson to me, and I paddled off.

It's harder to trace the Swedish influences on Roger Tory Peterson, for he did little personal writing like Olson or Stegner. Yet it is known that one of Peterson's greatest inspirations as a youth was a Swede named Yan. Yan was the hero of Ernest Thompson Seton's novel *Two Little Savages*, which was subtitled *Being the Adventures of Two Boys Who Lived as Indians, and What They Learned*. Yan loved nature and especially birds, and, like Peterson, he was misunderstood by his father and friends. Yan validated Peterson's own impulses, and *Two Little Savages* became Peterson's bible, read over and over. Peterson was also inspired by the book's two hundred illustrations. In the introduction to his landmark *Field Guide to the Birds*, Peterson credited Yan for inspiring the guide:

Those of us who have read Ernest Thompson Seton's semi-autobiographical story, "Two Little Savages," remember how the young hero, Yan, discovered some mounted ducks in a dusty showcase and how he painstakingly made sketches of their patterns.

This lad had a book which showed him how to tell ducks when they were in hand, but since he only saw the live ducks at a distance, he was usually at a loss for their names. He noticed that all the ducks in the showcase were different—all had blotches or streaks that were their labels or identification tags. He decided that if he could put their labels or "uniforms" down on paper, he would know these same ducks as soon as he saw them at a distance on the water.

Many of us, later on, when the sport of bird-study first revealed its pleasurable possibilities, tried to locate a book—a guide—that would treat *all* birds in the manner that Yan had suggested for the ducks.[16]

Failing to find such a guide, Peterson created his own, and it made him famous.

That Peterson was interested in his Swedish roots is attested by his visit to Sweden at age forty-two. He went to Uppsala, where his grandparents had lived, and searched through a graveyard looking for Petersons. He was touched when he found a gravestone for an Anna Sophia Peterson, the same name as his grandmother, though she had died in America. He was also touched by his visit to the Uppsala home of the great naturalist Carolus Linnaeus, whom Peterson greatly admired. It is fitting that both Linnaeus and Peterson had roots in Uppsala, for Uppsala was the Rome of the Vikings' religion, their main shrine for worshiping nature. In 1976 Sweden's king, Carl Gustav, traveled to Peterson's hometown of Jamestown, New York, to present him with the Linnaeus Gold Medal, the highest award of the Swedish Academy of Sciences.

Roger Tory Peterson was very similar to Linnaeus, and very Swedish, in how he combined a love of nature with a love of order. In the 1700s Linnaeus was hailed as the Newton of biology for developing the classification system for plants and animals. Two other Swedish scientists were so obsessed with measuring things precisely that we use their names for measurements, Anders Celsius, who first described the centigrade thermometer, and Anders Ångström, from whose name was taken the term for the wavelength of light, the angstrom. Peterson's obsession for birds was matched by his attention to order in his field guide. He started by making precise illustrations of birds, and then, as in an anatomy textbook, he listed and pointed red arrows to features that differentiated one bird from another. Then he offered natural history information. Millions of people for whom birds had been merely pretty colors found that through Peterson's guidebook a mere speck of color in the backyard could be transformed into a saga of continent-wide migrations.

Because Peterson's field guides won the trust of millions of people who originally had no environmental inclinations, he may have been environmentalism's most effective ambassador to the general public. Many people found it easier to care about a bird they had seen in their backyard than about a remote wilderness they had never visited or about the general idea of ecology. Peterson campaigned tirelessly for conservation, and not just for birds. Even on bird issues he communicated the idea that birds were part of an ecosystem, requiring habitats and vulnerable to human-made pollutants. Many thousands of people who thought they were only going to hear Peterson lecture on birds left as activists. As environmentalism struggled to gain respect in the 1960s, perhaps no one contributed as much respect as Peterson.

Other Scandinavian Americans have also made major contributions to environmentalism. In his later years, Charles Lindbergh traveled the world crusading for wildlife conservation, and he did more than anyone to make the World Wildlife Fund prominent in America. The Swedish-born Lars-Eric Lindblad founded ecotourism with his ship, the *Lindblad Explorer*. The Norwegian-Minnesotan Robert Bly, in both his poetry and social commentary, insisted on the bond of people to both nature and the human community. A new generation of literary naturalists has been prominent with Scandinavian Americans, most notably David Quammen, Peter Matthiessen, and Richard Nelson.

The breakthrough of environmentalism around 1970 was aided by one more Scandinavian that needs to be mentioned. This is not a person but a camera, the Swedish Hasselblad camera NASA selected for all the Apollo flights to the moon.

On the flight of *Apollo 8*, the first to circumnavigate the moon, astronaut William Anders, who later became U.S. ambassador to Norway, pointed his Swedish camera toward Earth and took the first-ever photo of earthrise, of a crescent Earth rising over the moon. This photo has been given much credit for doing what hundreds of books couldn't, for

Zen-shocking the world into environmental enlightenment. The Swedish camera showed the human race a very Scandinavian perspective on nature. The universe turned out to be a lot like a Scandinavian winter. It was beautiful, yes, but it was also brutally cold, utterly desolate, and depressingly dark, and in it humans were a tiny and very fragile thing, easily destroyed. Humility was the only possible attitude. No perfect universe was going to take care of us. Our survival required recognition that we were dependent on a community, not just a human community but the community of life.

A view of Earth from space provided for the human race what Listening Point had provided for Sigurd Olson. It was a place far away from human society, a place immersed in nature, a place where we could see the relationship between human society and nature in proper perspective. From the Listening Point of *Apollo 8*, the human race finally listened.

To See the Earth as It Truly Is

Through the green of the ponderosa pine forest, I glimpsed another world.

For several miles I had seen only forest. This forest went on for dozens of miles. It could have been a typical forest in Sweden. Indeed, the trail I was following was named for a Swede. In the wintertime, this trail was so buried in snow that few people even reached the trailhead. It was an appropriate place to be named for a Swede. Yet if you were paying attention as you walked the trail in summer, you would notice that this forest lacked the lakes and streams of a Swedish forest. When you reached the end of the trail, it was very obvious you were a long way from Sweden.

I reached the end of the trail and stood looking across miles of empty space to where the ponderosa forest started again. I stood looking a mile down into the Grand Canyon. I stood on Widforss Point, which was named for the same Swede the trail was named for, Gunnar Widforss. On the opposite rim of the canyon, in the ponderosa forest, was a small cemetery, and there, amidst the graves of pioneers and rangers, was the grave of Gunnar Widforss. On his tombstone, lines from Robert Browning attested to the rightness of his being buried amidst nature's beauty.

It is quite an honor to have a trail or an overlook point at one of the world's greatest natural wonders named for you. There are few Grand Canyon trails or points named for people, and almost all of those are named in honor of early explorers and pioneers. Gunnar Widforss came to the canyon decades after the explorers, but he was a pioneer of sorts, a pioneering artist. He was honored at the canyon because many people felt that no other artist had honored the canyon so well. The only other artist to have a Grand Canyon overlook named for him was Thomas Moran, who became famous and rich for his canyon landscapes. Widforss never won much attention in the art world, and he died penniless, but he inspired strong loyalties among those who knew the canyon best. Those who knew Widforss personally were especially loyal, for he had a gentle and generous spirit. But many who knew only the canyon and saw its many inept and false renderings in art recognized in Widforss someone who could do full justice to the canyon and the other southwestern scenes he painted. His paintings were purchased by prominent southwestern families like the Goldwaters as well as by rangers and other canyon residents. Today, after seeing the works of hundreds of artists who have tried to paint the canyon, often imposing their own personalities and art theories upon it, many canyon lovers feel that no one has matched Widforss at letting the canyon speak for itself. One of his biggest admirers is Bruce Aiken, an artist who for thirty years has lived inside the canyon, manning the pump house that supplies water to the rim. Aiken has become famous for his own canyon paintings, and he hails Widforss as his greatest inspiration. A few years ago Aiken was delighted to host Widforss's grand-nephew from Sweden who had never seen the Grand Canyon before and who was touched to find that the name Widforss was still admired there. An unknown Widforss admirer occasionally leaves a paintbrush on the Widforss grave.

It may seem unlikely that someone born in Stockholm should develop the truest vision of the American Southwest, a realm seemingly so different from Scandinavia. Yet Widforss was only one of four Swedish artists who became so enthralled with the American Southwest that they devoted their careers to exploring and painting it. The other three were Carl Oscar Borg, Birger Sandzén, and B. J. O. Nordfeldt. Today all four are greatly respected for their visions of the Southwest, and their works are prized by major museums and collectors. Their lives had much in common. They were all born in the 1870s, came to America as young men, and ended up as American citizens. They painted many of the same scenes. Yet they didn't belong to any common school. I can find only one reference to even two of them ever meeting each other. They lived in different places, painted with very different styles, and focused on different themes. But they shared a passion for nature that is very Swedish, and they shared the feeling that in the Southwest they had come home.

To understand why four Swedes felt such rapport with the Southwest, consider the contrast between the visions of Thomas Moran and Gunnar Widforss. Moran was born in England and was devoted to English romanticism. He was so devoted to the landscape paintings of J. M. W. Turner that he followed Turner's path around Europe, found the exact spot from which Turner had painted a scene, and painted it with the same style and color scheme Turner had used. When Moran later painted the Grand Canyon, he ignored the canyon's own colors and forced upon it the color scheme Turner had used for painting the Italian countryside. Moran also forced onto the canyon many other conventions of romanticism and deleted basic elements such as the geological strata that didn't fit his formula. This was actually the secret of Moran's popularity. The first American tourists to explore the desert Southwest were often disturbed by it. Their sense of natural beauty had been shaped by romanticism, and they defined beauty as a rolling green English countryside with gardens and streams or as sublime alpine peaks. To such eyes, the Southwest was barren, skeletal, ugly, and unnatural. Moran and many other artists felt more loyalty to art than to the land itself, and they pleased a public who wanted to be reassured about the strange Southwest.

When the Swedes discovered the Southwest, they found a landscape they had long been accustomed to. The Southwest might have sand instead of snow, heat instead of cold, canyons instead of fjords, mesas instead of granite islands, and hardy desert plants instead of hardy arctic plants, but in its grandeur, rawness, and inhumanity, the American Southwest was just like Scandinavia. The Swedes weren't bothered by an inhuman scale, by the lack of green, by a nature opposed to human purposes. They felt right at home. The Swedes arrived in the Southwest shortly after the railroad made it easily accessible and the American public began exploring it. The Swedes were among the first artists to make careers out of interpreting the Southwest. They

helped Americans to accept the Southwest on its own terms, as a grandeur that could be both harsh and loved. For Swedes accustomed to
long dark cold winters, it was hard not to love the southwestern light.

It was more than just a Swedish passion for nature that focused the
attention of four Swedish artists on the American Southwest. In 1893,
when Widforss and Borg were the impressionable age of fourteen and
Nordfeldt was fifteen, a Swede published one of the landmark works of
southwestern archaeology. Gustaf Nordenskjöld was the son of a famous Swedish polar explorer, and thus his book got as much attention
in Sweden as it did in America. Nordenskjöld was in Colorado recover-
ing from tuberculosis when he heard about a cowboy searching for lost
cattle who instead stumbled upon lost castles. Nordenskjöld sought out
the cowboy and thus found his way to Mesa Verde. He conducted the
first archaeological excavations of Mesa Verde, and his book made the
world realize that an impressive civilization had thrived in the Southwest. The first white Americans to explore Mesa Verde were looters
seeking artifacts for quick wealth, and, as with the four artists, it took a
Swede to teach Americans how to value their land for the right reasons. Carl Oscar Borg in particular became so fascinated by the Pueblo
tribes that he spent fifteen years living among the Hopi.

Gunnar Widforss first saw the American West on a cross-country
train trip that was supposed to take him to a California port to sail for
Asia. He didn't get past Yosemite. He started painting California
scenes, and his feeling for nature soon got the attention of Stephen
Mather, the first director of the National Park Service, who said, "He is
the only one who can paint the redwoods in watercolor."[1] Widforss felt
that only watercolor could capture the feel of light on rocks and plants,
and to this day he astonishes other artists with just what watercolor
can do. He managed to combine scientific detail with lyrical glow.
Under Mather's patronage, Widforss soon had a one-man show of national park scenes at the National Gallery, whose director declared,
"These are the finest things of their kind that have come out of the
West. He is possibly the greatest watercolorist in America today."[2]

When Widforss discovered the Grand Canyon, he found his home
for the next twelve years. No other landscape so enthralled his spirit
and challenged his art. He roamed all over the rims and packed his art
supplies down the trails in pursuit of all the canyon's secrets. His accu-
racy impressed the park naturalist, yet Widforss insisted he was only

trying to capture the canyon's grandeur. Knowing how much the canyon changed appearance through the day, he would work on a picture for the same hour day after day.

The El Tovar Hotel on the rim sold Widforss's paintings, and in return he got free lodging and meals, even when his paintings weren't selling. In the winter Widforss went to California or southern Arizona, but he always looked forward to returning to the canyon, where he was a beloved member of the park community.

If Widforss got lonely for the sound of the Swedish language, he didn't have to travel far to hear it. Just outside the park boundary was a Swedish town called Apex. The Santa Fe Railroad, whose main line ran from Chicago to Los Angeles, mostly through prairie and desert, needed a source of timber for ties, bridges, and buildings, and it turned to the ponderosa forests of northern Arizona. Discovering that Arizona cowboys knew nothing about cutting timber, the railroad brought in Scandinavians, mostly Swedes, and set up a town for them, including a schoolhouse. A locomotive named August Lindstrom, for the timber company president, roamed back and forth for twenty miles along the park boundary. Today Apex is a ghost town of collapsing foundations, abandoned railroad hardware, rusting stoves and washtubs, and huge piles of tin cans, warped shoes, and broken china. Several times I have picked through the china, looking for a plate brought lovingly all the way from Sweden, but all I saw was "Made in Illinois."

When Widforss was away from the canyon in 1934, a doctor warned him that a heart condition made it unwise for him to live at the seven thousand feet of the canyon rim. Widforss returned to the canyon anyway, and just as he was driving up to the rim, thrilled to see it again, he had a heart attack, crashed his car into a tree, and died.

Widforss wasn't the first Swedish artist to be given free room and meals at the Grand Canyon in exchange for his artwork. In 1916 Carl Oscar Borg came to paint the canyon and met Charles Brant, a Swedish American who was the manager of the El Tovar Hotel. Brant welcomed Borg into the grand wooden Norwegian Arts and Crafts–style hotel. Brant later wrote Borg that his canyon paintings had won extraordinary praise from the visiting Thomas Moran, who was usually scornful of rivals.

At age twenty Carl Oscar Borg literally painted his way to America. He won passage from Sweden to England by painting the boat on the way, and he won passage to America by painting decorations in the captain's quarters. Right from the start, Borg didn't fit in with American values. His Swedish work ethic got him fired from his first job as a house decorator because the labor union decided he was working too hard, making everyone else look bad. He then carved furniture for a company that shipped its products to England just to import them back into America as expensive English antiques.

Borg headed for California and became part of an art community, led by prominent author Charles Lummis, that envisioned the West saving America from material values, offering instead the values of natural beauty, simple living, and Native American spirituality. Borg, who felt that art was "a kind of religion, the worship of beauty in nature,"[3] had found both the right landscape and the right friends to fire his creativity. One of his strongest supporters was Antony Anderson, a Norwegian American and the art critic for the *Los Angeles Times*. Borg's art quickly evolved from stormy seas and Viking ships to desert mountains. Like Widforss, Borg was a realist who turned light into magic. Unlike Widforss, whose paintings seldom included people, Borg was focused on people and how they fit into the land.

Borg won the admiration and patronage of Phoebe Hearst, the heiress and mother of William Randolph Hearst, and she sent Borg on a long tour of Europe and Egypt in the company of another Swedish American, Gustavus Eisen, who was purchasing art and artifacts for her. Eisen was a prominent biologist who helped develop the fruit industry in California. In recognition of Eisen's role in creating Sequoia National Park, a mountain there was named for him. Borg was fascinated by the ruins of Egypt but appalled by the art scene in Paris, where cubism and every other modernism were raging. They had nothing to do with worshiping nature.

The outbreak of World War I forced Borg to return to America. He got an assignment with the U.S. Bureau of Ethnology photographing and etching Native American life in the Southwest. When he arrived at the Hopi mesas, he found the place that would be for him what the Grand Canyon was for Widforss, the center of his world. The Hopis seemed the embodiment of Borg's nature mysticism. They must have sensed a kindred spirit, for they accepted Borg into the Hopi community, initiated him into the snake clan, and allowed him to paint secret ceremonies. As he worked, he was surrounded by curious Hopi children. For the next two decades he worshiped nature by depicting amidst its mesas and canyons the people who knew how to belong there. "Here," he wrote of the desert, "one is much nearer the creator of all. Most people hate it and are afraid of it because it is a hard country and the inhabitants know what hunger and thirst are. . . . Here one is so near the heart of nature, undefiled and pure as it was from the beginning of time."[4] Borg tried to spend several months a year on the Hopi mesas, and he became known as He Who Returns in the Spring.

The rest of the year Borg returned to southern California, but he wasn't happy with the cultural momentum of the 1920s, when Hollywood and Wall Street seemed to be the only gods. For several years Borg worked as a Hollywood set designer, and although he was hailed as a pioneering genius, he quit in disgust at the growing dominance of profit and glitter over art. When the Great Depression hit, life was hard for all artists but especially for nature artists in an art world dominated by the abstract. Seeing the midwestern dust bowl and other wasted landscapes, Borg was disgusted by an America that "has almost ruined this wonderful country which had all they needed, just to make money and be richer than anyone else."[5] He foresaw doom for the Native Americans, because "the white intruder will come nearer every year. . . . The cars will come and hit the old Indians who cannot move out of the way fast enough. Then will come the buyers and sellers of land, as well as of souls. Then there is no speaking about the Great Spirit, but about gold and profits."[6]

In 1938 Borg returned to Sweden to live, declaring that at least he could paint the Laplanders, who were still safely "out of the hands of the merchants."[7] But in 1945 he returned to California. When he died, his ashes were scattered in the Grand Canyon.

Birger Sandzén was the only one of the four Swedes to pursue an academic career, and it insulated him from economic struggle, but since the college where he taught for almost sixty years was in the Kansas prairie, it left him just as isolated as if he was on the Hopi mesas or the Grand Canyon. Like Widforss and Borg, Sandzén said he preferred being shielded from the fads of the art world so he could draw his inspiration from nature. He chose Bethany College in Lindsborg, Kansas, partly because it was the Swedish college farthest west. From childhood Sandzén had been fascinated by the American West, and as soon as he finished art school he emigrated. "A free new country," he hoped.

"It should be heaven for a painter. Out there in the West a painter could develop a style of his own to fit the country."[8]

In Stockholm and Paris Sandzén received a first-rate art education, including lessons from the famous Swedish painter Anders Zorn, yet Sandzén declared that nature was his "Great Teacher." In Paris he did absorb impressionism, and critics would constantly compare his bold, bright, energetic brush strokes to van Gogh, yet Sandzén insisted that he didn't know about van Gogh until long after he had developed a similar style on his own out of a need to do justice to the bold formations and energetic light of the West and to the intensity nature stirred in him.

Sandzén spent his summers roaming the Southwest and the Rockies. Like Widforss and Borg, he made a special trip to Mesa Verde. But unlike Borg, Sandzén felt that to place people or ruins in a landscape painting was to detract from it. Sandzén sometimes felt privileged: "As a sketching ground the Southwest possesses unlimited possibilities . . . abundant material of every conceivable character."[9] And sometimes he felt overwhelmed. He found the Grand Canyon "incomprehensible . . . If one is going to paint the Grand Canyon, one has to be satisfied with only a few beautiful details if one is not to fail. It is absurd to try to grasp the great magnificence of it."[10] He could find splendor enough in a Kansas prairie or a sunflower. He could find intensity enough without bold colors, for his hundreds of prints and lithographs were still full of amazingly energetic forms. One art critic commented, "I wonder if any artist, other than Sandzén, will ever be able to flood a black and white print with as much sunshine as he has."[11]

Critics got a closer look at Sandzén than at Widforss or Borg, for his van Gogh style left him closer to the mainstream. Critics did recognize that his enthralled vision of the West was distinctly Scandinavian, for better or worse. Sandzén himself wrote to his brother: "One thing is quite clear to me: My decisive and distinctive Nordic artistic temperament does not precisely conform with Anglo-Saxons here."[12] Of a New York City show of Sandzén's work in 1922, the *New York Herald* said: "He paints with fiery, tempestuous colors quite unlike any native who has gone west to paint."[13] The *Christian Science Monitor* commented: "Here without mistake is the wild Nordic impulse, transplanted and recharged with the old vigor in the atmosphere of western America . . . [Sandzén] has startled New York like the banners of his ancestral Vikings. If anyone else has had such massive vision of the scenic West, it has remained cloistered, like Sandzén's, until now."[14] The *New York Tribune* complained: "It is the familiar crudity of the Scandinavian school that robs his sincere, sweeping paintings of the beauty that so strong a temperament ought to secure."[15] The *American Magazine of Art* found Swedishness even in his compositional eye: "Sandzén's art is elemental. . . . In the feeling for design, a strong Scandinavian trait as we all know, Mr. Sandzén does not forget form."[16] A Swedish art historian would summarize Sandzén's role: "Sandzén can be said to be the original transplanter of Scandinavian landscape poetry . . . to the rugged scenery of the Rocky Mountains."[17]

Living in a town as Swedish as Lindsborg, where Sandzén was deeply involved in the life of the community, it was easy for him to remain in touch with his Swedishness. For many years the art studio at Bethany College was a Swedish manor house, built as the Swedish pavilion for the 1904 St. Louis World's Fair and transplanted to Lindsborg. On campus today is a gallery built just to display Sandzén's work.

B. J. O. Nordfeldt was less isolated than the other three Swedes, for he was part of the Santa Fe art world in its blossoming years. He was also the most modernist in style. His emigrating parents brought him to Chicago, where he studied at the Art Institute, and he then returned to Europe to paint. In Paris he discovered Cézanne and Gauguin, and he would paint New Mexico through their eyes. Santa Fe was his Tahiti. He settled there in 1919, and for two decades he painted the land and the faces, the villages and the ceremonies of Native Americans and Hispanics. Critics noted that his abstract style didn't hide the deep respect he felt for his subjects. Considering that most American western landscape painting featured cowboys, pioneers, or soldiers heroically taming the land and the enemies of national destiny, Nordfeldt's respectful focus on nonwhites may have owed something to his Swedishness. Nordfeldt's style changed many times, perhaps under the varied influences in Santa Fe. He brought to Santa Fe another Swedish American artist, the Iowa-born Raymond Jonson, who studied with Nordfeldt in Chicago and who for twenty years would carry southwestern landscape painting as far into abstraction as it could go and still be recognizable as real earth. As different in style as Nordfeldt was from the other Swedes, Nordfeldt was very similar in feeling that the ultimate wellspring of life and art was not the human city but nature.

One famous Scandinavian American painter won his fame for depicting not nature but the American conquest of it. Olaf Wieghorst was born in Denmark in 1899 and arrived in America when the frontier was fading into legend. He sought out what remained of the legend, serving in the U.S. cavalry on the Mexican border and as a cowboy in New Mexico. Then he moved to New York City and became a mounted policeman. He painted cowboys, cavalry troops, and stagecoaches and was hailed as the successor to Remington and Russell. He also depicted the frontier by acting in two John Wayne movies.

More famous yet is another Dane, the Idaho-born Gutzon Borglum, who started out painting cowboy scenes and then found his genius as a sculptor of American heroes, culminating in Mount Rushmore. Carl Oscar Borg probably would have been appalled at the thought of carving a sacred Native mountain into a patriotic shrine. I can imagine him scolding those misguided Danes, whose nation was mostly cultivated while Sweden was mostly wilderness, for emphasizing the power of humans instead of the power of nature. As far as I know, none of the four Swedes ever allowed a cowboy into their paintings.

It wasn't just Swedes who felt rapport with the Southwest. On my visit to Helsinki, I became so fascinated with the paintings and murals of Akseli Gallen-Kallela, which are prominently displayed in Helsinki, that I made the trek out to his home and studio on a quiet lakeshore. His home, which included a round tower, was designed by Eliel Saarinen, whose son Eero designed the St. Louis Gateway Arch. After I enjoyed the *Kalevala*-inspired paintings on the ground floor, I climbed the tower stairs and discovered that this tower too was a gateway to the American West. A whole tower room was devoted to Gallen-Kallela's paintings of the Southwest. He had gone to America to install his show in Chicago, continued on to New Mexico, and ended up staying a long time in Taos. Though I was a bit amused to have come all the way to Finland just to see New Mexico landscapes, pueblos, and Native Americans, I really didn't feel any discontinuity between them and the *Kalevala* paintings downstairs, with their vision of a strong nature and the strong people who knew how to belong there. Apparently, Gallen-Kallela himself felt no discontinuity between Scandinavia and the American Southwest.

The Unforgotten Spirit

When *Robert Frost* declared that "the land was ours before we were the land's," he wasn't thinking of the Scandinavians of the Pacific Northwest. They belonged to their land right from the start. In fact, they belonged to their land even before they saw it. Many of them came to the Pacific Northwest because they already knew that they belonged there.

A large majority of the first Scandinavian settlers in the Pacific Northwest had originally tried to settle in the Midwest. By some standards, the Midwest was paradise. For Swedish and Norwegian farmers accustomed to stony soil and narrow fjord terraces, the Midwest's endless, flat, rich, stoneless, treeless soil was unbelievable. Indeed, many Scandinavians couldn't believe that any soil without trees could possibly be fertile. Yet even those who succeeded as farmers were often unhappy with the landscape. For people accustomed to forests, lakes, rivers, seashores, mountains, and fjords, the endless flatness was an unnatural landscape, as disturbing as the unblocked sun and wind that helped drive many settlers mad.

There were many who did not succeed as farmers. In the late 1800s the only remaining midwestern land was in the High Plains beyond the one hundredth meridian, where there wasn't enough rainfall to support farms. Even in better locations, midwestern farmers in the late 1800s were beset by drought, grasshopper plagues, financial panics, and monopoly railroads. It was even harder for settlers who were not originally farmers and were trying to learn basic agricultural skills. These inexperienced farmers included many Scandinavians, especially Norwegians, who back home had been fishermen, sailors, shipbuilders, and lumberjacks. While some of them found that the Great Lakes region offered opportunities to continue their old trades, many more, told that farming was the route to success in America, found themselves following the track of other immigrants to the Great Plains.

Even those Scandinavians who succeeded as farmers were intrigued by rumors that farther west there was a region a lot like home, a place with seashores, forests, mountains, and abundant lakes and rivers. Actually, by 1883 these were no longer mere rumors. This was the year the railroad reached Puget Sound. Until then, the Northwest had remained difficult to reach, and its population and economy remained limited. Between 1880 and 1890 the population of Washington State jumped from 75,000 to 357,000. Much of this growth was due to a publicity campaign conducted by the railroad to attract settlers. The railroad president, James J. Hill of Minneapolis, thought that Scandinavians were especially qualified for the rigors of northern pioneering. He had already hired a lot of Scandinavians to lay the tracks, and he praised them with a statement that often shows up in Swedish American museums and histories: "Give me enough Swedes, and I'll build a railroad right through hell." Actually what he really said was: "Give me enough Swedes and whiskey, and I'll build a railroad right through hell."

To Scandinavians who were floundering as midwestern farmers, the Northwest beckoned. It offered them an alternative to returning home, which many did. In the Northwest they could simultaneously stay in America and return home, return not just to a familiar landscape but to the familiar trades of fishing, sailing, shipbuilding, and lumberjacking. Yet it wasn't just a question of economics. The Northwest called to the souls of those who had grown up with a deep love for the sea and the way a ship carved through the waves, those who had grown up surrounded by forests and had felt naked on the prairie, and those addicted to the shapes and scents of wood being crafted into ships. Even many who were succeeding as midwestern farmers heard the call of home and packed up and headed farther west.

In her book *New Land, New Lives*, a collection of oral histories of Northwest Scandinavians, Janet E. Rasmussen found many who immigrated to America for economic reasons but who needed the consolation of living in a landscape like home. One example is Gustav Simonson, a Norwegian born on an island where sailing and fishing were the only way of life. At age eighteen he and a friend immigrated to Minnesota, but as village kids they were disturbed by a big city like Minneapolis. "All we thought was to get away from the cities and get out to God's country."[1] Yet after a few weeks of working on a farm, they headed for Duluth, the one midwestern place most like a Norwegian fjord, its steep slopes overlooking the tip of Lake Superior. They worked on a road project, but "it was up on a ridge and we could stand and look out over Lake Superior and see the boats coming and going. That made us homesick. So next spring come around, I gonna be on a boat. Probably the hardest thing for us to take was to be removed from the water. That was horrible." Simonson heard that Alaska had lots of fjords and fishing, and he started dreaming of going there. "We had not the slightest idea how big the country was." In a rickety car with no brakes, they headed across Dakota and Montana. When they reached Puget Sound, "I can tell you the first thing I did, I went into a restaurant and ordered a boiled salt mackerel. Salt mackerel in the old country was a delicacy." He was delighted to find so many Norwegians in the area. "You always ran into them and you had an affinity for looking up another Norwegian." Eventually he made it to Alaska, where he skippered a halibut boat. The crews of the halibut fleet in Alaska were 95 percent Norwegian, the skippers 99 percent Norwegian. "I was right at home. That felt good. It felt like I been back in Jerusalem."

In Oregon and Washington too Norwegians dominated the deep sea fishing fleets. No one else had experience at fishing far out on dangerous seas. The non-Scandinavian fishermen preferred the sounds, rivers, and coastlines. Scandinavian sailors also dominated the northwestern cargo fleet to the degree that it was nicknamed "the Scandinavian Navy." Much of the cargo they hauled was timber, which was also an industry filled with Scandinavians. Crosscut saws were nicknamed "Swedish fiddles." Scandinavians not only supplied the manpower for logging, they developed many new tools and ideas for it. The Anderson brothers, who built one of Washington's biggest logging companies, were appalled by the wastage of traditional logging practices, which left a lot of wood to be burned or to rot, and they imported special equipment from Sweden to make fuller use of trees. A lot of timber went into the shipbuilding industry, which was yet another stronghold

of Scandinavians. And for the farmers who had failed in western Dakota, the Northwest offered good land and no shortage of rain.

By the 1910 census, Scandinavians made up 25 percent of the population of Washington State, making them the largest ethnic group. In
contrast to the whole of Scandinavian America, where Swedes outnumbered Norwegians by about four to three, in Washington State the
Norwegians outnumbered the Swedes by about four to three. Oregon
had a smaller yet still substantial proportion of Scandinavians. Increasingly, as word spread back in Scandinavia, Scandinavians were immigrating directly to the Pacific Northwest. When the Alaska gold rush
started in 1892, Alaska became easier to reach and settle, and many
Northwest Scandinavians were drawn to North America's most Norwegian of landscapes. Few of them saw much reason to go off searching
for hidden gold when the seas were swimming with obvious riches.

If you want proof that the Pacific Northwest is the right land for
Scandinavians, you can see it all over the place if only you look with an
anthropologist's eye. In studying cultures around the world, anthropologists have noted patterns in the religious beliefs and symbols of
various peoples. It was the similarities of religious symbolism that
prompted Carl Jung to suggest his idea of the collective unconscious.
Many anthropologists stop short of saying religious symbolism is biologically programmed and attribute similarities in symbols to similarities in lifestyles. The rival explanation for such similarities is the theory of cultural diffusion, which holds that ideas are spread by contact
between cultures. The most dramatic proponent of the theory of cultural diffusion was the Norwegian Thor Heyerdahl, who sailed his reed
boat *Ra* from Egypt to Central America to prove that the pyramids and
sun gods of Central America could have been inspired by contact with
Egypt. While there's no doubt that Thor Heyerdahl knows a lot more
about sailing than the average anthropologist, only a Norwegian would
find the idea of everyone sailing around the oceans and bumping into
one another to be the easiest explanation for cultural similarities. It's
easier to believe that similar environments and lifestyles such as desert
farming inspire similar religious responses such as belief in sun gods,
rain gods, and soil fertility gods.

Just as there are similarities in the religious symbolism of Egypt and
Mexico, there are similarities in the pre-Christian religions of northern
peoples. The coasts of Norway and Alaska, the tundra of Siberia and

Canada, the forests of Oregon and Sweden promoted similar lifestyles and concerns. Fishing, herding, and hunting in a northern climate demanded gods very different from those involved with farming along the Nile. Nowhere is this difference more obvious than in the fact that an animal god that was almost universally evil for agricultural peoples was one of the leading deities for northern peoples.

You can find this god all over the Pacific Northwest, on totem poles, on masks, in art galleries and jewelry cases, on museum walls and T-shirts, in anthropology texts and children's picture books. In the Pacific Northwest it hasn't been long since Raven was worshiped as the creator of the world. Raven was an irresistible character for northern peoples, for he thrived in a climate that defeated most birds, thrived through remarkable intelligence, flexibility, and hardiness. If Raven was a trickster, both as an animal and as a god, untrustworthy and far from wholly benevolent, in this too he was a fitting symbol for the northern climate. Yet Raven was even further from being evil in the way he and his cousin the crow were evil for people who relied on crops, which ravens and crows will gladly devour. For northern peoples, ravens offered little direct competition for food, and thus ravens could serve as companions or models in the game of survival.

There's another reason why white Americans are inclined to see ravens as evil. A thousand years ago, a flock of giant ravens invaded Britain. Actually, the ravens were on the sails of the Viking longships. For the Vikings, the raven was sacred, representing divine wisdom and protection. These were not associations that occurred to British priests when the Vikings were sacking their churches. Things got even worse when the Vikings decided to settle in Britain and brought their religion with them. When Viking paganism started influencing Christian Britons, winning Raven a spot on peasant altars to Mary, the Christian Church fought back in its usual way by demonizing the pagan gods. Raven was depicted as the embodiment of evil and death. This anti-Viking propaganda campaign was so successful that today Britain still has an unusually dark view of ravens and of Vikings too, for that matter. The British view of ravens traveled to America, where it was perpetuated by Poe and Hollywood.

I doubt that many of the Scandinavians who came to the Pacific Northwest and saw raven totem poles knew enough about their own pagan past to recognize the god of their ancestors. But there was no better symbol of the good fit between Scandinavia and the Pacific Northwest. Gods embody a landscape and the lives of the people who live upon it. Raven embodied the spirit of the North. The raven totem poles stood facing the Pacific, remembering when ravens had roamed the North Sea, welcoming the descendants of those bold sailors to another land under Raven's protection. Of course, the Native Americans themselves weren't nearly so welcoming. In an ironic twist of history, the Viking invaders were now the Christians, and the people they invaded were the raven worshipers.

Yet some Northwest Scandinavians discovered that their raven-worshiping past wasn't very far beneath the surface. One of these was anthropologist and author Richard Nelson. Nelson was born in the very Norwegian town of Stoughton, Wisconsin. To this day, Stoughton's biggest public event of the year is Norwegian Constitution Day on May 17. Stoughton sends its high school Norwegian folk dance troupe traveling far and wide. "We grew up with a very strong consciousness of being Scandinavians," said Nelson, "and in our home 'Norwegian' was only half a word. The full word was 'good Norwegian,' and rarely did we hear it any other way."[2] As a child Nelson became enthralled with nature. In this he was encouraged by his family. He'd had a nature-loving uncle who shunned towns and lived in the Wisconsin north woods. "I think my love for nature came from my Swedish Norwegian mother, who had pictures and paintings of rural-woodsy scenes all over the walls. And from my Norwegian American father, who gently nurtured and supported my fascination with butterflies, then reptiles (a roomful), then the Alaska wilds." When Nelson later wondered why his family was so nature-oriented, he found the Scandinavian heritage a plausible explanation. "Is that genetic and therefore bedded back in Scandinavia? Is that why I've chosen as my home the southeast Alaska coast, which in so many ways is like Norway's coast?" Or perhaps it was culturally embedded. "Our entire milieu in Wisconsin was deeply affected by Scandinavian traditions in the sense that people from those countries brought with them a strong affinity for the outdoors: farming, fishing, hunting, boating, camping. I tend to look beyond my immediate family to the subculture I grew up in."

In college Nelson set out to study biology, but its quantitative approach failed to express his sense of affinity with nature. Then he discovered cultural anthropology, a more personal form of science that could even study the affinity between people and nature. When Nelson discovered the tribes of the Pacific Northwest, his life course was set. He has spent his career studying the people of the raven and their relationship with nature. He has lived with the tribes, heard their stories, attended their ceremonies, and gone fishing and hunting with them. The result has been several anthropological books, most notably *Make Prayers to the Raven*, which PBS made into a six-part television documentary. Nelson explored his own feelings for the Pacific Northwest and its people in his highly praised nature memoir, *The Island Within*. Nelson feels a great affinity for a people whose lives are completely immersed in nature. For them nature isn't a recreational getaway or an abstract idea or an aesthetic experience but a powerful reality in which everything has meaning for humans, in which humans must live with respect and humility. This nature is emphatically not the nature of romanticism, which prompted John Muir to scold Teddy Roosevelt to outgrow his boyish fondness for hunting. In the Far North, survival for humans requires the constant taking of animal lives. Much of Nelson's ethnography consists of studying tribal hunting traditions, and even here, especially here, in the midst of death the tribes behave with respect and humility. Even as Nelson pursues his own passion to identify with nature, he resists the temptation to romanticize the land and its people, and he is wary of the misuse of Native American traditions by New Agers. In the preface to *The Island Within* he explains:

> I was privileged to live and study among Native American people, and I have borrowed heavily from their teachings, not only for my work but also for guidance in the daily conduct of my life. I must emphasize, however, that I am deeply committed to the Euro-American culture into which I was born. I have not aspired to adopt the feathers of another people but to bring certain principles that have guided them into my life as a citizen of North America. . . . I have chosen the Koyukon way, as one among many, to express the fundamental canons of restraint, humility, and respect towards the natural world.[3]

Repeatedly in *The Island Within*, Nelson complains about the accident of his being "born into a culture that keeps the worlds of humanity and nature apart."[4] He gropes to heal that schism. He refuses to offer Native Americans as gurus for modern America, but he never stops envying their identification with nature, and he tries to find his own way back to it. Clearly, he has found a land and a sense of belonging that fit his Norwegian impulses. And presiding over that land, appearing over and over again in Nelson's books, is the raven, who after a thousand years was never entirely forgotten.

I suspect there were many Northwest Scandinavians for whom their pagan, nature-worshiping past was not so far under the surface. The Pacific Northwest offers a landscape that is ready to scratch that surface, a Mecca for hikers, skiers, river runners, wind surfers, and wildlife lovers. The spirit of that landscape has been given strong expression by its Native American cultures in their legends, art, and ceremonies. Only in the desert Southwest have Native cultures remained so intact and offered white Americans such strong symbols of a strong landscape. In Seattle, Native American designs are everywhere, and while some of them, like the logo of the football team, may be simply a matter of stylishness, the Native designs and themes you find in the art galleries reveal that whites are hungrily drawing upon Native inspirations. If you look at the artists' names on the Native-inspired artwork, you notice some Scandinavian names. The artwork includes a lot of ravens.

Another sign that the Pacific Northwest is the right place for nature worship is the fact that Seattle has become America's foremost venue for Richard Wagner's *Ring* cycle, which brings to life the mythology of pagan Scandinavia, or at least the Germanic version of it. People flock from all over America and the world to watch Wotan dispatch his two seer ravens to monitor the doings of the giants, dragons, heroes, and Valkyries. Many in the audience take the *Ring* as seriously as a religious ceremony. Many in the audience are Northwest Scandinavians. If you look around the lobby at intermission, you can see women wearing raven designs on their dresses and jewelry.

I'll offer one last piece of anecdotal evidence for how the pagan lurking within Northwest Scandinavians can be stirred to life. One year I attended the annual Scandinavian festival at Seattle's Nordic Heritage Museum. The museum is in the Ballard neighborhood, which was once a major port for fishing fleets and thoroughly Scandinavian. Once Ballard even had a neighborhood of Icelanders.

The festival included a Viking encampment, with people dressed in period costumes and demonstrating Viking crafts and staging sword fights. It also included a storyteller, a bearded older man who illustrated his tales from the sagas with carved wooden figures attached to boards he held up before his audience. The figures and the storytelling were so well done that I assumed that the storyteller, Roy Johnson, had long been immersed in his Nordic heritage. But as I talked with Roy I found out this wasn't true. Until the year before, he had been immersed in Native American culture. He had spent thirty years working as a school psychologist in Holbrook, Arizona. Holbrook is on the edge of the Navajo reservation and not far from the Hopi and Zuni reservations, so its schools are full of Native Americans, most of whom are bewildered by the choices between Native traditions and the ways of American society. On a daily basis Roy had to deal with the painful confusion and the casualties of their struggles for identity. Unlike many whites with authority over Native Americans who act as agents of assimilation into white society, Roy encouraged Natives to respect their own heritage. It sounded to me as if Roy had sought his own identity in Native traditions. He had been virtually adopted as a son by a Hopi man who lived on the Hopi mesas, and the Hopi man's two sons came to live in Roy's house, and Roy put them through school. Roy was fascinated by Hopi kachina ceremonies, with their evocation of natural forces, and he started carving kachina dolls. His Hopi friend was appalled that a white person would carve kachina dolls, which was properly done only by Hopis. In an attempt to expiate his sin, Roy tossed all his kachina dolls onto the fire, but his Hopi friend was even more horrified by this. Roy still felt compelled to carve Native figures, so to be safe he started carving ceremonial dancers from the Great Plains tribes. He carved for his own satisfaction, not to sell anything. When he retired and moved to Washington State, he was inspired by Northwest tribes, and he started carving their ceremonial masks. I didn't ask him if he carved raven masks, but you can't get far in the Northwest pantheon without doing Raven. One day, after all his years of carving, his wife asked him why he had never carved anything representing his own heritage. Roy was stumped. He answered that he actually didn't know anything about his own heritage, so he started investigating his own Swedish roots. When he read the Viking sagas, he was astonished to find what he had been searching for all along, a people with a deep identification with nature, a people with a strong sense of right and wrong conduct toward nature and toward one another, a people with legends and heroes as fascinating as anything in Native America. So here he was, with his Viking kachina dolls, telling stories from the sagas, conducting a ceremonial of sorts, conducting cultural therapy, trying to prevent young people from losing touch with their heritage.

After the festival I made a circuit of Puget Sound and visited the town of Poulsbo, which has the best Scandinavian look of any town in the Northwest. Poulsbo was once a Norwegian town, the home port of fishing fleets that ranged all the way to Alaska. A Poulsbo cod-fishing company and cannery became one of the largest on the Pacific Coast. The cod fishing gave out long ago, and today the cannery has been converted into a school of marine science. The Norwegians too have given out or at least been outnumbered by people moving in from Seattle or the naval bases nearby. Today you won't see many fishing boats amidst all the yachts in the marina. The Scandinavian portion of the town population is down to about 10 percent, about the same percentage as for the whole of Washington State, the influx of newcomers having diluted the 25 percent figure of 1910. Yet even as Poulsbo has become less and less Norwegian, it has looked more and more Norwegian. Back in the 1960s the downtown merchants committed themselves to a Scandinavian style of architecture. You can also find plenty of Scandinavian things in the shops and restaurants.

I went into the Nordic Maid gift shop, which sold mostly Scandinavian things. The maids in question were the Peterson sisters, whose brother-in-law had started the town's Norwegian look by retrofitting his pharmacy. I looked over the merchandise, but I wasn't inspired to buy anything. It was mostly the same items you found in every Scandinavian gift shop. But then, on the back wall, I spotted something more exciting. It was a nicely done watercolor of a raven perched on the branch of a tree, looking over a bay, with cloud-shrouded mountains in the distance. Right behind the raven was a totem pole carved with a raven's face and beak. Behind that was another totem pole, snapped off at the top. Both totem poles were leaning, indicating their abandonment long ago. Yet the raven was sitting there smiling, alive and well. Humans and their cultures could come and go, humans could forget what they once worshiped, but nature remained, with all its secret powers, patiently waiting to speak to those who knew how to hear and feel it. This, I thought, was the perfect souvenir of the Scandinavian Northwest. So of course I bought it. It would fit perfectly over my shelf full of Hopi crow/raven kachina dolls.

9

Adventures in Legoland

he two American towns with the most elaborate Scandinavian architecture are both in southern California. Yet perhaps any investigation of the Danish town of Solvang and the Swedish town
of Kingsburg should start in a third southern California town, Legoland. Legoland is a theme park built by the Danish toy company full of
miniature cities built out of 30 million Lego blocks. It is the offspring
of the original and very popular Legoland in Denmark. The California
version has more of an American emphasis, including Lego versions of
New York City and New Orleans. The Danish Legoland has a few
American landmarks, including a Lego Mount Rushmore, but it features Danish landmarks familiar to Danish children.

If you visit the town of Solvang right after visiting Legoland you
may have the Twilight Zone experience of feeling that you have just
shrunk to the size of Legoland, or that the fantasy streets of Legoland
have just come to life. Solvang is a fully realized Danish town full of
authentic Scandinavian architecture. There are Danish windmills turning in the breeze from the Pacific Ocean a dozen miles away. There are
steeples and clock towers copied from the famous ones in Copenhagen. There's a copy, if not quite full scale, of the Round Tower Ob-
servatory. Most buildings are done in the cross-timber/white stucco
style that in England is called Tudor. The roofs are copper or wooden
shingled or red tiled. Since there are no real storks in the area to carry
on the Danish tradition that a stork on the roof brings good luck, there

are hand-carved wooden storks on the roofs. Chimneys and gables and dormers and wooden scrollwork further the Danish look. The buildings are arranged around plazas and secluded courtyards, with gardens and cobblestone walks. And of course there is a Little Mermaid statue. There are Danish flags flying everywhere, and some of the shopkeepers wear Danish folk costumes. The dozen motels in town all have Danish themes, so you can choose from the Royal Copenhagen, the Viking Motel, or the Hamlet Motel. I didn't check to see whether the Hamlet Motel had a room number 2-B or not 2-B.

When I first drove into Solvang I was quite impressed by its architectural ambitiousness. Solvang far outdid my favorite Swedish and Norwegian towns, Lindsborg, Kansas, and Decorah, Iowa, which have modest Scandinavian touches to otherwise normal American downtowns. Solvang was quite a rarity in America for having a unified architectural theme of any kind. It spoke with an accent as strong as the Spanish of Santa Fe, the French of old New Orleans, and the colonial English of Williamsburg. And like those towns, Solvang is a strong magnet for tourists. The sidewalks and shops were swarming. A million visitors a year come to Solvang. A large portion of them come on daytrips or weekend getaways from Los Angeles. I had a hunch as to why they come. It is the same reason millions of Americans seek out Santa Fe and New Orleans. But before I drew any conclusions, I had to do some investigation.

As I strolled the streets and checked out the numerous shops, I soon noticed one contrast between Solvang and Santa Fe and New Orleans. There were no art galleries in sight. It didn't seem to be high culture that drew a million people a year to Solvang. Lindsborg and Decorah, which are both college towns and artist communities, have stronger cultural accents than does Solvang.

I soon decided that it wasn't even Scandinavian culture that drew a million people a year to Solvang. The shops, in contrast to their Scandinavian exteriors, had relatively little Scandinavian content. I saw only two shops that were dedicated specifically to Scandinavian merchandise. One of them was a chain store, Dansk Design, usually found in outlet malls, offering stylish housewares. In the other store the clerk declared proudly that everything there came from Denmark, but the first teacup I inspected declared "Made in England," and many other items came from Finland and Sweden. It was as if the clerk used "Denmark" as a generic word for anything Scandinavian. There were other stores that advertised "Scandinavian Imports" outside but had only modest selections amidst the usual American gift shop items. I'd say that both Lindsborg and Decorah offered a better selection of authentic Scandinavian arts and crafts, whether modern designs like Swedish glass and Norwegian sweaters or folk arts like Swedish Dala horses and Norwegian rosemaling. Most of the shops in Solvang were specialty shops offering porcelain figurines, clocks, clothes, candles, and other things you could have found at the malls back home in Los Angeles. It isn't the shopping that draws a million people a year to Solvang. But the shops make it clear that Solvang attracts the average American, with middle-class tastes and budgets.

Was it the food? There were half a dozen bakeries with genuine Danish pastries and other goodies and even more restaurants where one could enjoy Danish meals. The food succeeded in living up to Solvang's unique identity in the same way that the food in Santa Fe and New Orleans is uniquely southwestern or Cajun. Solvang is so serious about its Danish identity that it had a law banning fast food chains, even if they built in Danish style. Yet my hunch told me that the food in these three towns was only the symbolic, bodily satisfaction of a hunger that was mainly psychological.

Amidst all the symbols of Danish identity in Solvang, there were plenty of signs of identity confusion. I had lunch in the Red Viking Restaurant, which had a plausible smorgasbord yet an odd decor. Alongside prints and models of Viking ships, the walls held Spanish armor and weaponry, as if no one would know the difference between the Vikings and the Spanish conquistadors. Earlier, the man at the chamber of commerce had suggested I go see the historic Lutheran church with its hand-built wooden model of an "old Viking ship" hanging from the ceiling. The ship turned out to be a nineteenth-century sailing ship of the kind Danes had immigrated to America on. It seemed that the Solvang chamber of commerce was rather vague about Scandinavian history. The most widespread identity confusion in town was the sale of Dutch souvenirs. Many shops offered nothing but tourist trinkets, and the leading symbol of Solvang was the windmill. You could buy porcelain windmills, salt and pepper shaker windmills, and mugs and plates and tiles depicting windmills, and most of them said on the bottom "Made in Holland" or "Dutch Novelties." You could also find plenty of images of wooden shoes, tulips, and milkmaids in Dutch costumes. Some of the souvenirs had the word "Solvang" fired into the porcelain, but others merely had a Solvang sticker attached where you would otherwise find a sticker saying "Amsterdam" or "Pella, Iowa." Neither Solvang merchants nor tourists seemed bothered by this confusion. The merchants needed windmill merchandise, and of course windmills are a Dutch specialty. Most Americans probably didn't know the difference between Dutch and Danish, and, after all, both start with a *D* and belong to an unreal, fairy-tale world. Indeed, Solvang makes many concessions to being a fairy-tale town, including many references to Hans Christian Andersen. You could stay at the Storybook Inn and eat at the Little Mermaid Restaurant.

Yet I soon discovered that the residents of Solvang were rather touchy about suggestions that their town isn't real. They are especially tired of being depicted as a Disneyland theme park. Every time I asked merchants about the Danish theme, they would say defensively, "You know, Solvang really is a Danish town, full of Danes who are proud to celebrate their heritage." And they would proceed to tell me the town's history.

Solvang was actually founded with the goal of promoting Danishness. It was the brainchild of some Lutheran pastors and professors from the Midwest who saw California as a promising site for a Danish American colony. In 1911 they searched California and bought some rich farmland, calling it Sunny Field, which in Danish is Solvang. The centerpiece of the colony was a Danish folk school, Atterdag College. The concept of the folk school was started by a charismatic Danish bishop, N. H. S. Grundtvig, in the 1830s, a time of low Danish national morale in the wake of Napoleon. The folk schools emphasized Danish traditions and pride. Grundtvig was enthralled by the Vikings and had his pupils read the sagas and sing songs praising the Vikings. It was natural that Danish Americans, concerned with preserving Danishness, would make the folk schools their foremost tool. Though Atterdag College died out, its purpose lived on and began taking architectural form. In 1939 the new elementary school was built in Danish style, and a few years later a carpenter built his house in the form of a windmill. When a bit of the downtown was refitted from Spanish mission style into Danish style, it caught the attention of the *Saturday Evening Post*, which did a big story showing dancers in Danish folk costumes in front of Danish buildings. The result was a burst of tourism. Solvang residents were amazed to discover that the outside world was going to reward them for being Danish. They started transforming more of the downtown into Danish style and opening new shops and cafes. Solvang tourism got a boost from the 1952 movie *Hans Christian Andersen*, in which Hollywood ignored Andersen's real and melancholy life story and invented a charming one. (The movie won six Academy Award nominations, but even a hoaxed Hans Christian Andersen couldn't compete with P. T. Barnum, whose circus won best picture for *The Greatest Show on Earth*.) Solvang's Danishness also attracted real Danes. The original settlers were second- or third-generation Americans, but during World War II many Danes in exile, including government officials, made Solvang their home, and some of them stayed after the war. Real Danes have continued moving into town and starting businesses, reinforcing Solvang's Danishness. I heard quite a few Danish accents in the shops and cafes.

Even the non-Danes in town got into the spirit of it. I talked with Kathy Mullins, the non-Danish owner of the town bookshop, which upstairs included the Hans Christian Andersen Museum, full of displays about Andersen and his stories and rare editions of his books. Her bookshop had one of the country's largest selections of Scandinavian books, including hundreds of old books in Danish given up by locals who could no longer read their grandparents' language. Kathy told me that many of her Scandinavian books were bought by Scandinavian Americans who came to Solvang to connect with their roots. Kathy came to Solvang when her husband worked for Boeing at nearby Vandenburg Air Force Base. When Boeing wanted to transfer her husband back to Seattle, they opened the bookshop so they could stay. She now felt like an honorary Dane. She told me that many people in town were in touch with relatives in Denmark and had visited there, although as fourth- or fifth-generation Americans they didn't really identify with Denmark very strongly. I asked her if she ever got tired of the Danish act, and she said no, "It's a lot of fun."

It isn't just genuine pride that makes it unfair to accuse Solvang of selling its heritage for profit. It's also the fact that no one can manipulate a million people a year into going out of their way to pay a town hundreds of millions of dollars to act Danish. It's the tourists who have created Solvang and not vice versa, and they have demanded that Solvang exist because of what is lacking elsewhere. I am sure it is no coincidence that Solvang happened in the shadow of Los Angeles. There have been other towns elsewhere in the country, impressed by the success of Solvang, that have tried to turn themselves into Solvangs, often with minimal success.

Racine, Wisconsin, for instance, was one of the main destinations of Danish immigration, and today it has a Danish population far larger than Solvang. When I set out to find the Danishness of Racine, I followed a chamber of commerce map to a red dot that said "Danish Village." I was expecting some version of Solvang. When I arrived at the red dot I didn't see any Danish village, so I drove back and forth trying to find it. Finally, I noticed I had been passing a Danish bakery in the otherwise normal business street. I went in and bought a kringle, the ultimate Danish pastry, the size of a pizza. I asked the employees about the red dot on the map, and they said I was in the right place. I asked if there was anything else Danish in the neighborhood, and they pointed me across the street to a combination cheese store and Scandinavian gift shop. This was actually a logical combination for Wisconsin. Just as Denmark was the dairy of Europe, the Danes helped make Wisconsin the dairy of America. I went into the shop and asked the owner about the Danish village on my map. "At one time," she said, "the Racine chamber of commerce was trying to create a Danish tourist attraction by encouraging all the shops in this old Danish neighborhood to offer Danish items, but the effort fizzled out." Racine remains a gritty, industrial, Great Lakes port town, a world apart from Solvang. If Racine Danes feel any jealousy of Solvang, they hide it behind a contemptuous attitude. "Solvang," another Racine Dane told me, "is just a tourist trap."

Another Danish town trying to trap tourists is Elk Horn, Iowa. It did succeed in trapping the National Danish Immigration Museum, and it outdid Solvang by importing an authentic old windmill from Denmark. But Elk Horn is a long way from even a modest-sized city, and its trickle of tourists can barely support one motel. If the residents of Des Moines want to see windmills, then it's a shorter drive to the Dutch town of Pella, where the highly successful Pella Window Company is bankrolling the Solvangization of the town.

So why did Solvang happen in southern California, in such a peripheral spot in Danish American history? I believe it's because Los

Angeles is the capital city of American rootlessness. Even back in Tennessee and Kansas, Americans had a weak identification with their land and their communities, but by the time Americans were filling up California, American culture had taken on forms even less supportive of roots. Main Street America had turned into Freeway America. Downtowns were giving way to suburban shopping malls. Southern Californians didn't even have downtowns to kill but built an endless sprawl where no one had been born and no one expected to remain long enough to care about the future of the community. Los Angeles was the birthplace of McDonald's and Franchise America, which soon had every town in America looking exactly the same, every meal tasting the same, every mall selling the same merchandise, every theater showing the same glorifications of Los Angeles life.

Yet Franchise America seems to have left its citizens unsatisfied. They seem to be hungry for a world more personal, more authentic, more rooted. And thus Americans set off in search of something they barely know how to define. They pay admission to Disneyland just so they can walk down a nineteenth-century Main Street. They cruise the length of old Route 66, teary-eyed with nostalgia for abandoned motels and cafes that weren't designed and run by corporations. They flock to Native American villages to learn the secrets of how to belong to the land and to the tribe. And yes, they seek out the handful of towns that have managed to resist the onslaught of Franchise America, the Santa Fes and New Orleanses that are loyal to their own strong identities and that suggest the deeper roots of old Europe. Visitors to Santa Fe seem delighted to find that even McDonald's is forced to build in Santa Fe style.

And then there's Solvang, which completely banned McDonald's, at least from the town center. There is no clearer way of repudiating southern California culture. A million people a year come to Solvang just to find a town that feels authentic. Even if Solvang isn't authentically old or Danish, it still feels more authentic than Franchise America. People come here to feel, if only for a day, if only unconsciously, a sense of roots and community they can't find in Los Angeles. Even when they try to take home a bit of Solvang in the form of a cheap Dutch souvenir, there is still something authentic in this impulse. Perhaps it was just a coincidence that rootless Los Angeles selected a Scandinavian town to give it a taste of roots. But perhaps it wasn't a coincidence. Perhaps there was at least a vague recognition that Scandinavians knew more than Americans about how to belong to a community and to the land.

Scandinavian towns aren't the only ones trying to satisfy America's longing for roots. Communities that already have unique identities such as New England villages have risen up to keep franchises out. Towns that don't have much of an identity have set out to find one, and frequently their ethnic heritage is the most obvious resource. America is developing a lively industry that can be called ethnotourism. Towns that forty years ago were indistinguishable from other towns are now recognizably Dutch or Czech. Hundreds of ethnic festivals have sprung up. In big cities, these festivals draw large crowds of other ethnics, who come for the food, the music, and the momentary Solvang experience. The architectural part of ethnotourism doesn't work so easily on the East Coast, where immigrants inherited Yankee architecture and where neighborhoods changed ethnic identity often enough that people didn't bother trying to anchor their identity in buildings that they actually hoped their children would leave for wealthier neighborhoods. In a big city, retrofitting a few buildings would hardly make a scratch in the look of a neighborhood, but in a small town, a few ethnically accented buildings can transform the whole spirit of the place. In the Midwest and West, hundreds of small ethnic enclaves have largely retained their original identities over more than a century, and it's easier to believe that ethnic architecture, even if retrofitted, embodies their true heritage.

Sometimes ethnotourism attractions arise from the spontaneous enthusiasm of locals. Sometimes they are more calculated. I once dropped into the office of a professor of community planning at the University of Nebraska. On his desk sat a Dala horse painted with a "thank you" from the people of Oakland, Nebraska. It was he who had drawn up the master plan for turning plain Oakland into a Swedish village. He had provided them with a plan for decorating the town, a plan for selling Swedish gifts, a plan for staging a Swedish festival, and a plan for marketing themselves as a Swedish attraction. If Oakland had had a Pony Express station, he might have given them a plan for marketing themselves as a Pony Express attraction. Many of the Norwegian touches in Poulsbo, Washington, were the result of a master plan drawn up at the University of Washington. This is not to say that the people of

Oakland and Poulsbo weren't sincerely inspired by their Scandinavian heritage. Even when ethnotourism was planned as an economic development strategy, the way a town would plot to lure a dog food factory to help an ailing economy, there remained an understanding that the town had a genuine resource that was genuinely desired by a hungry public.

Ethnotourism can also go awry, much worse than by selling Dutch trinkets in a Danish town. The English theme town of Lake Havasu City, Arizona, has never escaped the nationwide ridicule it inspired when it was built in the 1960s around London Bridge, imported from London by a real estate developer. At least now the bridge actually has water beneath it instead of just sand, but the incongruity of red double-decker buses amidst cactus and scorching heat leaves many visitors feeling they must be suffering from sunstroke. But at least Lake Havasu City had a vision. Sedona, Arizona, could never make up its mind what to pretend to be. The downtown was done as an Old West town, but its most prominent building is the alpine Matterhorn Hotel. Just down the hill, an upscale shopping center was built to look like an old Spanish mission. Other buildings were done in Native American pueblo style. All over town, Old West, Spanish, pueblo, European, and modern buildings are intermixed randomly.

After visiting Solvang, I headed for the San Joaquin Valley and a weekend in Kingsburg. By chance, I arrived in Kingsburg two days after the funeral of the man who was responsible for turning it into a Swedish theme town. The flags in town, both the American and Swedish flags, were flying at half-mast.

Kingsburg wasn't nearly as architecturally elaborate as Solvang, but it still far outdid Lindsborg, Decorah, and Elk Horn. It had two windmills, which I guess were supposed to be Swedish windmills, though I honestly can't tell the difference between a Danish, Dutch, or Swedish windmill, if there is any difference. It had a water tower in the form of a Swedish coffeepot, an idea no doubt stolen from Stanton, Iowa. The downtown held Swedish-style buildings, emblems from each Swedish province, murals depicting Swedish country life, a large wooden Dala horse children could sit on, and Swedish folk music coming from loudspeakers. Even the Mexican restaurant had a sign in the form of a Viking ship. Two restaurants served Swedish food.

There was one Scandinavian gift shop downtown. When I entered, I saw a lady wearing an Augustana College sweatshirt, and I asked her if she had studied there. She was careful to make it clear she had attended the Swedish Augustana in Illinois, not that Norwegian Augustana in South Dakota. I soon learned that her Swedish grandmother had come from Gränna. It also turned out that she was one of only a few dozen people alive who could say they had grown up in Bishop Hill, Illinois, back when it was almost a ghost town, full of rotting buildings. Today Bishop Hill has been revived by ethnotourism. The lady told me she had lived in California for years, and she traveled to Kingsburg whenever she needed a dose of Swedishness. She seemed to be succeeding in passing on her loyalties, for her daughter told me she was now attending Augustana and that when she got married it would be in the park in Bishop Hill.

The shop owner, June Olson Hess, wandered over to listen to our conversation. She enjoyed asking customers where they were from and hearing their stories. Since Kingsburg was the only town in the West with a strong Swedish theme, it attracted a lot of people trying to recharge their Swedishness. I told her that her shop appeared to have more authentic Scandinavian items than the whole town of Solvang, which wasn't that much of an exaggeration. She said that most customers wanted things just like what their grandmothers had. She couldn't sell much modern design, like stylish glass candleholders.

I asked June about the "Mr. Kingsburg" who had just died at age ninety-one; I had noticed the headline of the local newspaper. She told me about Gordon Satterberg, who had been mayor for two decades and who had generated the energy for the often thankless task of turning Kingsburg into a Swedish Solvang.

The Satterberg family was unusual in having emigrated directly from Sweden to California. Most Kingsburg families had moved on from Swedish towns in the Midwest. The Anderson family, for instance, had emigrated from Sweden to New Jersey, but when lightning struck their house, injuring three of them, they decided to find a place without storms, so they moved to Kansas. There they got a letter from a friend in California describing its pleasant weather, and they started packing. Quite a few Kingsburg families came from Lindsborg, Kansas, such as the Gunnarsons, who arrived in San Francisco just in time for the 1906 earthquake. Several Kingsburg families were in San Francisco during the earthquake and moved to Kingsburg only after their houses and jobs were wrecked. On the other hand, the earthquake prompted the Petersons to move from Chicago to San Francisco, since a carpenter would find lots of work. Most families came to town for the good farmland surrounding it. Some came to Kingsburg for their health. In fact, the first Swede to come to Kingsburg, Frank Rosendahl, in 1885, bought his land from a woman, the sister of Mark Twain, who had settled there for her health. Rosendahl didn't intend to found a Swedish colony. He was a professional landscaper who had helped design Central Park in New York, and he picked Kingsburg as a place to establish a nursery. But he spread the word about Kingsburg in Swedish-language newspapers around America, and the response was so great that for a long time Kingsburg was 95 percent Swedish, prompting an original Anglo resident to complain that Kingsburg was "getting so darned full of Swedes that a white man couldn't get a job."[1]

When Gordon Satterberg's grandfather left his log cabin to go to America, he locked it up, leaving behind some clothes, furniture, and household articles. Many decades later Gordon returned to find the cabin, its lock, and its contents still undisturbed. Gordon was born in Kingsburg in 1907. I'll continue his story momentarily.

It was at just about this time that a scandal struck Kingsburg. A Mr. Berg opened a bakery right downtown, as if he expected hardworking Swedish Lutheran farmwives to walk right in and buy bread, publicly disgracing themselves as too lazy to make their own. Fortunately, the bakery had a back door. Every so often Mr. Berg heard a surreptitious knock there, and a hardworking Swedish farmwife would buy a loaf of bread and nervously dart back down the alley, glancing about to make sure she hadn't been seen. Even worse, Mr. Berg started serving ice cream and cold sodas, and the kids of the hardworking Swedish Lutheran farmers started hanging out in the bakery when they should have been home working and building moral character. One day some civic leaders confronted Mr. Berg and demanded that he stop corrupting the town.

The Swedes were fighting a losing battle against the evils of the outside world. There was the day a few years later when a traveling tent theater troupe came to town. Young Clarence Wigh disobeyed his parents' stricture against shows and went, but a moral crisis occurred when Clarence won the door prize, six pounds of hot dogs. He knew that his poor parents would be happy to have six pounds of hot dogs, but then he would have to tell them he had attended a show. I suspect that as Clarence walked home, he wrestled mightily with his con-science. When Clarence confessed, his parents were appalled. But they did eat the hot dogs, even if they tasted of moral compromise.

The Swedish Lutheran farmers had a moral dilemma of their own. At the time they started arriving in Kingsburg, the main crop in the area was wheat. But farmers were realizing that the land was far better for growing fruit, especially grapes. The Swedes planted some of California's first commercial vineyards. Then an Italian moved to Kingsburg and opened one of California's first wineries. Wine was not ex-actly promoted by the Lutheran religion. But the Italian was paying good prices, and some Swedish farmers started sneaking over to his winery to sell their grapes. Then the Lutheran God showed them a righteous path. A terrible heat wave struck, drying the grapes on the vine, shriveling them into hideous black things. The farmers saw only ruin, but someone decided to take some of the dead grapes to San Francisco and market them as "Peruvian delicacies." They were a huge hit. Thus the California raisin industry was born. The hell-bound sinners became respected raisin growers. At first it was a struggle, partly because corporate produce buyers were able to pay growers as little as possible. So the Swedes joined with other San Joaquin raisin growers to form a cooperative to enforce a fair price. The cooperative became the Sun-Maid Raisin Company, headquartered in Kingsburg. The Kings-burg raisin-processing plant is the largest in the world.

The Swedes' sense of ethics paid off again during the Great Depres-sion, when canneries all over California were forced to close. Many Kingsburg residents believe that the town peach cannery survived only because of the rather Swedish management style of A. W. Swenson. Locals who went to work in other canneries were shocked by the meanness of management and the angry indifference of employees. I will quote from one of Swenson's workers, Pauline Peterson Mathes, who later wrote the town history. Pauline's family seems to have been infected with the writing bug, for one relative became editor of *Better Homes and Gardens*, and a relative who stayed in Sweden, Harry Mar-tinson, won the Nobel Prize for literature.

In many communities, cannery workers were considered among the lower echelon of the townspeople, some of them being migrant workers going from one cannery to another. In Kingsburg it was different. Everyone worked in the cannery, from the socially elite to the lowest on the socio-economic level and there was no stigma attached. Everyone was treated alike. The writer thinks this was at least partially due to the leadership of Mr. Swenson. From the beginning, his was an enlightened leadership, far ahead of his time. . . . He always treated the employees as people, not just a herd of human beings . . . engendering a feeling in them that they were important to the successful operation of the plant. This, in turn, paid off in better and greater production by the employees. In recent years several books have been written indicating that if employees can be made to feel they are a part of a business, they will increase production. Mr. Swenson did it because he felt it was the right thing to do, and as we said before, he was ahead of his time.[2]

The Depression started an influx of outsiders into Kingsburg that lowered the percentage of Swedes until they were a minority. Kingsburg's most famous son would be an African American, Rafer Johnson, who won the 1960 Olympic decathlon. The minority status of Swedes made things more interesting when Gordon Satterberg tried to turn Kingsburg into a Swedish village.

Satterberg was probably typical of the people behind ethnotourism. He was genuinely passionate about his heritage, but he was also a practical businessman who saw an opportunity. As a pharmacist in downtown Kingsburg, where once you could buy everything you needed without speaking a word of English, he saw the stores closing as malls opened in nearby Fresno. He also saw the growing crowds in Solvang. Following Solvang's example seemed to be the only hope for saving downtown Kingsburg. Satterberg started by painting a building to look Swedish. He infected others with his enthusiasm, and more Swedish touches appeared, but many people in town, including Swedes, found the whole idea ridiculous. When the giant wooden Dala horse appeared downtown, it was often ridiculed, and one night it was kidnapped by three guys, including a Swede, who buried it in a vineyard. The city made a plea for its return, alive and unharmed, and after it was found the ridicule of it stopped, and people accepted it as a town mascot. Satterberg legislated some guidelines for redesigning the downtown, but almost every time a new building was planned or an old one was slated for remodeling, a big fight broke out over the Swedish theme. Even Swedes complained about the added expense of going Swedish, especially for businesses with little to gain from tourism. Mexican American businessmen were even less inspired to pretend to be Swedish. Finally, a Dutch American insurance agent threatened to sue the city if he was required to make his new offices Swedish, and after he built a thoroughly bland building a new ordinance was passed, with legal teeth, enforcing a Swedish style. By then the tourists were coming and new businesses were succeeding, so most people were willing to go along. Even the new Taco Bell was done in Swedish style, and the McDonald's has a large Dala horse out front. But the fighting never ceased. The Mexican Americans complained to June Olson Hess, who was in charge of the annual Swedish festival, that they weren't welcome to sell tacos at the festival. She answered that nobody forced them to sell Swedish meatballs at their ethnic festivals. Every year Kingsburg high school students were selected as king and queen of the Swedish festival, and the Mexicans complained that it was racial discrimination that Mexican kids weren't allowed to be the Swedish king and queen.

Maybe June was just depressed about losing her strongest ally in the struggle to make Kingsburg Swedish, or maybe I was just a sympathetic listener, but she went on and on about the petty infighting that went on every year behind the scenes of the Swedish festival, which visitors saw only as a fun celebration. But then, I'm sure that when Mickey Mouse takes off his costume after a hard day's work at Disneyland, he and Goofy argue about who's goofing off.

It was symptomatic of the difference between Kingsburg and Solvang that while Solvang is packed with Solvang postcard sales racks, I had to search all over Kingsburg to find a Kingsburg postcard. Most symptomatic of all was what I found in a Kingsburg antique shop. In Solvang there was an antique shop full of ornate old clocks, very stylish and expensive ways of marking time. In the Kingsburg antique shop for two dollars you could buy a more touching timepiece. I found a basket full of old matted photographs of Swedes dressed in their best clothes. There were no names on the photos, but most of them bore logos of photography studios in Stockholm. I could only wonder if these were early residents of Kingsburg or relatives who had been left behind.

Whoever they were, they were forgotten now. Any stranger could buy them as decorations.

No exploration of Scandinavian America would be complete without a visit to its most famous town of all, a town visited faithfully by far more people than visit Solvang. So many people are so devoted to this town that the AAA travel guide to Minnesota includes a listing for Lake Wobegon. The guide explains that Lake Wobegon can be hard to find.

By an unlikely accident, like the ones that befell Alice and Dorothy, I was granted admission into the dimension where Lake Wobegon exists.

I was in St. Paul when Garrison Keillor was giving a reading and signing of his paper-and-ink-so-fresh-it-was-a-joy-to-smell-it novel. The reading was held at a church just down the street from the Fitzgerald Theater, home of *A Prairie Home Companion*. By the way, I've never understood what Keillor is doing in a theater named in honor of a writer who was infatuated with the rich and with the poses of Jazz Age pop culture. I suppose that Fitzgerald is less inappropriate than Minnesota's other literary icon, Sinclair Lewis, who savagely ridiculed small-town life on the prairie. Yet a question is raised by the prominence of both Fitzgerald and Lewis. If they represent twentieth-century American literary culture, with its contempt for average America and with its posturings of sophistication, then exactly why are millions of sophisticated people flocking every week to listen to the doings of a small Scandinavian town on the prairie?

Personally, I think Keillor belongs in the Mark Twain Theater. Twain was a master of American folk humor, yet he used that humor for some very serious purposes. Twain launched laser-guided attacks on social pretense and social injustice, but when it came to the characters he cared about, his cynicism suddenly yielded to deep tenderness. Tenderness, compassion, and humanity are qualities seldom advocated in literary academia, which has made gods out of irony, alienation, and scorn. Keillor has Twain's sharp eye for social pretense, yet I think it's his tender eye for ordinary people that has touched an unsatisfied need in the public.

After the reading we removed to the pastor's study for cookies, tea, and the book signing. For crowd control Keillor announced one letter of the alphabet at a time, in reverse order, as if in democratic sympathy for those who through no fault of their own had always come in last, and for each letter he added some sample Norwegian names. For *T* he added Tollefson and Thorvaldson, and the *T*s lined up.

When he got to the *L*s, I recalled that Keillor had a Danish wife and had lived in Denmark for a while, so when I handed him my copy I explained that even though my name was pronounced like the Danish toy, it was actually Swedish and spelled with an *a* instead of an *e*. I added that originally it had been pronounced with a deeper *a*, like the Latin word for lake, but my great-grandfather settled just downriver from a town called Lagro, a misspelling of the French Le Gros, a nickname for a prominent and overweight Indian chief, so the locals started pronouncing Lago with a French "Le."

"Well then," Keillor said, "your name must have been spelled with an umlaut over the *a*."

"No," I said, "it wasn't."

"But," he said more insistently, his pen withholding judgment over the blank page, "if the Swedes pronounced it Laaago, they must have spelled it with an umlaut."

"Not as far as I know," I said. "I've been to our ancestral village and seen our family graves and the sign over our clothing store, and there were no umlauts."

There was no point in trying to reason with an ignorant Swede, so Keillor went ahead and signed my book, without an umlaut, and that was the end of that. Or so I thought.

Three weeks later I was listening to *A Prairie Home Companion* when suddenly I heard Keillor say my name. The detective Guy Noir was being hired by a man who had become rich and famous touring America as an Irish singer, but now a woman from his past had surfaced who knew that he was really a Swede from Iowa whose real name was Carlson, and she was blackmailing him. The woman's name was Linda Lego.

I supposed that shortly after the book signing, Keillor was writing the skit about Noir and Carlson, needed another Swedish name, recalled that dumb Swede with the altered name, and decided that because of the famous toy, people would regard Lego as a Scandinavian name, and so he went ahead and used it.

Well, I thought, since Keillor has sort of turned me into a character in his world, maybe this means I can look around the place a bit.

So I headed up the interstate toward St. Cloud. I exited onto a county highway and headed into the rolling countryside, past the lakes and woods and red barns and white cows and tidy Lutheran churches, through many small towns that weren't Lake Wobegon. I didn't know exactly where I was going, but I was trusting my intuition, since after all Lake Wobegon is all about trusting the human imagination.

Finally, at the crest of a hill, I saw a standard green Minnesota Department of Transportation highway sign that read "Lake Wobegon." But I didn't need the sign, for with one glance at the town I recognized that all its women were strong and all its children were above average. I recognized some of the buildings and the Statue of the Unknown Norwegian. Why, there was the Chatterbox Cafe, with some familiar-looking cars parked out front. I parked and walked to the door. When I stepped inside, I thought I recognized some of the voices. The waitress smiled at me and said, "You're not from around here, are you? How did you happen to find us?"

I started to introduce myself and explain, but as soon as I said my name, the whole room fell silent, the clinking of silverware ceased, there was a grinding of chairs on the floor, and I found that everyone was staring at me, apprehensively.

"Say," said a man I suspected was Mayor Clint Bunsen, "you wouldn't happen to be that Lego who goes around trying to blackmail people just because they're Scandinavian?"

"No. No!" I protested. "I was framed. I mean, my name was borrowed by . . . er, well, are you familiar with a guy named Keillor?"

The room was filled with a murmuring I wasn't sure how to interpret.

"You don't have to explain any further," said Mr. Bunsen, smiling. "I've been framed a time or two myself."

"Well," I said, "now that I've got your attention, I'd just like to say how pleased I am to be here. If I could ask, I've always wondered what you thought of Garrison Keillor. I think of him as a modern Mark Twain, and I think his large following says something significant about our culture."

"Don't you think you're spreading it on a bit thick," said a man who was spreading butter on his roll, "comparing Keillor to Twain? Maybe you're just trying to butter up Keillor so he won't sue you for infringement of intellectual property copyright. You don't think just anyone can drive into town and start writing about it, do you?"

"Well, no," I said, crestfallen. "It's just that I couldn't possibly write a book about Scandinavian America without including Lake Wobegon, and I had the good luck to be sort of turned into a character, which was almost like an invitation."

"Of course," said someone who might have been a Tollerud, "Guy Noir and his crowd don't come around here, and from what I've heard, it's a good thing. Now, what's this talk about Keillor's cultural significance?"

"Just think about it," I said. "All those millions of highly educated city people who spend their other evenings watching BBC literary dramas and deconstructing Woody Allen movies devoting Saturday evening to a low-tech medium and an even lower-tech town on the prairie."

"What gets me," someone interjected, "is all those opera people. They go from listening to the Met on Saturday afternoon to listening to bluegrass in the evening. People who would never go out to hear bluegrass or country, who would be socially embarrassed by it, will dutifully sit there and listen to anything Keillor hands them, figuring it must be good for them."

"But it's not the music that people are waiting for," I said. "Think of all the millions of people who got all the way through college without being offered a single novel that showed gentle understanding and forgiveness for its characters, the millions who are so schooled in alienation that they don't even know what it's like to belong wholeheartedly to a community, the millions who thought that happiness consisted of impressing others with their ironic and scornful wit at suburban cocktail parties and who can't understand why they are so lonely. There's a hunger that draws people to Lake Wobegon. And maybe it's no coincidence that the town where people find a sense of community and humanity is a Scandinavian town."

"Heck," said a Tollefson, "he couldn't have used an Italian town on the radio. Most of the communication between Italians is just wild hand gestures and facial expressions. We Norwegians only move our lips, so we're perfect for radio."

"That's true for the cooking too," yelled the cook from the kitchen. "All those Italian smells and flavors would get lost over the radio. But Norwegian food doesn't have any flavor to lose. Except for lutefisk, and that's a smell you're better off losing."

"A Scottish or Irish town might be too loud and merry for Minnesota Public Radio," said another Norwegian. "A Norwegian never would have invented an instrument like the bagpipes."

"If you used an African American town," said another, "you'd have rap music, and all those stuffy NPR programming directors would kick you out. But you gotta admit, it has to mean something that a whole century worth of Lake Wobegon kids have worried their parents by eagerly listening to black folks inventing ragtime, blues, jazz, rock and roll, soul, and rap."

I answered, "I never claimed that Scandinavians were good at self-expression, being lively, hugging their children, singing joyfully in church, or anything like that. But it's the glory of America that different groups can cure their cultural vitamin deficiencies from the strengths of other groups, and everyone ends up stronger. And I think it's a cultural deficiency that draws people to Lake Wobegon, and to Solvang; you know, that Danish town in southern California."

I must have said something wrong, for the cafe was filled with unhappy grumbling.

"Now that I think about it," said the butter-up man who had threatened me with a lawsuit, "I'll bet that you could sue Keillor for damaging your reputation. For someone writing about Scandinavians, nothing could be worse than being mixed up with a notorious blackmailer of Scandinavians. I'll bet no one has been willing to talk with you since. I'll bet Keillor didn't ask your permission either."

"It hasn't been a problem," I said.

"Well, somebody ought to sue him," said someone. "I tell you, hardly a week goes by when somebody in town doesn't get the notion to sue him." There was a murmur of agreement.

I was shocked. "You're kidding! But why? Is it because he makes fun of you?"

People looked around at one another, puzzled.

"Makes fun of us?" said Mr. Bunsen. "I'm not aware that Mr. Keillor has ever made fun of us."

"Is it the exaggerations? The ethnic stereotypes?"

Again, a puzzled glancing about.

"I don't know what you mean by that," said Mr. Bunsen. "No, it's because he tells the truth, the whole truth, and nothing but the truth, spilling our secrets and bragging about us to the whole country. It's not just that Norwegians aren't supposed to brag. It's that all these outsiders hear how wonderful our town is and keep showing up here. It's spooky enough when a total stranger steps out of his BMW with California license plates and greets you like he knows you. But when these southern Californians move into town, they just don't know how to fit into a small Norwegian town."

"Southern Californians moving into Lake Wobegon?" I said. "I had no idea."

"Hardly a week goes by without another one showing up and trying to order sushi and wine in the cafe or trying to drive L.A.-style on Main Street, with speeding, tailgating, red light running, and obscene hand gestures. They're driving real estate prices and taxes through the roof and building their weird houses on stilts on hills where they can see everyone in town and everyone can see them sunbathing in the summer. I'm not saying they're bad people. A lot of them were midwestern kids who just watched too much TV in the 1960s and decided they'd rather be surfers, movie stars, or hippies than boring midwestern kids, but now that they're spending half their days stuck in traffic and have families of their own, they've decided that maybe those small prairie towns weren't so bad after all, and they try to go home again."

"I think Mr. Keillor might quote Thomas Wolfe on that subject," I said.

"And all because of Mr. Keillor, the first town the Californians think of is Lake Wobegon. But they just don't know how to fit in."

"I had no idea," I said. "I hope you didn't think I was planning to move in. I just wanted to take a look around. I really appreciate your hospitality."

"Just do us one favor," said Mr. Bunsen. "Tell people about all those other nice towns on the prairie. Tell them that it's been a quiet week somewhere else."

"I'll do my best." I thanked everyone again and left.

As I was driving out of town, my attention was caught by some children playing on their front porch. I slowed down to look. Of course, I thought, of course the children of Lake Wobegon would play with Lego blocks. Lake Wobegon was a place where the human imagination was highly honored, and Lego toys respected the imaginations and abilities of children. With many American toys, the only challenge was to find the button to push, and then the toy played with itself. It occurred to me that Lego toys embodied Scandinavian values, which can be summarized with the word respect, an above average level of respect between human beings. Respect was what America turned to Lake Wobegon to hear and learn about.

The children seemed to be making a Danish windmill. Or maybe it was a Norwegian windmill. I really can't tell the difference.

10

With Liberty and Justice for All

T*here was* no better place than St. Peter, Minnesota, to have a good discussion about the Scandinavian style of democracy. St. Peter was the hometown of the first Scandinavian American to almost become president of the United States. In 1906 John Albert Johnson won reelection as governor of Minnesota with such massive bipartisan support that Democrats nationwide took notice and started promoting him as a commonsense alternative to William Jennings Bryan, who had twice failed to win the presidency and was planning to try again in 1908. While Bryan was a master at stirring passions, both for and against him, Johnson was a master of conciliation and a thoughtful reformer. Former president Grover Cleveland supported Johnson's nomination. Though Bryan won the 1908 Democratic nomination, Johnson won enough votes at the convention to be considered a front runner for the 1912 nomination. But Johnson's sudden death in 1909 left Woodrow Wilson to win the presidency.

I was sitting in a St. Peter cafe on a Sunday morning talking with another Johnson, Ruth Johnson, a member of the Minnesota state legislature. Ruth wasn't related to John Johnson, but like him she had Swedish roots, as the town itself did. Before being elected to the state legislature, Ruth had been an associate dean at Gustavus Adolphus College in St. Peter. King Gustavus Adolphus led Sweden to its peak as a European power in the early 1600s. The college's Swedish identity was displayed not just in its name but in a Swedish flag in the center of campus and in a science building named for Alfred Nobel, an arboretum named for Linnaeus, a music building named for Jussi Björling, and a library named for Folke Bernadotte, a Swedish diplomat assassinated while on a peacemaking mission in Palestine in 1948.

I asked Ruth if Minnesota, the most Scandinavian of states, with twenty-one of the twenty-five governors since 1893 having Scandinavian roots, had anything about its political life that could be called distinctly Scandinavian.

Definitely, she replied. In the daily workings of Minnesota state government she observed the stereotypical Scandinavian aversion to conflict. This polite style was called "Minnesota nice." Ruth was an authority on the Scandinavian preference for conciliation over conflict, for as dean she had acted as a college ombudsman. Ombudsman, she explained, was a Swedish word and an old Swedish idea that worked so well in Sweden that it was copied all over the world. In America, someone with a complaint against the government or a corporation might first think of going to a lawyer and filing a lawsuit. In Sweden, they go to an ombudsman, who is charged with investigating and resolving conflicts. While Minnesota had no shortage of divisive issues, Ruth was convinced they were handled better there than elsewhere.

I was less interested in the style of politics than in the substance. I was intrigued by the similarities between the social priorities and policies in Minnesota and Scandinavia. I supposed it was no coincidence that the U.S. state with the most Scandinavians was also the state with the political culture most like twentieth-century Scandinavia. On list after list of social well-being and democratic-minded practices, Scandinavian countries top the world, and Minnesota tops the fifty states. For instance, both Minnesota and Scandinavia lead various rankings of healthiness and longevity, which may reflect genetics but which certainly reflects a strong commitment to public health care. Both Minnesota and Scandinavia lead various rankings of educational quality, illustrated by Minnesota having the highest high school graduation rate in the United States and by Scandinavians being the world's leading per capita book buyers. Voter turnout in Scandinavia greatly eclipses voter turnout in America, but Minnesota often leads the United States in voter turnout, reflecting the fact that Scandinavian Americans have long voted in larger proportions than Anglos and most other ethnic groups. Scandinavians are committed not just to the democratic process but to democratic results, illustrated by how Scandinavia has the world's highest proportion of women in national legislatures, and you can find a similar regard for fairness in various Minnesota policies and results. Scandinavia leads the world in per capita donations to poor nations, and Minneapolis is near the top of United States cities in charitable donations. Minnesota's liberal tendencies are evident not just in public policy but in Minnesota being, for the last two thirds of the twentieth century, the state that most frequently voted for the Democratic candidate for president. At first glance, Minnesota's political liberalism is paradoxical, for in their personal, fiscal, and moral values, Minnesotans can readily be called conservative. Yet this seeming paradox is true of Scandinavia itself, which combines conservative personal lifestyles with liberal social policies. Part of the explanation may be that Scandinavians, having missed the American experience with King George III, which left America officially distrustful of government, are more willing to view government as a trustworthy tool for pursuing personal and social goals.

Ruth was happy to endorse my suggestion that Minnesota was the noblest American state. She said it was a common experience for Minnesota state legislators to attend national conferences on education, health care, the environment, labor relations and women's issues, to find that other states were struggling to formulate policies that had long been standard in Minnesota.

Minnesota's high standards are not simply a result of Democratic big government social engineering schemes. Frequently, private institutions have set the pace, and Minnesota state government has simply tried to keep up. In health care, the Mayo Clinic has set such a high standard that Minnesotans don't even realize that the rest of their health care system is far above average. In education, Minnesota's flock of top-ranked liberal arts colleges, five of which have Scandinavian roots, has embarrassed the state college system into trying to live up. In environmentalism, it was citizen activism that in 1891 dragged the Minnesota state legislature into establishing America's second state park system. In the arts, Minnesota corporations have a strong tradition of supporting private cultural institutions; towns across America have gotten a whiff of Minnesota public-mindedness when Target has opened a store in town and started making generous donations to local arts organizations. In summary, Minnesota's liberal politics can be seen as an attempt to fulfill private, preexisting expectations about the quality a society should have.

Like me, Ruth was inclined to attribute Minnesota's political identity to its Scandinavian heritage, its core Scandinavian values about society. But I had to admit, there were some good objections that could be raised against this assumption. Before I get into this question, it's time to try to define Scandinavian political values a little better.

Scandinavian political values need to be viewed in the context of the millennia-old debate of political philosophers as to the highest value in organizing society: the individual versus the group, rights versus responsibilities. In the twentieth century, both fascism and communism have given horrifying proof of the savagery of societies that disregard individual rights in the name of the collective. On the other hand, the principles of human rights didn't protect the masses in capitalist nations from being preyed upon by ruthless oligarchs and by nightmares like the Great Depression. As a young, restless, ethnically diverse nation, America already suffered from its lack of rooted communities where people felt a strong sense of mutual obligations, and the American political dialogue tended to ignore the whole question of mutual obligations and frame everything in the language of individualism, in terms of rights. Liberals argued for the rights of workers; conservatives argued for the rights of businessmen. Anyone who suggested that workers and businessmen had moral duties to one another was unlikely to be comprehended. Environmentalists argued for the rights of owls and trees when they could have argued for the responsibilities of humans to the earth. Every issue, from social security to minorities to abortion, was argued in terms of whose rights took precedent.

When the Great Depression crippled the democracies and both fascism and communism were on the march, many democratically minded people were desperate to find a societal model that avoided the worst sins of both capitalism and totalitarianism, and they decided that they saw such a model in Scandinavia. Scandinavians seemed to have found a healthy balance between freedom and community, valuing both civil liberties and community responsibility for basic human needs, pursuing both capitalist affluence and egalitarian sharing. Americans obtained this image of Scandinavia through the 1936 bestseller, *Sweden: The Middle Way*, by Marquis Childs, the Washington correspondent for the *St. Louis Post-Dispatch*. In a lonely world for democracies, where Hitler and Stalin bragged louder every month and the New Deal was still groping for a way out of the Depression, Sweden offered an example of a nation that was deeply loyal to democratic values yet experimenting creatively with how to combine the best elements of both capitalism and socialism. The Swedes were proceeding with remarkable pragmatism, disregarding the ideologies of both the Left and the Right. While other Western liberal parties seemed convinced that nationalizing every industry in sight was the road to utopia, the Swedes seemed more interested in harnessing the capitalist engine to a social conscience. President Franklin Roosevelt became so eager to identify his New Deal with developments in Sweden that he dredged up some obscure Swedish leaf on his family tree and declared that he was the "only President to have Swedish blood in his veins."[1] Roosevelt made sure he attended the three hundredth anniversary celebration of the New Sweden colony in 1938, and he lavishly praised the Swedish people and their contribution to America. The New Deal would pay back Scandinavia for its encouragement, for when Scandinavia was invaded during World War II, FDR's speechwriter, the playwright Robert E. Sherwood, would write a Pulitzer Prize–winning play, *There Shall Be No Night*, which rallied sympathy for Finland, and one of FDR's war propagandists, John Steinbeck, would write a novel, *The Moon Is Down*, which rallied sympathy for Norway.

During the cold war years, Sweden remained an attractive role model for people who found both communism and capitalism out of balance. Perhaps inevitably, American liberals tended to idealize Sweden, not seeing the endless debates behind Swedish social policy, the difficult trade-offs, and a tax burden so staggering that even loyal Social Democrats complained bitterly. Even the Swedes' Scandinavian neighbors wondered out loud if the Swedes weren't overdoing it. In an ironic turnabout from the nineteenth-century peasant exodus to America, now it was wealthy Swedes who sought shelter in America. This American idealization of Sweden culminated in the Vietnam War draft dodgers who sought shelter in Sweden, expecting some sort of commune, only to find an obsessive work ethic and a strong corporate culture.

Conversely, American conservatives felt compelled to discredit Sweden. Some of them honestly didn't understand how a society could freely choose socialistic values, and they looked for some hidden dictatorship behind it all and pitied the Swedes who preferred security over the chance to become billionaires. The conservative attack on Sweden culminated in a 1960 speech by President Eisenhower blaming Swedish socialism for the world's highest rate of suicide, alcoholism, and general gloominess. Perhaps Eisenhower's Swedish American wife rebuked him over this, for he later publicly apologized to the Swedes. Nevertheless, such exaggerations became standard ammunition for conservatives who couldn't stand the idea that capitalism should have a heart or that socialism could be driven by a capitalist engine. Conservatives simply ignored the fact that Scandinavian corporations were regularly outgunning American corporations in the world marketplace. (If there are any conservatives out there who are skeptical about the prowess of Scandinavian corporations, just give me a call on your Ericsson or Nokia cellular phone and we'll discuss it.)

Swedes found much to puzzle over and laugh about in the American debate over them. But I believe that the basic image of Sweden as "the middle way" was essentially correct. Through their unique history, environment, and culture, Scandinavians have ended up with a healthier balance between freedom and community, the individual and the group, rights and responsibilities. After the fall of communism, one Swedish conservative politician declared that Sweden shouldn't be proud of being the middle way between success and failure. Yet when the prevailing models of capitalism are a Britain built on severe class stratification and an America built on severe individualism, the world still has much to learn about how to combine capitalism and humane values, and no one has been working on this problem longer and more diligently than Scandinavians.

I also believe that Scandinavian social values, this balance between freedom and community, have been transplanted to America and have shown up in the lives of Scandinavian Americans and made important contributions to American society. The political tradition of Minnesota is evidence for this thesis.

But, as I admitted to Ruth, there were some good objections to this idea. First, Minnesotans came from the nineteenth-century Scandinavia of monarchies and social stratification, not the twentieth-century Scandinavia of universal human rights and social services. Second, from the time they arrived in America, from the time of Abraham Lincoln to the time of Teddy Roosevelt, Scandinavian Americans were solidly Republican. Third, there are other political units loaded with Scandinavians such as North Dakota that are even more staunchly Republican than Minnesota is reliably Democratic.

Of these three objections, the second is almost self-refuting, for the Republican Party of Lincoln and Teddy Roosevelt was the pioneer of civil rights, of environmentalism, of opposing predatory capitalism. Only when the Democrats took over that role did Minnesota switch to the Democrats.

As for the first objection, one possible answer is that Minnesota liberalism had no Scandinavian roots after all and evolved here in America due to strictly American causes. But this flies in the face of the whole experience of Scandinavians in America. If Scandinavian Americans had been shaped by their experiences in America alone, they should have been the most conservative of ethnic groups, the very last ethnic group to worry about social injustice and reform. Scandinavians entered the American mainstream more easily than almost anyone else, largely avoiding the syndrome of immigrants spending at least one generation as a despised underclass. As Protestants, they escaped the religious bigotry that afflicted Irish Catholics. As northern Europeans, they escaped the ethnic bigotry that afflicted eastern and southern Europeans. By not settling in cities, they escaped becoming cogs in a tough industrial system. By becoming farmers, they became instant landowners, which in Europe usually meant you were a guardian of the status quo. Often within a few years of their arrival, Scandinavian Americans tasted prosperity, building pleasant houses and bank accounts and ambitions to have their sons rise high in an amazingly open American society. So why worry about reform? It's true that farmers were exploited by monopoly railroads, and the prairie saw waves of agrarian populism. But in other prairie states these waves of populism soon died down; in Minnesota, populism became the dominant theme, a theme shared by personalities as different as Paul Wellstone and Jesse Ventura. It's true that Minnesota was more industrialized than other prairie states and thus had a larger labor movement, but many eastern states were far more industrialized and unionized than Minnesota, and they never developed Minnesota's high social standards. Minnesota was so charged with liberal energy that it, along with Wisconsin, which was also loaded with Scandinavians, became the powerhouse of the Progressive movement.

Another way to explain the similar politics of Minnesota and Scandinavia is to suppose that one place inspired the other. You can suppose that Scandinavian social democracy inspired Scandinavian Americans, but this ignores the fact that the Scandinavian Americans most involved in reformist politics were second-generation Americans, the generation most eager to ignore and repudiate its roots. Conversely, some historians have suggested that American democracy inspired Scandinavian reform, but this ignores the fact that Scandinavian social democracy went far beyond any model from America.

It seemed to me that the easiest way to account for the political similarities of Minnesota and Scandinavia is to accept that they derive from deep-rooted social values that can be traced back into Scandinavian history, perhaps as far back as Viking days. These values didn't disappear the moment Scandinavians immigrated to America. Evidence for this comes from the sociological bestseller by Harvard professor Robert B. Putnam, *Bowling Alone: The Collapse and Revival of American Community*. Putnam sought to find quantitative indexes for the elusive concept of community, measuring participation in everything from politics to sports leagues. He added these indexes up into a "social capital" ranking of the states, and he found that "one surprisingly strong predictor of the degree of social capital in any state in the 1990s is . . . the fraction of its population that is of Scandinavian stock."[2] This may be as close as we can get to proving that Scandinavian social values were transplanted to America and have made a definitive difference here.

It may be true that democratic values weren't being well served in nineteenth-century Scandinavia, but the monarchies and social stratification of nineteenth-century Scandinavia may not be as definitive of Scandinavian social values as were the monarchies and class structures of other European countries. Because Scandinavia bypassed feudalism, with much of its farmland remaining in the hands of free farmers, Scandinavia didn't have as extreme a class polarization as did Britain, where the Industrial Revolution was built atop the fault line left by feudalism. In a previous chapter I speculated that Marxism had minimal appeal to Scandinavians because it didn't fit their view of nature and society, but perhaps a further reason is that Marxism was addressed to feudal Europe. In Scandinavia, class polarization wasn't the dominant, insoluble social reality. While other liberal political parties in Europe were conducting various forms of class warfare, the Scandinavian Social Democratic parties were not primarily class parties but offered a vision of a family-like "home of the people" that appealed to the middle class.

One can go further and suppose that the very reason some Scandinavians immigrated to America was because their democratic impulses weren't being well served in their own kingdoms. A good case study for this thesis is the career of Charles Lindbergh's grandfather.

In the 1850s August Lindbergh was a brave yet frustrated reformer in the Swedish Parliament. He was a committed democrat opposed to the privileges of class. He sought to protect servants from beatings by their masters. He waged a decade-long campaign to outlaw the whipping post as a punishment for crime. He worked for universal suffrage. He was bitterly opposed by the Swedish elite, who finally managed to discredit him by implicating him in a scandal at the Bank of Sweden, where Lindbergh served as a director. Disgusted, Lindbergh immigrated to Minnesota. There he kept a low political profile, but he seems to have inspired his son with his democratic convictions, especially his dislike of oligarchy. His son became a U.S. congressman in 1906 and an important supporter of Teddy Roosevelt's campaign against oligarchs.

And what about the objection that a Scandinavian enclave like North Dakota is staunchly conservative? North Dakota is the most rural of the farm states, while Minnesota has one of the largest metropolitan areas in the farm states, so perhaps this contrast points us back to the impact of industrialization and urbanization. In Scandinavia, much of the energy for social reform came from the challenge of industrialization. Minnesota faced a very similar challenge, while North Dakota didn't. It seems that the only theory that can combine all of these facts is the idea that when Scandinavian community values were confronted with industrialization, they produced a similar response, and thus Scandinavia and Minnesota evolved in similar ways. Yet in *Bowling Alone*, Robert D. Putnam found that the political differences between Minnesota and North Dakota made very little difference in their "social capital" ranking, the two states regularly ranking side by side, near the top, in everything from good education to low crime and low TV watching.

As if this whole discussion isn't complicated and problematic enough, I should add that there are some who want to give Lutheranism the major credit for both Scandinavian social values and for the development of modern social democracy. Certainly one can make a good case for the good fit between Lutheran values and many Scandinavian character traits such as modesty, honesty, hard work, and thrift. Yet if I was Lutheran I would be quite eager to avoid equating Lutheranism with national destiny, for then Lutheranism would get the blame for the destiny of the founding and leading Lutheran nation, Germany. German social values are quite different from Scandinavian social values. The common roots of Germany and Scandinavia in ethnicity, language, and religion make it all the more remarkable how different their courses in recent history have been. Another problem with crediting Lutheranism for social democracy is that the growth of social democracy coincided with a growing secularism that left the Scandinavian countries the least religious countries in Europe.

I suppose that after all my flattery of both Minnesota and Sweden, a Minnesota Swede like Ruth Johnson couldn't help agreeing with my thesis that the nobility of both places was rooted in a common seed of cultural values.

Later on, I found further evidence for my thesis in the lives and work of ten prominent Scandinavian American social reformers. They came from many states and backgrounds, and their careers ranged from poet to vice president, from journalist to Supreme Court chief justice, but they showed a remarkable consistency of values, that Scandinavian balance of freedom and community. They devoted their lives to implementing these values into American society. They were deeply sympathetic to the outcasts of American society and outraged at a society that could exploit and brutalize its own citizens. They worked to build a society that treated its people with respect and helped them fulfill their needs. Yet they were also deeply distrustful of authoritarianism, rejected the temptations of Marxism, and championed the American tradition of civil liberties.

In the lives of these ten men, you can again see the relative absence of social barriers against Scandinavian Americans. Within the third generation, Scandinavian Americans had reached every position of power in American society except the presidency. For most of the second half of the twentieth century, the U.S. Supreme Court was presided over by the Scandinavians Earl Warren and William Rehnquist. For the quarter century starting in 1964, the Democratic Party only once neglected to include a Scandinavian on its national ticket, and even in that off year it offered a Norwegian for first lady, Eleanor Stegeberg McGovern. So the question arises again: if Scandinavian Americans like Earl Warren and Hubert Humphrey were less victimized than other ethnic groups, why did they become so concerned about the victims of American society? Ironically, it may be that the very reason Scandinavian Americans haven't reached the presidency is because they were too concerned about the victims of American society, more concerned than was the rest of America.

I am not suggesting that Scandinavian American political leaders have been uniformly liberal. I have already implicitly acknowledged otherwise by naming William Rehnquist alongside Earl Warren. The Rehnquist Court disallowed the Warren Court's willingness to force social reform onto American society. But the scarcity of prominent Scandinavian American conservatives like Rehnquist only confirms the point that if Scandinavian Americans had been shaped by their experience in America alone, they should have been overwhelmingly conservative. That they have been otherwise may prove that, as the harshest critics of Earl Warren and Hubert Humphrey always insisted, there really was something un-American about them.

To help elucidate the experience and values of Scandinavian Americans, I will borrow the words of one of the most perceptive observers of twentieth-century America, Eric Sevareid. As a protégé of Edward R. Murrow, Sevareid was a pioneer of broadcast journalism, first through radio reports from the front lines of World War II and then as the philosopher of the *CBS Evening News*. Sevareid may have done more than anyone to help American journalism fulfill its potential as the conscience of a democracy.

In 1946 Sevareid published an acclaimed intellectual autobiography, *Not So Wild a Dream*, in the tradition of *The Education of Henry Adams*. Sevareid had written his first book at age eighteen, detailing a 2,250-mile canoe trip he and a friend made from Minneapolis to Hudson Bay. Sevareid, the grandson of a Norwegian immigrant, said the trip was inspired by the Kensington Runestone and the idea that the Vikings could have reached Minnesota from Hudson Bay. In his autobiography, Sevareid said that his political inspiration too came from something Scandinavian, his hometown of Velva, North Dakota, which he saw as the ideal democracy, the right balance of freedom and community:

Perhaps it was our common dependence upon the wheat that made all men essentially equal, but I do know now, having looked at society in many countries, that we were a true democracy. . . . A man might affect pretensions, but he could not pretend for long. We lived too closely together for that. There were, of course, differences in degree of material wealth. . . . But no man lived in fear of another. No man had the power to direct another to vote this way or that. . . . This was an agrarian democracy, which meant that there was no concentration of capital goods, which meant in turn, since we had no all-powerful landlords, that no class society based upon birth or privilege had a chance to develop. If this was a Christian democracy, still, no virtue was made of poverty; the Scandinavian is too hard-headed for that. But to be poor was no disgrace. If the man of the house in one of the families that lived close to the edge fell ill and could not work, my mother and other mothers carried them baskets of fresh things to eat. It was not charity, not condescension to ease the conscience; it was neighborliness.

Later, I read all the exalting literature of the great struggle for a classless society; later, I watched at first hand its manifestations in several countries. It occurred to me what men wanted was Velva, on a national, on a world, scale. For the thing was already achieved, in miniature, out there, in a thousand miniatures scattered along the rivers and highways of all the West and Middle West. I was to hear the intelligentsia of eastern America, of England and France, speak often of our Middle West with a certain contempt. . . . They have much to learn, these gentlemen.[3]

Sevareid concluded the book with a declaration that the democratic values of Velva were the answer to the crisis and hopes of a world burnt by fascism and squaring off between Russia and America. If a Main Street banker dared to claim that a small North Dakota town held the answers to the world's troubles, he would be ridiculed for provincialism. But Sevareid is quite serious in declaring that only if America models itself after Velva will it succeed in its new role as world leader:

There was still time for America to tip the balance and work its fashion upon the future. It could still work greatly to create a world in its own great image, but if the result was to be one to capture the allegiance of the confraternity of goodwill, America would also have to work greatly upon herself. All that America truly meant, all that Americans had perished for, would be devoid of consequence or portent unless the image of society that America showed the world was that of the little Velvas as I had known, remembered, and cherished them.[4]

Thirty years later, on the American bicentennial, when Sevareid's autobiography was reprinted as an American classic, he made no apologies for his advocacy of Velva. It was not nostalgia or naïveté. His whole television career consisted of urging America to be more like a Scandinavian town on the prairie.

It was a Danish American journalist who played a central role in starting the American Progressive movement. Shortly after Jacob Riis published *How the Other Half Lives* in 1890, he was visited by a young man who was just starting a political career. The young man later wrote that Riis's book was "to me both an enlightenment and an inspiration for which I felt I could never be too grateful. . . . I had called at his office to tell him how deeply impressed I was by the book, and that I wished to help him in any practical way to try to make things a little better. I have always had a horror of words that are not translated into deeds."[5]

If Jacob Riis was a man of words, the young visitor, Teddy Roosevelt, was definitely a man of deeds. Without Jacob Riis, the deeds of two Roosevelt administrations might never have occurred.

Riis was born in Denmark, the son of a newspaperman, and immigrated to America at age twenty-one, partly to forget an unhappy love affair and partly because he believed America was the land of opportunity. Instead, he found a land of horrific slums. Riis never found Velva. The main thing he noticed about democratic values in New York City was that millions of poor immigrants had no value to American society. "One half of the world does not know how the other half lives, nor does it care. The half that is on top cares little about the struggles and even less about the destiny of those underneath, as long as it is able to hold them down and keep its own seat."[6]

After many laboring jobs and mistreatments, Riis got a job as a reporter and began publicizing the misery of the slums. Riis became America's first photojournalist, pioneering the use of flashbulbs to take indoor photos of slum life. His resulting book, *How the Other Half Lives*, caused a national uproar. It wasn't just the grim photos; it was Riis's moral outrage, the accusation that America had betrayed its promises.

Teddy Roosevelt and Riis became strong friends and allies. Roosevelt credited Riis for helping him consolidate his political musings into the conviction that government needed to curb the power of the rich and make America, in Roosevelt's words, "an economic and industrial as well as a political democracy."[7] Roosevelt came to national prominence as New York City's crusading police commissioner, and much of his agenda was shaped by Riis. With Riis rallying public support and Roosevelt doing the political fighting, they accomplished many reforms. Roosevelt's success earned him the governorship and then the presidency. Roosevelt repeatedly offered Riis important government posts, but Riis preferred to remain a man of words.

Two years before Teddy Roosevelt became president, another Scandinavian American man of words, Thorstein Veblen, gave the Progressive movement its theoretical foundations.

Veblen viewed American society through the eyes of an outcast, not because he ever dwelled in a slum but because of his odd, alienated personality. Veblen's inability to fit in got him cast out of the economics faculty of Stanford and then the University of Chicago. He lasted for seven years at the University of Missouri, where my father later taught.

Feeling apart from American society has been the common experience of new immigrants. If it's true that a lonely Norwegian fishing village generated a stronger community bond than did a big European city or a feudal estate, then Scandinavians were left especially sensitive to the lack of community in America. Immigrants sought to fill this lack in various ways. They clung to their churches. They flocked to join fraternal lodges, which offered not just secret bonding ceremonies but financial aid for the sick and old; each Scandinavian nationality started its own lodges, such as the Sons of Norway. They found solidarity in both labor unions and corporations. They strived for financial success not just for its own sake but because it bought respect in American society.

Somehow, Thorstein Veblen got an extra large dose of alienation, partly because, as the son of a Norwegian immigrant, growing up in a tight Norwegian community in Minnesota, he didn't start speaking English until he started college, and partly because of his own psychology. Instead of yearning to join American society, he perceived it as a monstrosity. With the detachment of an anthropologist studying a bizarre tribe and with the wicked satire of a novelist, Veblen wrote *The Theory of the Leisure Class* in 1899, and it made him an unlikely celebrity. Unlike traditional economists, who depicted the economy as the sum of agents rationally pursuing their own self-interest, Veblen depicted an economy grossly distorted by primitive cravings for status and power. The rich accumulated mansions and yachts and limousines like reptiles trying to display mating superiority. It was Veblen who coined the phrase "conspicuous consumption." Veblen's abhorrence of blatant displays of superiority was a very Scandinavian reaction. And it wasn't just in their private lives that the rich made gods out of status and power; they made major business decisions to satisfy those gods, even if they inflicted harm on the overall economy. At a time when American folklore hailed financiers and industrialists as masterful generators of wealth, Veblen depicted them as the worst enemies of capitalism, which would function more smoothly without them.

Veblen became a hero to three generations of reformers. Progressives invoked Veblen to argue that reform was not just a matter of compassion but of rationality, of removing disease from the economy. New Dealers invoked Veblen to refute charges that they were socialists; they were just trying to save capitalism from itself. Sixties radicals, inspired less by economic distress than cultural alienation, observed that prosperity had only further exposed the pathology of a society that valued conspicuous consumption above anything else.

However angry Jacob Riis was about poverty, however skeptical Thorstein Veblen was about capitalism, and however much communists wanted to invoke them to justify revolution, neither of them had any sympathy for the Marxist scheme of creating utopia by replacing capitalist dictators with proletarian dictators.

On one of his national lecture tours, Riis lectured in Galesburg, Illinois, and he was heard by a young man who was calling himself Charlie to hide his Swedish background. Only when Charlie started publishing poetry did he decide it was okay to be Swedish, and he started signing his work Carl Sandburg.

As a poet, Sandburg modeled himself after Walt Whitman, both in his free verse style and in his advocacy of American democracy. During the Civil War Whitman sought to rally public support for democratic values, and in Sandburg's own time of crisis, the Great Depression and World War II, he became an important voice of encouragement to a troubled nation. His lecture tours were packed; President Roosevelt urged him to run for Congress; and MGM paid him a fortune to write a novel from which it could make a patriotic epic. Later on, academia rejected civic poetry, or at least poetry that admitted there might be anything good about America, and Sandburg's reputation fell, and poets wondered why the public and men of power paid no attention to them. Sandburg, in his role as advocate of democracy, probably achieved more civic influence than any poet in American history.

Sandburg wasn't satisfied with a democracy that offered only civil liberties, and Jacob Riis helped him realize what else was needed. Sandburg had already watched his father being ground down by the monopoly railroad for which he worked as a blacksmith. Perhaps Galesburg was less inclined than most of America to settle for such injustice. Galesburg had started out as an offshoot of the Oneida commune, and it was located only twenty miles from Bishop Hill, which also started as a utopian commune. Before the Civil War, Galesburg was a sanctuary on the Underground Railroad. When the Gilded Age railroad arrived, it was quite a contrast to the tattered socialist ideals of Galesburg and Bishop Hill, but it offered a lot of jobs and turned Galesburg into a center of Swedish immigration. The first Swedish newspaper in the United States was published there. Carl never forgot how, when Galesburg railroad workers tried to strike, company thugs shot them dead in the street.

Seeing Jacob Riis impressed Sandburg that a career as a crusading journalist and public orator could have a huge influence. Sandburg started writing a column for the Galesburg newspaper, exploring the progressive ideas in the air. Then he moved to Chicago to become editor of a politically minded literary magazine. Thorstein Veblen was teaching in Chicago then, and Sandburg's wife enrolled in his economics class. Sandburg developed a public lecture on Walt Whitman and hit the lyceum circuit. Whitman gave him a good excuse to advocate the Common Man. On a lecture trip to Wisconsin, Sandburg encountered the thriving Wisconsin Progressive movement, which had just elected Robert La Follette to the U.S. Senate and would soon elect several Socialist Party mayors in Milwaukee. A young Jewish girl growing up in Milwaukee then, Golda Meir, would learn her American-style socialism there and later implement it as prime minister of Israel.

Sandburg made a big impression on the Wisconsin Socialists, and they hired him as an organizer. Three years later Sandburg was appointed the personal assistant to Milwaukee's first Socialist mayor. Two years after that, Sandburg's boss was the Socialist nominee for vice president under Eugene Debs.

But Sandburg wanted to return to Chicago, and to writing. A brand-new Chicago magazine called *Poetry* encouraged his talent. Soon Sandburg was a nationally acclaimed populist poet. To pay the rent he wrote for the *Chicago Daily News*, including movie reviews, making him the Roger Ebert of the day. When World War I broke out, Sandburg was sent to Stockholm to get the news direct from Germany and Russia. He was delighted to set foot on the soil of his forefathers. He struck up a friendship with Per Albin Hansson, the editor of the newspaper of the Swedish Social Democrats who later became prime minister. "We understood each other thoroughly," Sandburg recalled, "the Wisconsin movement in which I had been an organizer having operated with much the same theory and viewpoint as the Swedish party affiliated with the trade-unions."[8] When Sandburg got home, his fresh pride in his Swedishness prompted him to change his new baby's name from Mary to Helga.

In the 1920s, Sandburg communed with another man of the people, Abraham Lincoln. Sandburg had long been interested in the art of biography, and as a youth he had planned to write a biography of a Swedish king he admired. Lincoln had been a living presence in Galesburg, the site of one of the Lincoln-Douglas debates. Sandburg's biography of Lincoln's prairie years came out just before the Wall Street crash, and since Sandburg turned Lincoln into a bit of a socialist reformer, his book gave the New Deal an old hero. Sandburg's biography of Lincoln's war years came out just before Pearl Harbor and gave the country a reminder of a successful democratic crusade. Sandburg's Lincoln biographies, and the Pulitzer Prize he won for them, gave him stature among people who ordinarily didn't read poetry. In the depths of the Great Depression, Sandburg wrote his most affirmative poetry, proclaiming that America would yet summon out of its people's strength and its great history a humane and proud destiny. As Hitler marched, Sandburg publicly denounced Charles Lindbergh, the leading spokesman for neutrality. After Pearl Harbor, Sandburg sought to be for Roosevelt what Whitman had been for Lincoln.

For the 150th anniversary of Lincoln's birth in 1959, Congress held a joint session to hear Sandburg memorialize Lincoln. When Sandburg died in 1967, six thousand people gathered at the Lincoln Memorial to memorialize Sandburg. The guests included President Johnson and Chief Justice Warren.

In the backyard of Sandburg's boyhood house in Galesburg, there is a granite boulder named Remembrance Rock beneath which Sandburg's ashes are buried. The name of the rock invites more than just remembrance of Sandburg. *Remembrance Rock* was the title of his novel on American history. When it was published in 1948, reviewers compared it to *War and Peace* for its length and historic sweep, though few complimented Sandburg for having a novelist's eye for character and story line. It was symbolic that Sandburg would name his own grave for his epic story of America. Sandburg loved America, loved it with an immigrant's love in which even his own Swedish name wasn't as important as being included in America. Inclusion was the essence of the American Dream, the unbelievably generous idea that anyone could come from anywhere, from countries where they had been excluded, and here they could be as good as anyone else. Inclusion was what motivated Sandburg's political efforts, his demand that capitalism include everyone in its potential.

Remembrance. I remember how as a child I had a recording of Sandburg reading his poetry. I listened to it many times. I was fascinated by his kind spirit and his love of language, the way his rich voice caressed every word as if he was rubbing a magic lantern. One long poem so impressed me that I played the record over and over, copying down a few lines at a time until I had the whole thing.

Remembrance is why I drop by Sandburg's home when I go through Galesburg. It's not that there's anything new for me to see. Next door to his home is a small museum with displays about his life and work, and I read the displays again, remembering things I had forgotten. It's amazing how readily we forget even the most important things. Sandburg couldn't remember his own father's name. Carl's father had changed his last name on coming to America, and Carl never knew what the original name was or exactly where his father was born. When Sandburg went to Sweden in 1950 and tried to find his roots, a researcher gave him the wrong name and the wrong place, and this erroneous story went into Sandburg biographies. The museum has the right name, Danielson, and a map of Sweden showing his hometown. It is, in fact, just down the road from Gränna. Sandburg's father, August, left for America in 1869, the same year as my great-grandfather August. Perhaps they were on the same ship. I don't remember.

Remembrance is also why the visitors register at Sandburg's home always includes visitors from Sweden. Being so close to Bishop Hill, Sandburg's home is on the trail of Swedes searching not for roots but for branches. Many of them know only that some relative sailed for America long ago, and they have no hopes of locating actual relatives, but they still feel the pull of Remembrance Rock.

In the 1930s a new generation of writers continued Chicago's reputation as the capital of leftist literature. It included Richard Wright, Saul Bellow, Studs Terkel, James T. Farrell, and Nelson Algren. As a Swede and a chronicler of social outcasts, Algren was hailed by Malcolm Cowley and other critics as the successor to Carl Sandburg. But Algren had grown up in tougher times, and he and his work had a much tougher edge.

It seems that Algren was doomed to identify himself with misfits. As a kid he started calling himself "Swede" after the Chicago White Sox player Swede Risberg, only for Risberg to become infamous for throwing the 1919 World Series.

When Algren graduated as a journalist from the University of Illinois in 1931, jobs were impossible to find. He became one of the legion of hopeless people drifting around the country on freight trains. He decided to become the literary equivalent of Jacob Riis, showing America its darker side. He got more of an initiation than he bargained for, for when he tried to steal a typewriter he ended up spending months in a rural Texas jail. Back in Chicago he started producing stories and novels portraying the underclass with grim honesty. While Steinbeck's Joads were innocent victims, Algren's drug pushers, gamblers, gangsters, thieves, drunks, prostitutes, and killers were all trapped in self-destruction. Yet Algren offered compassion to them and a sociological scorn to the society that generated such traps of degradation alongside opulence. When Algren's novel *The Man with the Golden Arm* won the first National Book Award in 1949, Eleanor Roosevelt presented the award to him. Yet Algren got another lesson in American values when Hollywood gypped him out of payment for the movie version, paid Frank Sinatra a fortune to star in it, and replaced a suicide with a happy ending.

Like many intellectuals in the 1930s, Algren was attracted to communism, but as someone who cared more about people than about ideas, he was soon disillusioned by the communist disregard for individuals. He did sign enough party-line petitions that J. Edgar Hoover personally ordered an investigation of Algren. When, after Pearl Harbor, Algren was drafted into the army, he was at first disgruntled at the idea of fighting for capitalism, but when he discovered that his FBI file meant he was being left behind when the rest of his unit shipped out, he demanded to serve his country, and he did.

Algren's most unlikely contribution to human equality was his encouragement of the woman who fell madly in love with him, Simone de Beauvoir. Though Beauvoir wouldn't leave Paris (or Jean-Paul Sartre) for him and he wouldn't leave Chicago, she declared herself his wife, and they went on a honeymoon cruise down the Mississippi River to New Orleans. When she died forty years later, she was buried alongside Sartre, but she was wearing Algren's ring. Beauvoir loved Algren's compassion for the oppressed. She told a biographer that it was Algren with whom she first discussed her hopes of writing an essay about the oppression of women. Algren encouraged her to develop her idea into a book, and as a model he gave her a copy of *An American Dilemma*, the seminal study of American race relations by the Swedish sociologist Gunnar Myrdal. He also gave her a book by Gunnar's wife, Alva Myrdal: *Nation and Family: The Swedish Experiment in Democratic Family and Population Policy*. Writing in 1941, when it seemed possible fascism would erase democracy, Alva Myrdal offered Sweden as a model of how public policy could promote democratic values in family life. After showing how Swedish public policy had helped improve the status of women, she then raised the big question: why were women worldwide treated as inferior, even by women themselves? Alva Myrdal declared that this was a social contrivance as unnatural and unjust as racial discrimination in America, and it needed to be challenged and changed through social reform.

Beauvoir couldn't get started on her essay on women, but then Sartre took her on a long lecture tour and vacation in Sweden. She received a letter from Algren saying she had inspired him to write a masterpiece, *The Man With the Golden Arm*. Beauvoir was planning to fly to Chicago in a few weeks, and she was chagrined that she had no comparable inspiration to report. So she started writing her essay on women, what became the seminal feminist study, *The Second Sex*. She wrote to her Swede that she was in Sweden writing the book he had believed in. The book even included a mention of Sweden's "very important feminist tradition . . . invoking old Swedish tradition."[9]

Algren was in Paris for the publication of *The Second Sex*. Beauvoir credited Algren's moral support for getting her through the storm of criticism against her. For years afterward, whenever someone publicly criticized Beauvoir, she and Sartre would joke that they would "send Algren to punch his nose."[10]

When Gunnar and Alva Myrdal arrived in America in October 1929 for a year of studying American society, they got more than they expected. Two weeks later, the stock market crashed. The Myrdals got to observe a young democratic society struggling with a massive social breakdown. While the Myrdals were perplexed by some things such as the popular belief that the crisis would soon fix itself, they also developed great respect for the strength of democratic values in America.

The Great Depression put the people and values of many nations to a severe test, and both America and Scandinavia can be proud of their responses. While other nations were being hypnotized by psychopaths preaching the rule of the strong, America chose a president who could barely lift himself out of his wheelchair, and who placed human compassion before doctrine. In the same year FDR was elected, the Social Democrats began their long reign in Sweden, also placing compassion before doctrine. If anyone should have been tempted by Hitler's Nordic superman mythology, which even used Viking symbolism, it was the Scandinavians, but the fascist parties in Scandinavia remained tiny. When Hitler invaded Denmark and Norway, their Jews were defiantly evacuated to Sweden.

Along with Franklin Roosevelt, America elected two Scandinavian American governors who became key partners in Roosevelt's reforms. In Minnesota there was Floyd B. Olson, and in California, Culbert Olson.

When Eric Sevareid was a student at the University of Minnesota, Floyd B. Olson was his hero. Sevareid was involved in a student protest against compulsory military training, and when the university president barred the protestors from using the campus auditorium, Governor Olson showed up and addressed the students from the front steps, endorsing their opposition to the warlords of capitalism. In a campus mock convention, Sevareid helped nominate Olson for president.

In fact, there was speculation that President Roosevelt would choose Olson as vice president in 1936 to bolster his strength among agrarian populists. This was remarkable not just because of Olson's reputation for radicalism but because he wasn't even a Democrat. In Minnesota in the 1930s the Democratic Party placed a distant third behind the progressive Republicans and the radical Farmer-Labor Party.

Floyd B. Olson was the son of a Swedish mother and a Norwegian father and learned his sympathy for the underdog while growing up on the poor north side of Minneapolis. He worked his way through law school and became county attorney, earning public respect by fighting political corruption. When the Depression hit, the 1930 election offered Americans their first chance to formulate a political response. Olson responded by running for governor with declarations that capitalism had failed, that the system should go to hell, and that he wasn't a liberal, he was a radical. Yet when in office, Olson proved to be a pragmatic reformer. He angered conservatives by enacting a graduated state income tax, strong labor laws, and a ban on farm foreclosures. But he also angered radicals by ignoring his own party's platform calling for public ownership of banks, railroads, and factories. When Roosevelt became president in 1932, Olson became one of the staunchest supporters of the New Deal. It might well have been Olson and not Henry Wallace who became FDR's agrarian populist vice president, but once again, as with Governor John Johnson, Minnesota lost its chance when Olson died of cancer in 1936.

In California it was a Danish Olson who brought home the New Deal, but it came later, in 1938, for California found itself paralyzed between the Right and the Left. A Republican governor, ignoring the unemployed when he wasn't persecuting them, gave John Steinbeck lots of material for *The Grapes of Wrath*. Meanwhile, the Left proposed a series of dubious pension schemes, the most famous of which was EPIC (End Poverty in California), proposed by the novelist Upton Sinclair, whom the Democrats nominated for governor in 1934.

Culbert Olson had supported Sinclair for governor, and when Olson ran for governor in 1938, his rhetoric was enough to get him accused of being a communist, but on being elected he proved to be, like Floyd B. Olson, a pragmatic reformer seeking state versions of New Deal ideas.

Culbert Olson attributed much of his political philosophy to having been born in Utah, where the Mormons emphasized community over economic competition. Olson didn't expect that being a liberal non-Mormon would be a barrier to a political career in Utah; in 1916, the same year Olson got elected to the Utah state legislature, Utah supported Woodrow Wilson for president and elected one of the first Jewish governors in U.S. history. As chairman of the Judiciary Committee, Olson became a key partner in the new governor's progressive agenda. In 1920 Olson nearly won the Democratic nomination for the U.S. Senate. Yet 1920 was the beginning of a conservative era in America, and this was part of the reason Olson decided to abandon his political career and move to California to practice law.

The economic crisis reawakened the liberal crusader in Olson, but he found he couldn't get as far with New Deal reforms in California as Floyd B. Olson did in Minnesota. California was the ultimate address of the American Dream, which held that everything would take care of itself and that if you were poor it was your own fault.

The same year Californians elected Olson governor, they elected a Swedish Norwegian attorney general, Earl Warren. Like Carl Sandburg, Warren learned about the vulnerability of the individual in America by watching his father being mistreated by his railroad employer. When Warren's father joined a strike, he was blacklisted and had to leave his family and travel ninety miles away to get a job with another railroad. In college Earl Warren got involved in progressive politics. When Warren ran for governor against Olson in 1942, he ran as a progressive Republican in the tradition of Teddy Roosevelt.

Many years later, Republicans would feel that Earl Warren had betrayed them on the Supreme Court; Eisenhower called his appointment of Warren "the biggest damn fool thing I ever did."[11] (One has to wonder if Eisenhower's frustration with Warren was one source of his famous tirade against Sweden.) Warren's answer was that he had served the same philosophy throughout his career. Starting as a district attorney, he had actively sought ways to use the authority of government to help victims. If in his three terms as governor he was generally moderate in his policies, it was because as governor his job was to make compromises. As chief justice of the Supreme Court, his job was not to compromise but to uphold principles. Still, as governor his liberal sympathies were obvious in his proposing state health insurance, establishing a fair employment commission, integrating the California National Guard, reforming prisons and mental hospitals, increasing support for education, and opposing corporate influence.

Warren's huge reelection margins convinced the national Republican Party that he could help them carry the West, so he was nominated for vice president under Tom Dewey in 1948. In 1952 he was a favorite for the presidential nomination, until Eisenhower decided to run.

When Eisenhower appointed Warren chief justice in 1953, the Supreme Court was deliberating the case of *Brown v. Board of Education of Topeka, Kansas* and was badly divided. Under Warren's leadership, the Court soon made a unanimous ruling outlawing racial segregation in public schools. This was just the beginning of an era of society-changing rulings. The Warren Court outlawed discrimination in housing, banned laws against interracial marriage, protected the voting rights of minorities, outlawed school prayer, curbed government agencies from doing anything they wanted in the name of national security, expanded government powers to regulate businesses, strongly supported labor unions, required reapportionment of legislatures to insure one person/one vote, and, in the *Miranda* case, protected the rights of the accused.

By the time Warren retired, America was full of billboards demanding "Impeach Earl Warren." Even among sympathizers there was room to debate whether the Warren Court had intruded upon the authority of other branches of government. But Warren's legacy was an America that showed greater respect for its people, an America with a better balance between rights and responsibilities, an America that was more Scandinavian.

History might have turned out differently, and Earl Warren might have been elected vice president in 1948, if not for the actions of another Scandinavian at the other national political convention that year. President Truman, needing the support of southern Democrats for his reelection bid, offered no support for a civil rights plank in the Democratic Party platform. But the young mayor of Minneapolis, Hubert Humphrey, was determined that the Democrats make a strong commitment to civil rights, and he took the podium to address the convention. With oratory that was compared to William Jennings Bryan's classic cross-of-gold speech, Humphrey declared: "To those who say that we are rushing this issue of civil rights—I say to them, we are 172 years too late . . . The time has arrived for the Democratic Party to get out of the shadow of states' rights and walk forthrightly into the bright sunshine of human rights."[12]

To everyone's surprise, the convention voted for the civil rights plank, setting the party and the national agenda for the next quarter century. The southerners responded by walking out of the convention and then running Governor Thurmond for president. But some analysts gave the civil rights plank and Humphrey credit for bringing blacks and disaffected liberals back to Truman and thus winning the election for him. Humphrey got himself elected to the U.S. Senate that fall after unifying the Minnesota Democrats and the Farmer-Labor Party.

Like the name Warren, the name Humphrey does not reveal Scandinavian ancestry. When Warren was running for state attorney general, an aide presented him with a family pedigree he could boast about, going back to the Warrens of Colonial Virginia. Warren told him he should have traced the name Varren. The name Humphrey really did go back to Colonial Massachusetts on Hubert's father's side, but his mother, Christine Sannes, was born in Norway. She was brought to America as a child by her seaman father, who had expected to become a sailor on the Missouri River but ended up farming along the same South Dakota creek where Rölvaag would set *Giants in the Earth*. Christine's parents were delighted when she married a Yankee. Christine took young Hubert on long visits to her parents' house, where Norwegian was spoken routinely. It wasn't from the reserved Christine that Hubert got his talkiness. Earl Warren, by contrast, received his full share of Scandinavian reserve; when he was posing for campaign photographs, the photographer had to coach him into smiling.

Humphrey's political views were defined by the Great Depression and the New Deal. Bank failures caused his parents to lose their house and forced Humphrey to leave college and work for many years in the family pharmacy. Humphrey was impressed by how even a small, hardworking prairie town could be crushed by inhuman economic forces. He was heartened by the radio voice of FDR offering a caring and capable federal government. When Humphrey wrote his master's thesis in political science, he defended the New Deal against charges that it was a form of totalitarianism. He asserted that the founding fathers had envisioned a balance of order and freedom, creating "one of the great compromises of human history—a compromise between centralized power and individualized liberty."[13] But, he said, the rise of industrial capitalism brought an unexpected imbalance, an extreme concentration of power in the hands of the rich that could only be balanced by a moral government that acted on behalf of the community. Within limits set by the Constitution and by "the essential features of the capitalistic economy," America needed to improve its political democracy into a social democracy.

Twenty-five years later, Senator Humphrey was the only American public official invited to a summit of social democratic leaders held at the home of Tage Erlander, Sweden's prime minister. Also present were the prime ministers of Norway and Denmark. Humphrey felt enough in sync with their values and goals that he was planning to attend the summit again the following year, 1964, but it occurred to him that since President Johnson was considering him for the vice presidency, maybe he'd better check with Johnson first. Johnson was horrified that Humphrey would associate with those radical Scandinavians, so Humphrey didn't attend again.

When Humphrey joined the Senate, *Time* magazine put him on the cover as the "No. 1 prospect for Liberalism in this country," and he would live up to this billing. Many of the Democratic accomplishments of the 1960s were originally Humphrey initiatives of the 1950s: Medicare, the Peace Corps, the Job Corps, the Nuclear Weapons Test Ban Treaty, the Civil Rights Act of 1964. It was to win the support of liberals that Johnson selected Humphrey as vice president. It was also Humphrey's undoing. Though as an ardent anticommunist Humphrey was a willing spokesman for Johnson's Vietnam policies, the disastrous course of the war and the radicalization of youth left many Democrats regarding Humphrey as a voice of the establishment and American imperialism. Yet conservatives hadn't forgotten his liberal identity, and when Humphrey ran for president in 1968, Richard Nixon blamed the values of Humphrey and Earl Warren for all the trouble America was in. Third-party candidate George Wallace ran more against Warren than against Humphrey. The defeat of Humphrey and the retirement of Warren a few months later marked the end of an era, the liberal middle third of the century, and the beginning of a conservative final third in which even Scandinavian American Democrats would learn not to try to turn America into Scandinavia.

Humphrey's leadership in revitalizing the Minnesota Democratic Party inspired several talented men to enter politics, including Eugene McCarthy, who became senator and, in 1968, Humphrey's rival for the

Democratic presidential nomination; the Swedish Orville Freeman, who became governor and a cabinet member under Presidents Kennedy and Johnson; and the Norwegian Walter Mondale, who became vice president eight years after Humphrey left.

Walter Mondale's great-grandfather emigrated from the Norwegian town of Mundal and immediately went to work for American democracy by joining Lincoln's army. The Mondales settled in a small Norwegian town in Minnesota, and they retained enough of their heritage that Mondale's father still spoke fluent Norwegian. Mondale's father was a Methodist minister and "an old social gospel liberal." Mondale was close to his father and was inspired by him to enter politics and promote social gospel liberalism. Yet Mondale's Norwegian upbringing presented one barrier to a political career. Norwegians aren't supposed to brag. "You know," Mondale told the St. Olaf College scholar Odd Lovoll, "when I grew up you got spanked for two things. One was stealing, and the other was bragging. And which was the greater crime, I don't know. But in politics, basically the first thing you do is brag, see? To run for political office was hard when I first started, boy, I was so shy. And I had been taught so much not to brag or show off, you know, to be nice and deferential. Don't be pushy and vain."[14]

This very Scandinavian admonition against bragging and arrogance, this rule that no one should claim to be better than anyone else, translates into a very egalitarian form of politics, a spanking repugnance against seeing citizens being treated as inferiors. Mondale's political career consisted of spanking America for acting un-Norwegian.

Like Humphrey, it was Mondale's fate to get lost in another man's shadow. Starting when Mondale was a student at Macalester College and his political science teacher was Hubert Humphrey, Mondale was Humphrey's protégé. When Humphrey became vice president, Minnesota governor Karl Rölvaag, the son of the novelist, appointed Mondale to Humphrey's Senate seat. Later Mondale disappeared into the shadow of Jimmy Carter, who selected Mondale as vice president for the same reason Johnson selected Humphrey, to reassure northern liberals about a southern Democrat. But Carter alienated both conservatives and liberals, the first by sinning against the American Dream in suggesting that conspicuous consumption wasn't good for America. That Americans were still committed to the frontier myth was unmistakable in Carter's 1980 reelection defeat by someone who literally stepped right out of a cowboy movie, Ronald Reagan. Disaffected liberals found another Scandinavian to support for president that year, independent candidate John Anderson, a congressman from the Swedish enclave of Rockford, Illinois.

When Mondale ran for president four years later, America was in no mood to be scolded about its selfishness. Mondale lost every state except Minnesota.

The Democrats couldn't seem to learn their lesson about associating with Scandinavians, for four years later they nominated yet another one for vice president, Texas senator Lloyd Bentsen, great-grandson of a Danish immigrant who settled in South Dakota in 1884 only to head for the warmer Rio Grande valley. Once again the Democrats got slaughtered, but they did carry Minnesota. In 1992 Bill Clinton finally obeyed the lesson about associating with Scandinavians, but, being a sneaky kind of guy in regard to women, Clinton did sneak two Scandinavian women into the White House, Tipper (Carlson) Gore as second lady and Janet (Rasmussen) Reno as attorney general, alongside Lloyd Bentsen as treasury secretary.

At least Humphrey and Mondale left their mark on one campaign for human equality. It was Humphrey, through President Truman, who arranged for the first woman to be appointed a U.S. ambassador. Minnesota's Eugenie Anderson became ambassador to Denmark. It was Mondale who selected the first woman nominee for vice president.

Remembrance. It was 1976, the American bicentennial, a good year to consider the sweep of American history. I was part of a large crowd outside the Eero Saarinen chapel in my hometown. The chapel had four equal sides and four doors to symbolize that people came to faith from many directions. The architect may have been Scandinavian, but the design was a good symbol of American democracy. The chapel could also have said that the American nation came together from every direction, from every nation and race and class and religion. That day we had come together to hear another Scandinavian say something about America. Walter Mondale was campaigning for vice president, and the hill beside the chapel happened to make a good outdoor amphitheater.

Though Mondale would win that election, the Democratic Party was now greatly baffled by its paradoxical relationship with the American Dream. American liberalism upheld the American Dream of inclusion for all, rejected the American Dream that the endless capitalist frontier would take care of everything by itself, yet assumed that an ever-growing capitalist pie would always give them surplus money to crusade with. Conservatives had never forgiven liberals for besmirching the myth of the eternal frontier, but only when they could plausibly claim that the budgetary cost of liberalism was crippling the economy, only when a nongrowing pie meant that government-induced inclusion for one group meant exclusion for another, only then did conservatives really succeed in portraying liberalism as the outright enemy of the American Dream. Worse, 1960s radicals had even rejected the dream of inclusion for all, deciding that America was an inhuman machine you shouldn't want to join. Whereas for Humphrey freedom for African Americans meant inclusion, 1960s radicals wanted African Americans, Native Americans, and Third World peasants to fill the role of the romantic noble savage defying the evils of civilization. When the radicals eventually took over university humanities departments, even Walt Whitman himself couldn't show up on campus and read one of his America-loving poems without being branded a bourgeois patriarchal fascist.

If by 1976 it was clear that America wasn't going to become a social democracy like Scandinavia, it was also becoming quite believable that America might just succeed at its dream of inclusion for all, of welcoming people from every direction, every nation and race and class and religion and gender, and bonding them into a real community. To an ethnocentric world suddenly thrust by modern communications and trade and weaponry into close contact with all of itself and facing the choice of democratic values or self-destruction, America had become the crucial, microcosmic test of human fate. If it turns out that we do succeed as a species, then some of the credit belongs to the kids of Velva and Galesburg and Mundal, Norway, who insisted on *both* liberty *and* justice for all, who challenged America to rise from selfishness and, in Ted Sorensen's words, ask what you can do for your country.

• • •

Postscript: When I was writing the first draft of this chapter in 1998, St. Peter, Minnesota, was devastated by a tornado.

The tornado tore right through the Gustavus Adolphus campus, damaging every building, toppling the spire from the chapel, and ripping out almost every tree. The tornado tore right through the oldest neighborhoods, wrecking hundreds of homes, including the home of Governor John Johnson. The next day on CNN, I saw Ruth Johnson with Governor Carlson, inspecting the damage. A few weeks later I got a firsthand report when I crossed the scholarly path of Roland Thorstensson, a Gustavus Adolphus teacher of Swedish. He showed me photos of the wreckage, but he reported that the town and the surrounding community had rallied wonderfully. In fact, he repeated the comments of some of the insurance company adjusters who had come to St. Peter from the Gulf Coast states. The adjusters were accustomed to dealing with the aftermath of hurricanes in the South, where it was routine to see the National Guard patrolling against looting and chaos, where victims were often enraged at nature's betrayal of them, and where threats of lawsuits were often the instant response to disagreements over compensation. The adjusters said of St. Peter that they had never seen a community respond so well to a natural disaster. To begin with, the people of St. Peter simply stoically accepted that this was the way nature worked. Then they set about the recovery effort with a remarkable spirit of cooperation. When people disagreed with insurance compensation offers, they responded not with angry threats but with careful negotiation. The southerners said that the rest of the country could learn a thing or two from these small-town Minnesotans.

11

Vikings on a Sea of Sand

E *ight and* a half centuries after Fate decided that the Spanish and
not the Vikings would bring Europe to America, the Vikings and
the Spanish had an unlikely crossing of paths in the Utah desert.
In 1776 the Spanish Fathers Escalante and Dominguez, in exploring
routes between Santa Fe and California, emerged from a narrow canyon through the Wasatch Mountains and found a great basin with a
huge lake. That canyon, the river flowing through it, and the town that
later sprang up at the spot where they camped that night would be
called Spanish Fork. In 1855 three emigrants from Iceland arrived in
Spanish Fork, the first of nearly four hundred Icelanders who would
make Spanish Fork the first Icelandic settlement in the United States.
Quite possibly some of the Icelanders were direct descendants of Leif
Eriksson, and in getting to Utah they had shown plenty of Viking fortitude, but that the Icelanders should settle in a town named Spanish
Fork in a nation full of place-names honoring Columbus was a lesson in
the ironic forks of history.

The irony of Icelanders coming to the desert is visible in Spanish
Fork today in its Icelandic Monument, built in 1938 in the form of a
lighthouse. I went by it at night just to see its light guiding ships that
exist nowhere but in the long memories of the Icelanders. The lighthouse is capped by a Viking ship weather vane that responds to the
cool dawn mountain breezes coming out of Spanish Fork Canyon.

Alongside the lighthouse is an Icelandic flag and a garden of Icelandic poppies. A plaque honors the first fifteen immigrants, who had typical Icelandic names like Thordur Didriksson and Magnus Bjarnason. The year before my visit to Spanish Fork, the president of Iceland came there to celebrate the one hundredth anniversary of the Iceland Day Festival, one of the oldest Scandinavian festivals in America. When the festival started in 1897, Spanish Fork boasted both Lutheran and Mormon churches that gave services in Icelandic, an Icelandic Sunday school, an Icelandic library, the Icelandic Mercantile and Manufacturing Company, and the Icelandic Social Hall.

The Icelanders of Spanish Fork are but a small part of a chapter of Scandinavian American history that comes as a surprise to many. Scandinavians played a major role in the Mormon pioneering of the West. To people who know Mormon Utah as the political antithesis of liberal Minnesota, the Scandinavian enthusiasm for Mormonism may seem like a disproof of my thesis that Scandinavian Americans have displayed the same core social values displayed in today's Scandinavian social democracies. But I suggest that Scandinavian Utah is only further evidence for my thesis. If we review the early history of Mormonism, we see that while the rest of pioneer America was embracing the myth of rugged individualism, the Mormon Church was emphasizing the importance of community and cooperation to the extent of launching America's most ambitious experiment in communism. I'll suggest that Mormon community values were a good match for Scandinavian values, even if these values were expressed quite differently in Utah than in Minnesota.

It was probably inevitable that America would become a religion. America was already a civic religion, a superior destiny both economically and morally. This civic religion alone lured millions of Europeans to leave home. In the vision of Joseph Smith, America became a theological destiny as well. After Christ preached to the Israelites and was crucified, he showed up in America to deliver a further gospel to the ancient Americans. Smith reported that it was to America that Christ would soon return to rule his kingdom on Earth, which would be prepared by Smith's followers.

Smith's revision of Christianity was already controversial enough to stir up animosity against him, but then he added polygamy, theocracy, and sobriety. Even worse, the Mormons had the un-American notion that economic competition shouldn't be the highest principle of a society.

After the Mormons had been driven out of several states, they settled in Illinois at just about the time the first Scandinavians were homesteading there. Something about the Scandinavians must have impressed Smith, for he decided to send missionaries to Scandinavia to bring hardy farmers to the Illinois prairie. But history forked again. Smith was killed by a mob, and his successor, Brigham Young, decided to lead the Mormons to Utah, where no one would bother them. Scandinavian converts would end up heading for terrain far different from the fabled America prairie. When Eric Jansson and his own group of religious dissenters arrived to found Bishop Hill in 1846, the Mormons had just abandoned their town of Nauvoo a few dozen miles away.

The Mormon missionaries arrived in Denmark at a fortuitous moment, for the Danish Parliament had just established freedom of religion after centuries of Lutheran monopoly, and the Mormons harvested the accumulated dissatisfactions with Lutheranism. More potently, they harvested the lure of America. Mormonism was the only religion for which conversion equaled immigration. Converts were supposed to come to America to help build Zion. If converts couldn't afford the passage, then the church's Perpetual Emigration Fund would help pay their way. If a woman pledged herself to a polygamous marriage, her Utah husband would pay her way. Such arrangements only fueled skepticism about the sincerity of conversions, but since most converts worked hard to pay their own way, suffered ostracism by family and friends, and passed through the fertile American Midwest on their way to the desert, there's evidence enough to grant that most converts were true believers. We need only recall the power of America as the promised land. Because of this power, the Mormons found it easier to win converts in Europe than in America. Often enough, converts didn't realize until arriving in America that Mormons were a vilified sect there. In their naive admiration for all things American, converts might suppose polygamy to be just another innovative democratic institution.

Between 1850 and 1900, some 30,000 Scandinavians immigrated to Utah. Half of them were Danish. In Sweden and Norway, the Lutheran Church arranged to ban Mormon missionaries, but it was easy enough for them to sneak in from Denmark. By 1900 Scandinavians made up 34 percent of the foreign-born in Utah, and Scandinavian stock made up 16 percent of the total population. In 1870 only Wisconsin had more Danes. In 1910 only four states had more Swedes.

The missionaries had their greatest success in the poorest farming areas, which implies an economic motivation. It was easy for the Scandinavian establishment, which was embarrassed by the Mormons' success, to ridicule converts as backwards peasants. About one-third of the converts renounced Mormonism and never emigrated. But in 1869, events helped the Mormons. The completion of the transcontinental railroad in America made the trek to Utah much easier, and bad harvests in Scandinavia made it easier to leave. Once in Utah, more converts defected, sometimes out of unhappiness with Mormon doctrine or authoritarianism, sometimes out of dismay at the desert they were expected to settle, and they headed back home or at least to those prairie wheat fields they had passed through on the way. James Borglum, the father of Gutzon Borglum, the sculptor of Mount Rushmore, abandoned Utah for Nebraska. But Scandinavians tended to be less shocked by a hostile environment than were other ethnic groups, and plenty of them stayed. The Scandinavian willingness to tolerate a hostile environment only increased the eagerness of Mormon leaders to recruit more Scandinavians.

The best farming areas in Utah were two high mountain valleys, the Sanpete and the Cache. When the first settlers there proved unable to cope with winter, Brigham Young decided to send in the Scandinavians. They succeeded in creating the breadbasket and the dairy of all Utah. Young wanted to discourage any loyalties to anything but the church, including ethnic loyalties, so for years he ordered the Sanpete Danes to cease conducting church services in Danish, but they defied him and continued holding Danish services into the 1920s. A Utah Danish-language newspaper lasted until 1935.

The Swedish converts tended to be skilled artisans, and they preferred settling in Salt Lake City, enough to create a "Swede Town" neighborhood.

While the rest of the American frontier was being settled by loners or lone families or railroads or mining corporations, the Mormons turned the settling of the Great Basin into a community project. Teams of settlers, supported by the resources of the whole state, headed to promising locations not to enrich just themselves but to benefit the whole state. These efforts succeeded brilliantly, establishing some four hundred communities. In 1874 Brigham Young sought to institutionalize the Mormon principle of cooperative economics by launching the United Order. Over two hundred communities set up cooperatives, usually just a store, factory, or farm, but some communities wholly abolished private property, ate in communal dining rooms, and shared their benefits equally. Previous American attempts at communal living had been limited to solitary units. The Mormon statewide effort won the praise of radical labor unions and helped inspire Edward Bellamy's utopian novel *Looking Backwards*. The American press attacked the United Order as traitorous, further proof that the Mormons were un-American. Even in Utah, the United Order was controversial. Scandinavians supported the United Order more strongly than did other ethnic groups, and often they were its leaders. But the United Order soon foundered on the same human nature that usually ruined communes. In some communities it lasted for years, but more often it was soon decommissioned into more private forms of enterprise.

Given this history, you might wonder why Utah became the political opposite of Minnesota. Actually, Utah's reputation for political conservatism is a recent development. Utah voted for Bryan, Wilson, FDR, Truman, and Johnson, and it even gave John F. Kennedy 45 percent of its vote. In 1968 Utah gave less support to George Wallace than did many northern states, including Lincoln's Illinois. Utah made a major contribution to the New Deal in the person of Marriner Eccles, FDR's chairman of the Federal Reserve Board who converted FDR to Keynesian economics and the need for government leadership in economic life, something the Mormons had been practicing for decades. What sets Utah apart from Minnesota is a long history of persecution by the federal government. Mormons might support socialistic practices if they were sponsored by and benefited the church, but they had a gut reaction against the expansion of federal authority over their kingdom. Increasingly, the Democratic Party meant expanding federal authority. In the 1960s the Democrats became associated with social forces eroding religious and community and family life, and Utah broke sharply with the Democrats. It wasn't that the Mormons were philosophically opposed to a strong central authority, for they already had the strongest central authority in America, which offered its own social services. Only in Utah was the federal government viewed as a dangerous rival to an already existing authority. Perhaps a touch of Utah's anti-Washington passion informed the career of political columnist Jack Northman Anderson, the Utah-raised grandson of Swedish and Danish converts whose investigative reporting frightened several presidents and even J. Edgar Hoover.

In 1850 two Icelanders studying trades in Copenhagen converted to Mormonism and returned home to spread the word. This was the start of Icelandic Utah. Brigham Young sent the first Icelanders to Spanish Fork on the assumption they'd be happier among fellow Scandinavians, not realizing that those fellow Scandinavians were the Danes who had ruled Iceland for centuries and who were much resented by Icelanders. The Icelanders discovered that they had traveled thousands of miles to democratic America just to be treated as inferiors by the Danes of Spanish Fork. So the Icelanders set up their own neighborhood across town from the Danes. The Icelanders had an especially hard time adjusting to Utah. Whereas the Danes could continue being farmers, the Icelanders were mostly fishermen, and they had to learn new skills. They banded together to help one another. They were left with a deep nostalgia for Iceland, a nostalgia that has kept the Iceland Day Festival going strong for over a century.

I stopped at the house of Lil Shepherd, president of the Icelandic Association of Utah and member of the Spanish Fork city council. Like many of the original Icelandic families in town, she still lived in the old Icelandic neighborhood. Generations of intermarriage had disguised some old Icelanders behind English names like Shepherd. There were few pure Icelanders left. No one was sure how many Icelandic descendants there were in Spanish Fork, but perhaps it was a clue that when the president of Iceland visited, two thousand people turned out to hear him speak.

Lil showed me photos of the president's visit, including him standing at the graves of her ancestors. She said her ancestors would have been astonished at such an honor. She said that the president was clearly moved by the hundreds of Icelandic flags on the graves of the immigrants. In Iceland, Spanish Fork was a familiar place, if only because Iceland's Nobel Prize–winning novelist Halldór Laxness had written a novel about the emigration. The president thanked the

Americans for their loyalty to Iceland, which was remarkable, considering that there had been little contact between Spanish Fork and Iceland for a century. Lil had taken the lead in ending this isolation by organizing a tour of Iceland that became an emotional reunion with long-lost relatives. Now this tour was an annual event. The president must have been proud of his Mormon offspring, for he invited the Mormon Tabernacle Choir to visit Iceland.

The loyalty of the Spanish Fork Icelanders to a land few of them had visited or even received a letter from seems distinctly Icelandic. I talked with four other Icelanders in town, and all of them emphasized how tight-knit the Icelandic community was. They attributed this to the pioneer experience, but I'm convinced it goes back to Iceland itself, which places a strong emphasis on community solidarity. At the home of Phyllis Ashby, the historian of the Icelandic Association, I browsed through albums of photos and articles from a century of Iceland Day celebrations, including the 1955 emigration centennial parade, which included twenty-seven floats depicting aspects of Iceland such as the sagas and the Althing. We talked about community solidarity in Spanish Fork. She said that the pioneers were so poor that they had to help one another, sharing skills and goods. "If one man had a cow and his neighbor didn't, they both had milk." If an Icelander died, everyone went to his funeral, whether they knew him or not. It was "one large family." Another person told me that when he was growing up, his elders talked of Iceland "as if when you died and went to heaven, you went to Iceland." Other Spanish Fork residents didn't always appreciate the cult of Iceland, but the Icelanders answered them with their T-shirt slogan: "We love America. We ought to. We discovered it." The Icelanders were irked that the new school in their neighborhood hadn't been named for Leif Eriksson.

A couple of days later I talked with a sociologist from Brigham Young University who had studied Iceland, and he agreed that community solidarity was very Icelandic. He recalled how when Christianity was gaining ground in Iceland and creating tension between Christians and pagans, the Althing held a vote between the two religions, and when the Christians won, the pagans were readier to convert than to be social outcasts or troublemakers. "Iceland," he said, "was the only nation ever to change religions through a democratic election." In Viking days, the worst punishment wasn't death or prison but banishment. Indirectly, through the banishment of Leif's father, Erik, the Icelandic social bond led to the discovery of America. In today's Iceland, the social bond meant a society free of crime and neglect.

On his visit to Spanish Fork, the president of Iceland attributed the success of the desert Icelanders to a character formed on an equally isolated island where people had to work hard and cooperatively to survive forces of nature that were "much greater than all of us. . . . The soul of the Icelanders who came to Utah had been transformed by those forces. The farmers and fishermen were able to survive in their new homeland because of the discipline from the old country . . . the backbone of the Icelandic heritage."

From Spanish Fork I headed for the Sanpete Valley less than an hour away, where the largest town, Ephraim, was holding its annual Scandinavian festival. Compared to Spanish Fork, Ephraim was an upstart, having started its festival in 1976. When Ephraim was first settled, it was almost totally Scandinavian and became known as "Little Denmark." Throughout town today are names like Larsen, Jensen, and Olsen. The local joke goes that one day in church the bishop called upon brother Petersen to rise, whereupon a hundred men stood up. The bishop then explained he meant Peter Petersen, whereupon half the men sat down. In truth, to solve the name problem, hundreds of people went by nicknames like "Pete Poker." The local joke goes that when a stranger came to town looking for Peter Petersen, Petersen turned him away because he had forgotten his real name.

In the tidiness of their houses and lawns, the Scandinavian towns of Utah do seem more like Minnesota towns than the typical southwestern town with its junkyard decor. The Ephraim festival is held on the tidy green lawn of Snow College, which was named for Erastus Snow, who was in charge of the Mormon mission to Scandinavia. The quickness of Scandinavians in starting a college meant that today Snow College is one of the oldest two-year colleges west of the Mississippi River. At the entrance to the college library is a stone slab elaborately carved in Viking style. Inside the library, you can find proof that the saga tradition is still alive in Utah. The Cache Valley produced the prominent poet May Swenson, who wrote celebrations of nature. The Sanpete Valley produced Virginia Sorensen, whose children's books won the

Newbery Medal and whose novels about the Sanpete Valley won praise from New York critics. Sorensen was fond of her Sanpete background but also troubled by Mormon Church practices.

Aside from a lot of flags, some good food, and a concert of Scandinavian music by the college orchestra, the festival had a minimum of Scandinavian content. Still, I was impressed just to see the five Scandinavian flags flying in Utah, flying over a full day of meals, music, historic tours, games, crafts, Native American dances, a parade, and a rodeo. Only at the end of the day did I learn that there might be a secret story behind the five flags.

After the festivities I drove out to the Ephraim pioneer cemetery. On the way out of town I passed the more recent cemetery, which had a beautiful green lawn and trees and elegant monuments. The pioneer cemetery was a stark contrast. Though it was surrounded by green fields, the cemetery was mostly bare cracked dirt, dirt so badly settled that many coffins were clearly outlined. The headstones, made from the local limestone, which was especially brittle, were so eroded they were not only illegible but collapsing. Headstone rubble lay everywhere. I supposed that watering was being deliberately withheld to prevent further erosion of both headstones and soil. A few families had planted gravel lawns and granite headstones. But after a day that was supposed to honor these very pioneers, this neglected landscape made me wonder.

The cemetery had a large information board, and someone was copying a poem from it. He turned out to be from Brigham Young University. For his sociology master's thesis, Todd had spent a year studying Ephraim, actually continuing a study done in the 1920s by a BYU sociologist named Nelson. Professor Nelson had compared three Mormon pioneer towns and concluded that Ephraim had a stronger community identity than the others. Todd had concluded that this community bond was just as strong today as it was eighty years ago, despite the slackening of the pressures that first bonded Mormons together, pressures like persecution and frontier survival. Todd didn't dismiss my suggestion that this Ephraim solidarity had Scandinavian roots, but he did insist that the displays of ethnicity I had seen today were not what they might seem. They were a recent development and somewhat artificial. Few people in town had been to Scandinavia or had much real interest in it. Locals who attributed their religious values to their ethnic heritage would be shocked by the real, very secular Scandinavia. Not only was the festival weak in actual Scandinavian content, but some of its poses were ridiculous, such as the suggestion that the rodeo was Scandinavian because Laplanders had reindeer roping contests. Todd attributed the festival to an event that happened one Saturday in 1952. The Mormon authorities in Salt Lake City had sent a demolition crew to Ephraim, filled the Ephraim Mormon Tabernacle with dynamite, and blown it up.

Until that day, Ephraim had derived its identity from the Mormon Church. It wasn't a Danish town but a Mormon town serving the infallible visions of the elders in Salt Lake City. The soul of the community was the Ephraim tabernacle, full of elaborate carvings and murals, built by the devoted hard work of the townsfolk's ancestors. Ephraim was shocked when Salt Lake City announced that the tabernacle would be demolished. It was true that the tabernacle needed repairs badly and lacked plumbing and electricity. Admittedly, the Salt Lake City authorities were no more insensitive to historic preservation than was the rest of America at that time. But the people of Ephraim felt betrayed. A century of loyalty to Salt Lake City had been rewarded with utter disregard for their community. It was even worse that the tabernacle would be replaced by a chapel, which had less significance than a tabernacle. It was as if Ephraim was being spiritually demoted. After their protests were ignored, the people of Ephraim watched in horror as their tabernacle exploded and collapsed into rubble.

In fifty interviews Todd did for his study, the tabernacle came up again and again, and it was obvious Ephraim had never forgiven Salt Lake City. The demolition had led people to question the authoritarian character of the church and the competence of its leaders. Perhaps the long Sanpete defiance of Brigham Young's orders to stop using Danish was evidence that Scandinavian Mormons were less accepting of authority all along; Todd told me it was unheard-of for Mormons to defy Brigham Young. If Ephraim retained any resentments over the Danish language battle, they were dynamited back to life. In any case, after the demolition, Ephraim was determined to go its own way. If the Church wasn't going to honor their identity, they would do it for themselves. But this raised a question: exactly what was the identity of Ephraim? The most obvious thing that set Ephraim apart was its Scandinavian heritage. Ephraim seized upon its Scandinavian roots to differentiate itself from Salt Lake City and became fanatical about historic preservation. Snow College set up one of America's first programs in preserving old buildings. It was to raise money to save the abandoned United Order co-op building that the Scandinavian festival was launched. It was at least symbolic that Ephraim terminated its Fourth of July celebration to put all its effort into the Scandinavian festival, which it holds on Memorial Day weekend, when the rest of Utah is honoring its war heroes. Outsiders like me never suspect they are seeing an act of rebellion.

· · ·

I was staying at a campground in the next-door town of Manti. On the hill above the campground was the night-lit Manti Temple, one of the first temples the Mormons had built. In Ephraim I was told that a Norwegian had been in charge of building the temple roof. He had never designed a roof before, but he was a shipbuilder, and there was an old Viking tradition of hauling longboats out of the sea in winter, turning them upside down, and using them as shelters and meeting halls. In Stockholm, the roof of the city hall council chambers would be designed like an upside-down Viking ship. So the Norwegian built the roof just like he would build a ship. Later on, I learned that the roof builder was actually Swiss.

The campground was full of people cheering for cultural confusion, for the persistence of old identities. Actually, they were cheering about an NBA playoff game between the Utah Jazz and the Los Angeles Lakers. The Los Angeles team was called the Lakers not because there are any lakes in Los Angeles but because they used to be a Minnesota team, and when they moved to Los Angeles they retained their old name, however misplaced it had become. The Utah team was called the Jazz because it used to be a New Orleans team. You might think that a Mormon state wouldn't want to be associated with America's most bawdy, boozy party town, but the Scandinavian festival parade had included far more tributes to the Jazz, to African musical spirit born in a French town, than it had included tributes to Scandinavia. What a mixed-up country we are. We haven't lost our old identities, only misplaced them. As a cheer rang out for misplaced identities, I thought of how appropriate it was that Leif Eriksson's upside-down ship should be the temple for worshipping America the promised land.

12

It's Been a Quiet 150 Years
in Bishop Hill

t's been a quiet 150 years in Bishop Hill, but the last week has actually been kind of busy.

This morning the town square and sidewalks are packed with at least ten thousand people. We are glancing up and down the road, unsure of which way the motorcade is coming from. Secret Service agents in sunglasses and blank expressions are standing in the street, glancing at us. We are awaiting the arrival of the king and queen of Sweden.

As people drove into town they may have been puzzled by a sign saying "Bishop Hill, 150." Since people were coming to celebrate the 150th anniversary of the founding of Bishop Hill, they may have first taken this sign as a reference to the anniversary. But the sign is the standard green highway sign found at the edge of every town in America. In the western states, these signs list both the population and the elevation. Here in the Midwest, they list only the population.

On the day it was founded in 1846, Bishop Hill, Illinois, had a population of some 1,200. The whole population arrived en masse after a 160-mile walk from Chicago. Chicago was the end of a boat trip through the Great Lakes and the Erie Canal from New York, which was the end of a hard voyage from Sweden on freight ships built to carry pig iron.

The group's leader, Eric Jansson, named the new settlement after his hometown in Sweden. Jansson was a charismatic religious leader who had so antagonized the Swedish Lutheran Church elders that they repeatedly had him arrested. Jansson, a peasant's son, was plowing the field one day when he had a vision that God had a special mission for him. He should spread the message that divine grace was available not through any church hierarchy or sectarian doctrine or rite but solely through the Bible and the perfecting of the human heart. Jansson started preaching in people's homes and winning a loyal following. Tired of persecution, he decided to lead his followers to the religious freedom of America. At that time only handfuls of Swedes were living in America, but the exodus of Jansson's group was the beginning of the migration of 1.3 million Swedes.

The Janssonists arrived in Illinois too late in the autumn to plant crops or build a town. They spent the winter in crude dugouts in the bank of a ravine. Nearly one tenth of them died. But in the spring they started years of building. Like many visionary communities in pioneer America, Bishop Hill was a commune, based on a mixture of idealism and necessity. The Janssonists built several large buildings combining public space and private apartments. The largest building, Big Brick, was four stories tall and two hundred feet long, and it held ninety-six apartments. They set up a church, school, hospital, bakery, dairy, brick kiln, store, blacksmith shop—everything they needed to be a self-sufficient community plus businesses, like broom making, to draw in money from outside. Yet even as they prospered, they started feeling the usual tensions that wrecked other communes plus unique tensions over Jansson's messianic leadership. The freedom Jansson sought in America didn't seem to mean freedom for his followers. When an outsider married Jansson's cousin and wanted to take her away from the colony, Jansson refused, and the outsider assassinated Jansson. Some of Jansson's followers waited for him to rise from the grave after three days. He didn't. Less than four years after the colony began, it lost Jansson's sense of purpose, and it would slowly fade away. The commune was finally dissolved in 1860, the assets were divided up, and Bishop Hill became just another farm town. A century later, the once-stately colony buildings sat abandoned and decaying. Only a hundred people still lived there. The kids were bused to school in the nearby town of Galva and were ashamed to admit they were from shabby Bishop Hill. Galva had been developed by the Bishop Hill colonists to be their railroad depot for shipping out their products and receiving new colonists, but Galva had grown into a prosperous town of three thousand while its parent town had faded away.

Three trends in the outside world intervened to save Bishop Hill from final collapse. In the 1960s Americans awoke to the need for historic preservation. Today Bishop Hill is an Illinois State Historic Site, with two of the buildings maintained by the state, others by the local historical organization. In the 1970s Americans developed a fresh interest in ethnic roots. By the 1980s young urban Americans were deciding that small-town life, which their parents had fled for the cities, might not be so bad after all. One by one, abandoned Bishop Hill buildings were turned into museums, shops, and cafes.

If Jansson and his followers had ever been told that the king and queen of Sweden were going to show up in their town in a few minutes, they would have been horrified. They would have run for their horses or their guns. They had gone to a great deal of trouble to get far away from the king and queen of Sweden. As hard as their journey was, as much as they must have missed home, every further mile between them and the Swedish authorities was a good mile. They were rejecting not just the Swedish authorities but Sweden itself. They weren't going to all this trouble just to be Swedes living in America. They wanted to become Americans. That was the whole seductive idea of America, that you could shed your past identity and become someone new. If they had immigrated to England, they would have had to remain Swedes, Swedes residing in England. But in America they could become as completely American as anyone else. They didn't come to America to be Swedish Americans. They came here to completely forget about Sweden.

Which leaves me wondering: exactly what are we ten thousand people doing here?

I had already conducted a semiscientific poll on this question. I'd had to park nearly a mile from town, at the tip of a long line of cars beside the highway, and as I walked in I surveyed the license plates. A majority were from Illinois, but there were a large number from Iowa, many from other midwestern states, and some from all over the country. Like the original settlers, people had gone to some trouble to get here. It was safe to assume that very few of these pilgrims were natives of Bishop Hill making a homecoming. No doubt some of the Illinois plates were area residents who came for the spectacle, regardless of whatever country the royalty was from. But there was clear evidence for a stronger loyalty. Quite a few cars had Swedish flag decals or other announcements of Swedish identity such as the bumper sticker: "You can tell a Swede, but you can't tell him much." Yet some of these drivers were expensively serious about their pride in Sweden: many of these stickers were on the bumpers of Volvos and Saabs. The proportion of Volvos and Saabs here was far higher than you'd find in a typical midwestern parking lot.

I would guess that a majority of the people in Bishop Hill today had never been to Sweden. But for Swedish Americans Bishop Hill had come to serve as an outpost of Sweden, an easier way to visit their homeland. The Bishop Hill shops and restaurants catered to this need, offering Swedish products and food.

One of the shop owners told me there were old-timers in town who disliked the trend of Bishop Hill trying to be a miniature Sweden. They said that the colony founders wouldn't have approved of the Swedish flag flying in the town square near the monument to the colonists who had served the American flag in the Civil War. The old-timers wanted the founders to be seen entirely within the context of American history, as pioneers and patriots. As Christians, the founders certainly would have objected to Midsummer Day festivities being conducted in the town square, with flowered heads dancing around a Maypole, a remnant of pagan times. Perhaps the old timers weren't entirely happy about the king and queen dropping in either.

I did know of one person in the crowd who was ambivalent about seeing the king and queen. Myself.

When I was a child my father studied at MIT, and we lived in Lexington, just down the street from the town green where the American Revolution began, the green with the famous statue of the minuteman. I saved my allowance and bought a set of toy Revolutionary War soldiers. In my battles, there was no question that the Americans were the good guys. The British were the bad guys because they had a king.

Maybe this lingered in my mind when, at age twelve, I was standing in the crowd outside Buckingham Palace, looking at the guards, when suddenly a Rolls Royce appeared with the queen of England recognizable inside it. As she passed by I decided that she looked just like any ordinary person, not godlike, not even wicked, just ordinary. I couldn't see what all the fuss was about.

I still can't comprehend why Americans are so fixated on the British royal family. Nor is this fixation anything new. Mark Twain complained that when the transatlantic telegraph cable was opened in 1866, we had to hear all about the British princess having a cold. I thought we'd had a revolution so we wouldn't be bothered by these silly pompous people. After I read that the tradition of the audience standing up for the "Hallelujah" Chorus at performances of Handel's *Messiah* was started by a British king standing up, whereupon all his subjects were obligated to stand, I made myself conspicuous by remaining seated. If someone had questioned my propriety, I would have explained that it was un-American to stand, it was an oath of obedience to foreign royalty. I would have cited the 1908 debate as to whether American athletes at the opening ceremonies of the London Olympics should dip the American flag to the British royalty like everyone else would. For a century now, American Olympic athletes have conspicuously refused to dip the flag to royalty, though of course royalty is a bit harder to find these days.

So why was I looking forward to seeing the king and queen—for the third time in the last seventeen hours? Okay, so the first two times had been unplanned. I had arranged my workweek to end at 5 P.M. at Augustana College in Rock Island, an easy hour away from Bishop Hill and its Saturday morning celebrations. Then I heard that the king and queen were going to appear at Augustana College at 5 P.M. on Friday.

Augustana, the oldest of the Swedish-founded colleges, has one of the most attractive campuses of the Scandinavian colleges, with hills, woods, elegant old architecture, stained-glass windows, and a wooden bell tower, except for its view of the ugly industrial warehouse district separating it from the Mississippi River. Considering how flat most of the Midwest is, it is notable that half of the Scandinavian colleges are perched atop river bluffs with grand views. The blandest location and view is the Danish college in the middle of Des Moines, Iowa, which defiantly calls itself Grand View College.

The crowd gathered outside the college library, whose long staircase offered a suitably grand entrance for royalty. The king and queen were inside, touring a collection of thousands of books donated to the college in 1860 by the king's great-great-granduncle.

The king and queen appeared and the crowd cheered and the band played. On the program it said: "Please stand as Royal Couple enters."

Since there weren't enough seats to begin with, I was already standing, so I was spared a conflict over my democratic principles. I could have sat down on the grass, but I didn't.

The band played the Swedish national anthem, and I glanced around to see if anyone besides the royal couple was singing the Swedish words. Some older people were, and a few students, perhaps language students. According to the program the last two lines of the anthem were a refrain of "Oh, I would live and I would die in Sweden." I imagined the king looking at the silent crowd as he sang these lines and thinking: *Deserters. Sons of traitors. How can you call yourself Swedish?*

We tried singing the American national anthem, and I wondered if the king perceived the last line about the land of the free and the home of the brave to be a rebuke to the unbrave who stayed in Sweden.

After the predictable speeches and presentations of gifts, the royal couple walked off to tour the Swenson Center, a national archive of Swedish immigration. The rest of us headed for the picnic tent.

That evening, while the king and queen were cruising on a Mississippi River steamboat, I heard on the news that in the morning they would stop at the Jenny Lind chapel in the village of Andover on the way to Bishop Hill. I had a friend back in Flagstaff, Arizona, a professor of environmental journalism, who was from Andover and whose uncle's barn was now the crafts shop in Bishop Hill. From her I knew that the chapel was named for Jenny Lind not out of celebrity worship but because Lind donated the money for it, another of her charitable deeds. The chapel didn't have a steeple because the wood for it was used for coffins during a cholera epidemic. So of course I had to be at the Jenny Lind chapel. At least there would be someone back home whom I wouldn't be embarrassed to tell I had followed the king and queen of Sweden around Illinois like a groupie.

In Andover there were more speeches and music, and the king and queen were given the key to the city, er, village, the only one Andover had ever given to anyone. When the royal couple went inside to tour the chapel, I didn't wait for them to reappear. I wanted to get to Bishop Hill in time for their royal arrival there. Apparently I was enjoying all this royalness.

The crowd in Bishop Hill also seemed to be eagerly anticipating all this royalness. Certainly the anniversary gained special importance from the royal couple coming all the way from Sweden. They had come not just for the sake of Bishop Hill but because the founding of Bishop Hill had been officially designated as the beginning of mass Swedish immigration to America. They were touring a dozen sites important to that immigration. They had just come from Minnesota, where at Gustavus Adolphus College they had been welcomed by thousands of children lining the sidewalk and waving Swedish flags. In their wake, they probably left a lot of people feeling more Swedish.

Which was odd, considering that the king and queen of Sweden aren't even Swedish.

The last truly Swedish king died in 1818. At the height of Napoleon's power, Sweden sided against him, with disastrous results. Napoleon routed the Swedish army, and the Russians seized Finland away from Sweden. The Swedish Parliament blamed the king's incompetence and deposed him and then implemented a more democratic constitution. They replaced the king with his uncle, who was childless. For a crown prince they selected one of Napoleon's foremost generals, Jean Baptiste Bernadotte, who couldn't speak a word of Swedish and wasn't Lutheran. At least he renamed himself Karl Johan and behaved like a Swede, annoying Napoleon by ignoring French interests. You would think that in the six generations since, the Bernadottes would have had enough chances to marry Swedish women that by now they would have blonde hair and blue eyes, but to me the king still looks French. He isn't making any progress toward looking Swedish either, for his queen is a German born in Brazil.

To summarize: Ten thousand Americans, who fought a revolution so we could forget about kings, are gathered in a town established with the goal of forgetting about Sweden, waiting for a French guy and a Brazilian woman so that we can fondly remember a country most of us have never seen.

I assure you that Swedish Americans are no more confused about our identities than any other Americans.

I have another question. If the Scandinavians are such democratic people, why do Sweden, Norway, and Denmark still have royalty? But I don't have time to consider this question, for the crowd is breaking into applause. A line of Volvos is approaching the town square. My heart is warmed by the sight of genuine Swedishness arriving in Bishop Hill. I am referring, of course, to the Volvos.

It seems that the Volvo dealer in Rock Island volunteered some of his cars for the royal couple. Perhaps the dealer is a Swedish American proud to contribute his services, but I can't help imagining the pitch his salesmen can now make: "This is a historic, royal limousine. The king and queen of Sweden rode in these very seats. It's well worth the extra price." The customers may be Italian or Irish Americans with only the sketchiest images of Sweden. They'll try to imagine the king and queen and envision a handsome tennis star or a blonde seductress or a brooding existentialist. This sales pitch may backfire and discourage a Republican businessman who doesn't want to be associated with a gloomy, tax-paralyzed socialist welfare state.

The king and queen emerge, and the crowd cheers. The governor of Illinois greets them. All three disappear into the Steeple Building, a three-story, columned, Greek Revival building with a clock tower on top. The clock has always had only one hand, an hour hand, because good Christians don't need to concern themselves too much with temporal things, and Swedes don't need minute hands to point out the need to work hard. The clock was built in 1859 by the original colonists and is run by a set of three-hundred-pound weights that dangle through a shaft to the ground. After touring the museum inside, the three emerge onto the balcony facing the square. The governor publicly welcomes the king and queen and talks about the contributions Swedes have made to Illinois and America. Then the king speaks, briefly, in English, about the historic importance of Bishop Hill and the pride of Swedes in their American cousins. He announces a grant of 100,000 kroner from the Swedish government to help restore Bishop Hill. The crowd is left wondering how much this is in dollars but cheers anyway.

Then the balcony becomes a reviewing stand. The parade begins. I stand on my toes to see, but I feel like shrinking with embarrassment. The king and queen have doubtless reviewed or ridden in many grand parades gleaming with European elegance. This parade is strictly small-town Americana, reminiscent of every county fair parade and homecoming parade in any American town. There are rhinestone horses and antique cars and tractors, the usual civic club floats, high school marching bands with baton twirlers, and a Bishop Hill band that is about what you would expect from a town of 150 people, which is to say they are awful. Really awful. Probably the worst band the king and queen have ever heard. Is this our demonstration of what Swedes have accomplished in America in 150 years? Yes, there are floats showing events in Bishop Hill history, and for a town this size they are well done, but they don't seem much different from the local history floats found in thousands of other American small towns.

But what had I expected to find in a small town in the middle of the American prairie? I could hear the old-timers scoffing at me for coming here expecting to find Stockholm.

After the parade, the king and queen go to tour a few more buildings before leaving town. They walk right in front of me, and the smiling queen looks right at me and waves. I am delighted. I have been blessed by the popes of Swedishness. With the rest of the crowd, I applaud enthusiastically.

When the king and queen leave, the crowd sets about exploring the town. All the museums and shops are packed. The Colony Store posts a doorman outside to regulate entry. The cafes all have lines, so I check out the food booths in the square. I don't see any Swedish food and end up buying hot dogs from the Galva High School marching band booth. The many crafts booths offer the same sort of Americana you could find anywhere else. I am disappointed to find that some of the shops offer nothing Swedish, only typical midwestern crafts and antiques.

I walk over to the state historic site visitor center, which features the paintings of one of the original colonists, Olof Krans. They are primitive in style, but this seems appropriate to their subject, scenes of pioneer Bishop Hill, of field work and village life. Sharing the gallery is the work of half a dozen contemporary Swedish artists. Their work is very sophisticated. It ranges from painting to ceramics to glass to fiber to wood carvings. Much of it is obviously inspired by nature. One woman made "fossil ceramics," ceramics imprinted by leaves, including leaves taken from the garden of Linnaeus. On her artist's statement she said: "Nature as designer is my greatest source of inspiration." The fiber artist said: "I want nature to speak, trying to re-create an awareness that we are dependent on Mother Earth, living Nature, the prerequisite of all life! My colors are inspired by Nature, the colors you can find in green grass and trees, in the blue sky, the sea, in yellow, maturing fields of wheat and in grey stones."

Standing near me are two women who look a bit familiar. I realize that they look familiar because I have just been staring at their photos.

It's the fossil ceramicist and the fiber artist. I compliment them on their work and say I hope they are having a good visit to America. They say they are indeed. I comment on the contrast between their work and that of Olof Krans and say I hope they have a chance to show their work in busier and more sophisticated venues, like Chicago. They say it is a great honor to be exhibited in Bishop Hill. I say it was an honor to be visited by the king and queen, but I wish they didn't have to see that silly parade. Oh no, say the Swedes, they are sure the king and queen *loved* the parade: it was such a wonderful picture of life in America. Bishop Hill is charming because it is so authentically American.

I think of how Swedes are noted for their diplomacy.

In the afternoon, after concerts and speeches in the town square, I figure out that there are several busloads of Swedes in the crowd. They are touring famous sites in Swedish America. Locally, they would also visit the home of Carl Sandburg. I talk with a few of them. By way of introduction I mention that my great-grandparents were from Gränna. Maybe I was subtly saying that I am one of them. They seem more interested in me as an American. When they ask where I live, I assume they are unfamiliar with American geography and simply say near the Grand Canyon, one of the few things in America they should have heard of. It turns out that they know plenty about the American West, and not just from cowboy movies but from reading history books. When someone asks if I know any Indians, I say sure, lots of them, and this seems to make me someone special. Being from Gränna seemed to be about as impressive as an American bragging he's from Peoria, but living in Arizona and knowing real Natives, now *that* was really something. Once again I try to apologize for the stupid parade, but they don't seem to know what I mean. They tell me, enthusiastically, that the parade was just so authentically American.

I finally figure it out. It should have been obvious enough. The Swedes hadn't come here looking for Sweden. They didn't need to shop for Swedish crafts in the Colony Store or take home a jar of imported Swedish lingonberry jam in order to feel connected to Sweden. They had enough Sweden where they came from. One Swede mentioned that it was funny to come all the way to America to see the king and queen, as he had never seen them before, except on television. There were plenty of opportunities to see them if you wanted to, but it wasn't that important.

The Swedes had come here looking for America. The real America. They had seen plenty of America in American movies and television shows, but they were never quite sure about the boundary between fiction and reality. They had seen images of pioneers, small towns, town squares with Civil War statues and American flags, and parades with rhinestone horses and baton twirlers. Now they were seeing the real thing, and it was just like in the movies, only they were part of it. They would have been fascinated if it was a parade in any small town in America, but it was even better because it was a parade in a Swedish small town in America. These were their cousins parading around with American flags, and their cousins really meant it, they were just like any other Americans, just as validly American as descendants of Englishmen who came on the *Mayflower*. Their cousins were part of the energy and power of the most fascinating and irritating country on Earth. Other Americans would never think of the cousins as Swedish, just Americans. Even a few years after the Swedish immigrants arrived in Bishop Hill, they became American soldiers fighting for the American ideal that no ethnic group should be deprived of equality. They had earned a Civil War monument just like everyone else's. The whole town of Bishop Hill was a monument to the whole idea of America.

The Swedish visitors had learned about Bishop Hill in history class and in novels. I gathered that Bishop Hill was much better known in Sweden than in America, even among Swedish Americans. When Swedes became Americans, they were taught that their pioneering towns were Jamestown and Plymouth and Boonesboro. America was full of pioneer towns for Americans to honor. But Sweden had only one town to remember as its beachhead in America. It did seem to bother some Swedes that a crackpot like Jansson got credit for Swedish emigration. Still, the Swedes were glad that we remembered Sweden. I suspected that this celebration gave the Swedes an exaggerated notion of how well we remembered Sweden. They probably would have trouble believing that in only two generations, Swedes could totally forget about Sweden.

I'm not sure it occurred to the Swedes that this celebration made their cousins different from any other Americans. For Americans, to celebrate ethnicity is to accent what distinguishes one American from another. But to outsiders, our ethnic diversity is what makes us most American. Every American had somewhere to remember. Remembering that your ancestors chose to come here from somewhere else was the highest tribute you could pay to America. The Swedes seemed happy to witness this utterly American ritual of remembering.

In the evening the diminished crowd gathers at the baseball field next to the town square to watch a historical pageant about Bishop Hill. We sit on wooden bleachers that are badly decayed, planks sagging, broken, or missing. The bleachers rest upon a natural slope into which 150 years ago the colonists built their dugouts to survive the first winter. At that time there was no flat field here, only a steep ravine. The colonists filled in the ravine, partly to bury the cholera germs that had decimated them and partly to create a level platform on which to construct Big Brick, the communal housing unit. Big Brick, long abandoned, burned down in 1928. Now the life-and-death struggles of the pioneers, their egalitarian ideals, their yearning to become Americans have become this: a baseball field. The wilderness that threatened the pioneers with chaos and death is now a well-mowed lawn whose bases and boundaries represent the careful order and rituals of a society. The baseball field finally forced me to admit it: this isn't Sweden but the small-town America of homespun parades and Sunday-afternoon baseball games in the park. The Swedes had made it, they had become real Americans.

The next morning I return to the town square to watch the Sunday service led by the pastor from the town of Bishop Hill in Sweden. He talks about how the two Bishop Hills represent a strong affinity between Swedes and Americans.

Later I wander over to the one place I hadn't visited yesterday, the cemetery. I notice a group of a dozen people entering the cemetery just before me. They don't seem to be randomly looking around but heading for a known goal. I wander more randomly. Some of the headstones are too worn to read, but others tell of people born in Sweden in the 1820s and buried here in the 1870s. Then there are people born in Bishop Hill in the 1860s and living into the twentieth century. There are veterans of the two world wars who went back to Europe to cleanse it of the authoritarianism their ancestors had fled.

When I walk past the group of people, they are gathered around one grave, posing for a picture. The woman taking the picture calls out to me to ask if I'll do them the favor of taking their group photo so that she won't be left out of it. I say sure. I look at the headstone. It's the grave of Eric Jansson. I ask them where they are from. They say they are from all over the country. They are using this occasion as a family reunion. But it's not really a reunion, as few of them have ever met before. I ask where their family started out, and they say, "Right here! We're the descendants of Eric Jansson."

I take the camera and look through it at a dozen smiling Janssonists. I am concerned about the angle of the sun, so I take photos from several angles. Then they produce other cameras. I frame the pictures carefully: it has become my responsibility to record a historic event. From Bishop Hill, Eric Jansson's children had spread out all over America and forgotten one another, and at last they had returned and remembered. I too had returned and remembered. Maybe I should be in the photos too. More than metaphorically, all Swedish Americans are descendants of Eric Jansson. This has been a family reunion for ten thousand people.

The king and queen had come to the reunion like they were members of the family. Apparently, the Janssonists had been happy to see them after all. I suppose the king and queen had seen the crowd like family, like wayward children who had made good.

I handed the memory-filled cameras back. We said good-bye to Eric and headed for the cemetery gate to disperse once again to every corner of America, but this time with remembrance.

13

Melting Pot Stew, with Raisins

There's a reason why Vesterheim, the premier Norwegian American museum, is located in a small town in a remote corner of Iowa, fifty miles from the nearest small city or interstate highway. It's the same reason why the Czech composer Antonin Dvořák spent a summer in the nearby town of Spillville. It's the same reason why the premier Danish American museum is in an isolated Iowa town of only seven hundred people. You might think that a Danish museum would do better fifty miles away in Omaha, Nebraska, one of the largest concentrations of Danish settlement. You might think that a Norwegian museum belonged in Minneapolis, the leading Norwegian city.

Perhaps I can best illustrate the reason Vesterheim is located in Decorah, Iowa, rather than Minneapolis by recalling an experience I had in Minneapolis. I stopped into a West African restaurant in a lively student neighborhood adjacent to the University of Minnesota. Many of the neighborhood restaurants were ethnic. None of them were Scandinavian. My restaurant was one of several African restaurants on the same street. Not knowing anything about West African food, I ordered blindly and was baffled when they brought out what seemed to be a large thin sponge and a plateful of mysterious blobs. I stared at the sponge, trying to decide if it was decorative or meant to absorb juice from the blobs. I studied my fellow diners and noticed one of them tearing off pieces of sponge and wrapping up blobs and eating them. This at least established the sponge as a kind of African pancake. I never did determine exactly what the blobs were, even if they were animal or vegetable. But as I returned to this restaurant again, I came to think of the neighborhood as a realm of African food and French pastries.

A few years later I went to see a new exhibit at the American Swedish Institute across town portraying the life of Swedish immigrants in the Twin Cities. Many of the old photos showed a neighborhood called Cedar-Riverside after the two main streets there. These names sounded a bit familiar to me, but I couldn't place them. Apparently, the Cedar-Riverside neighborhood had been the center of Scandinavian life. All the shops and restaurants were owned by Scandinavians, with signs in Norwegian or Swedish. You would walk down the street and hear more Danish than English. Several Scandinavian-language newspapers were published there. You could buy books in Swedish, attend one of six Norwegian churches, and trust your money to the Scandia Bank. In the evening there was always something going on at Dania Hall, which contained meeting rooms for clubs and an auditorium for entertainment. There was a thriving world of specifically Scandinavian American entertainment. You could hear singers in Swedish and comedians in Danish or dance to Thorstein Skarning and his Norwegian Hillbillies. Some performers became nationally famous, at least within their ethnic group. Cedar-Riverside had been the equivalent of the great ethnic neighborhoods of New York City.

I finally realized that Cedar-Riverside was the student neighborhood I had frequented for years. The African restaurant had probably once been Olson's Grocery or Hansen's Saloon. The next time I walked down that street I looked for traces of its Scandinavian past, but aside from the name atop Dania Hall, there were none. Actually, a few blocks away was Augsburg College, founded by Norwegians. I had never suspected it was the sole, well-rooted remnant of a ghost neighborhood. I'll bet that many of the students hanging out in the Cedar-Riverside cafes today didn't suspect they were in the groceries frequented by their great-grandparents.

The residents of old Cedar-Riverside, or at least their children, moved to the suburbs, moved in next door to Irish or Germans. Today there is no Norwegian neighborhood in the most Norwegian of cities. The leading Minneapolis Norwegian newspaper, the *Tidende*, which at its peak had a circulation of 33,000, ceased publication in 1935. Its remaining circulation was absorbed by the *Decorah-Posten,* which meant that big-city Norwegians had to get their news from a small town in Iowa.

I once set out to explore the most famous Swedish neighborhood of Chicago, Andersonville. Knowing that Chicago had become the second largest Swedish city in the world after Stockholm, I was expecting Andersonville to reflect this scale, so I allocated a whole day to exploring it. I was done in a couple of hours, and this included lunch in one Swedish restaurant and dessert in the other one. I guess I should have been impressed that there was any Swedish restaurant there at all. Like Cedar-Riverside, Andersonville was a stop on the road to American success. For many families, the brick row houses of Andersonville were a second stop after the wooden shacks and tenements of Swede Town along the Chicago River west of downtown. Today, Andersonville was serving the same Ellis Island role for more newcomers. There were a lot of Mediterranean and Asian groceries and restaurants. In the Swedish Bakery, most of the clerks were black, and most of the customers were Middle Eastern. I did find a real Swede in Erickson's, a small Swedish grocery store with an ancient neon sign saying "Fish Shop and Delicatessen" and a decor seemingly just as old. Ann-Mari Nilsson had been born in Sweden and ran the shop with her daughter. She told me that quite a few Swedes came to Andersonville expecting to find Swedish Americans, but there were very few still living in the neighborhood. Most had moved on to the suburbs, not any one suburb but diffused all over. Most of the Swedish organizations that once existed in Andersonville were now defunct. It was hard to find Swedes in the world's second-largest Swedish city.

The main reason I had budgeted a day for Andersonville was because of the Swedish American Museum Center there. In the photo I had seen of it, it looked like Vesterheim, which could easily absorb a few hours. But the Swedish museum wasn't nearly as impressive as Vesterheim.

So why did a world-famous Czech composer cross half of America to spend the summer of 1893 in a small Iowa town a dozen miles from Decorah? Dvořák had been appointed director of the New York Philharmonic, but he was getting homesick. He decided to use the summer to return home so he could speak his own language, hear Czech songs, and eat Czech food. But Dvořák had a friend from Spillville, Iowa, who told him he didn't have to go to the trouble of crossing the ocean to be at home among Czechs. Dvořák spent a happy summer in Spillville, speaking Czech and hearing favorite Czech songs, playing the local church organ daily, and, according to local legend at least, composing the *New World* Symphony.

Iowa is full of towns settled primarily by one ethnic group. When available farmland was taken, a town stopped growing, and the ethnic group was left to practice its own customs undisturbed by other influences. The Danish kids in Elk Horn weren't as likely to be teased about speaking Danish as were the Danish kids in Minneapolis. If you couldn't speak Czech, there was no point in complicating your life by trying to settle in Spillville. Even upwardly mobile Norwegians in Decorah didn't have any suburbs to move to.

I used to wonder why anyone would leave the beautiful landscapes of Norway for the flat, boring American plains. Then I actually visited Norway and saw the farms perched on ledges in fjords or littered with rock piles. I realized that to a Norwegian farmer, 160 acres of flat, thick soil without rocks was an unbelievable paradise. Still, it must have been nostalgia for home that prompted Norwegians to make Decorah their first settlement west of the Mississippi River, for Decorah is in one of the few spots in Iowa with any resemblance to Norway. It's in a steep river valley, with cliffs, springs, waterfalls, and thick forests.

It was the 1925 centennial of the first Norwegian immigrant ship to America that prompted Norwegian Americans to get organized about preserving their past. They founded an association for scholarly research, based at St. Olaf College in Minnesota. They founded Vesterheim, a Norwegian term meaning "home in the west," as a public museum. Starting from a collection of artifacts at Decorah's Luther College, Vesterheim grew into the nation's largest museum dedicated to any single ethnic group. Its main building is a former hotel, still elegant, and it includes several other buildings of exhibits, classrooms, a cafe, and a book and craft store. Out back is a gathering of pioneer buildings.

Not all Norwegian Americans were happy about the founding of Vesterheim. It came at a time when many ethnic groups were feeling overwhelmed by the dilemmas of assimilation into American society. Many immigrants had watched their children or grandchildren grow up with complete disregard for their native language, religion, and traditions. For some, Vesterheim meant that Norwegian traditions were now a thing of the past, something that survived only in museums, not in homes, churches, and schools.

One autumn when I spent a weekend in Decorah, I got a chance to consider the issue of assimilation.

After wandering through the museum, I explored their bookstore and came upon a newly published novel called *On the Way to the Melting Pot*. Actually, it was first published in 1917, but this was the first English translation. It hadn't taken this long to get translated because it was by some obscure Norwegian author. It was written in Eau Claire, Wisconsin, by an author, Waldemar Ager, who spent most of his life in America. Ager insisted on writing in Norwegian because he was a leading advocate of resisting assimilation. He felt that the key to preserving Norwegian culture was preserving the language. He of all people couldn't publish his novel in English. But by 1917, publishing in Norwegian meant that a lot of Norwegian Americans were incapable of reading his novel, especially the ones who most needed to hear his message.

The back cover compared Ager's novel to Sinclair Lewis's *Main Street*, which came out three years later. Like Lewis, Ager was deeply skeptical about American materialism and social climbing, but Ager thought that immigrants had even more to lose when they were seduced by American values. Desperate to be accepted by Americans, immigrants would cast aside their whole rich spiritual and cultural heritage. Ager wrote his novel as a warning about the costs of assimilation.

As I was paying for the novel, I asked the cashier why the police were setting up barricades on the street in front of the museum. She said there was going to be a street festival that night. "A Norwegian festival?" I asked, glad for my luck. No, she said, just a festival in honor of the street. The city had just finished redoing the main street and sidewalks, and after all the inconveniences to the public, it was time to celebrate.

Well, I thought, that was still fine. I could spend the rest of the afternoon sitting on a bench outside reading my novel, and then I'd have a chance to celebrate Decorah with the Norwegians. As I stepped outside I did notice that the street and sidewalks and antique lampposts looked new.

I found a bench in front of the Viking Realty Company. In the window behind me was a model Viking ship. Above me were Norwegian, American, and Iowa flags. I was right across the street from the Viking

State Bank, which used a Viking ship in its logo. Many of the stores bore Norwegian names, like Erickson Photography.

The translator's introduction to Ager's novel pointed out that 1917 was a moment of truth for Norwegian Americans. With the outbreak of World War I, immigrants were under pressure to prove that their loyalty was to America and not to a foreign country. It made Americans very nervous that some of their neighbors were still speaking German, and no one else could tell what they might be plotting. It wasn't just German Americans who were harassed. Using any foreign language called your loyalties into question. Even worse, some Americans couldn't tell the difference between German and Norwegian. The governor of Iowa even issued a proclamation forbidding churches from conducting services in any foreign language. The slow melting pot had become a pressure cooker.

The novel began with pots on a stove. A Norwegian woman was awkwardly trying to prepare an American-style meal to celebrate her child's baptism. When another Norwegian woman made Norwegian food for her child's baptism, it caused much gossip about how old-fashioned she was. When the American meal was served, the cook's husband had to instruct the puzzled Norwegian guests on how to eat it. The discussion turned to the survival of Norwegian customs. A plumber married to an American woman said: "'My wife is proud of what Norwegian she has learned, but your wives are proud of the Norwegian they have forgotten.'"[1] He complained that in school Norwegian kids learned all about Jesse James but couldn't name the village their fathers were born in. Someone countered that it was bad enough they were scorned for not speaking English; they shouldn't let their children be scorned too. The minister said that before long, church services would have to switch to English to keep young people involved.

From what I had read in history books, the minister's mild comments about language in church services didn't do justice to the bitter fights that actually occurred, splitting whole denominations and leading to the founding of new churches. The churches that insisted on using Scandinavian languages eventually held only old folks, and then they closed. It was the 1894 split in the Danish Church that left us with two Danish colleges, Dana College in Nebraska welcoming assimilation, and the Grundtvigian Grand View College in Iowa resisting it, although there were theological issues involved too.

One of the diners was a newcomer, a house painter named Lars Olson. Through his naive eyes we see American society and the efforts of Norwegians to adjust to it. While Lars was working as a clerk in a local clothing store he saw how Americans would sacrifice everything for commercial success. The store owner wouldn't join any church for fear of alienating other congregations, but he donated to all of them. If a customer was a Democrat, then the store owner pretended to be a Democrat. He always offered a phony smile and flattery, and he was just as dishonest about his prices and the quality of his goods.

Lars lived in a boardinghouse run by the Norwegian Mrs. Nelson. Her son Henry was the hero of the high school football team and had been for many years now, for he never studied hard enough to graduate. The school was happy he kept flunking because its football success gave it status in town. When Henry finally graduated at age twenty, he felt that his diploma gave him too high a social status for him to do manual labor, but the merchants considered him unfit for a commercial job, so he just sat around the house watching his mother work. Like a lot of kids of immigrants, he was embarrassed by his mother's old-fashioned, low-class ways. She didn't speak English, and Henry refused to speak Norwegian.

Lars was of high moral character, and he carefully saved his wages so he could return to Norway, with money he couldn't have earned there, to marry his sweetheart. But he started hanging out in saloons, since that was the only place he could speak Norwegian. There he met other Norwegians who had tried finding fellowship in civic or church groups only to find a language barrier. Now many of them were spending all their money on drink. Some had become alcoholic wrecks. Even men of good education, skill, and social standing back in Norway were floundering in America. Lars was more careful about drinking, but one night when he heard Mrs. Nelson singing a Norwegian hymn his mother used to sing to him, he went to the saloon and got utterly drunk.

Speaking of saloons, there was a bar right next to Vesterheim, and employees were busy setting up a beer garden in the street. The Winneshiek County Cattlemen's Association was setting up a grill. Right next to them, unwisely close if you ask me, the Ostrich Meat Association set up a table with a sign saying "The *Healthy* Red Meat." Next to them, the Dairy Council parked its "Moo-Mobile." Speakers and microphones were being set up for live music. Before long, dozens of antique cars started showing up at the end of a road rally and filling up the next block.

I returned to my book. When Edith Perkins, the daughter of one of the wealthiest men in town, took a fancy to Henry, her handsome football hero, Mr. Perkins decided it was time to put Henry in his place. He invited Henry over for tea, which Henry and his mother regarded as a great social triumph. But Mr. Perkins only gave Henry a humiliating scolding about what a lazy oaf he was and kicked him out of the house. Chastened, Henry decided it was time to make something of himself and got a job digging ditches. The other workmen were Norwegians, so Henry started speaking Norwegian. In the evenings he started studying Lars's Norwegian newspaper, the *Decorah-Posten*. He even accompanied his mother to Norwegian church services. But his mother wasn't happy with this trend. She had been proud to have an American football hero for a son, but now he was just another Norwegian common laborer. It was humiliating.

Meanwhile, Lars was doing his best to seem like an American gentleman, buying classy clothes, teaching himself English, calling himself Louis. He had taken a fancy to Sophie Omley, the college-educated daughter of his boss at the painting company. She was Norwegian, but her father was grooming her to marry a Yankee. Lars began worrying about whether his marriage proposal should be in English or Norwegian.

At dinnertime, I headed for what appeared to be a popular restaurant. I studied the menu for something Norwegian but saw nothing. I decided that fish would serve as a proper Norwegian meal. Looking around, I didn't see anyone else eating fish. I overheard people talking with embarrassment about today's Luther College football game. Luther had lost to tiny Martin Luther College from Minnesota. There was also talk about the Vikings, that is, the Minnesota Vikings football team.

Mr. Omley didn't approve of Lars's interest in his daughter Sophie. He had spent $800 on college and music lessons to turn Sophie into a lady worthy to marry an American gentleman. A Norwegian house painter just wouldn't do. Mr. Omley set out to sabotage the romance, and he succeeded. Lars quit working for him and became a clerk in a furniture store. He wrote to his long-neglected sweetheart in Norway asking her to come marry him. She wrote back that since he was now a fine American gentleman, did he really want a simple Norwegian farm girl? Lars swallowed his pride and sent for her.

Meanwhile, Mr. Perkins, during a visit to an exclusive resort where moneyless, affected, spoiled European "barons" and "counts" tried to charm his daughter Edith for the sake of her money, reconsidered what kind of husband he'd prefer for her. He decided he'd prefer a simple, honest lad. He remembered the football hero he'd treated so rudely. Since Perkins owned the company for which Henry worked, he'd heard reports of Henry's advancement to foreman of a crew that had defied the engineer's predictions and built a road through a marsh. Perkins decided to send Henry to study engineering in college, cultivating him for perhaps more than just an engineering job.

On my way from dinner back to my bench, I stopped to watch the assembling and decoration of a twenty-five-foot-long cookie. A reporter from the local paper was taking a photo of it, and someone thanked him for showing up to cover his daughter's softball game. The local paper was a thin weekly. I thought of how far away were the days of the *Decorah-Posten*, the greatest voice of Norwegian America. It had lasted almost a century, finally dying in 1973. It had sustained itself by absorbing the circulations of all the other dying Norwegian newspapers. At one time or another, there were at least two thousand Scandinavian-language newspapers in America. The power of the Scandinavian press is obvious when you visit the American Swedish Institute in Minneapolis, housed in the mansion of Swan Turnblad, publisher of the largest circulation Swedish newspaper. His paper died in 1940. Today, only a handful of Scandinavian-language newspapers remain, with a very small readership.

Lars put on his most fashionable clothes to go meet his fiancée arriving from Norway. As the train pulled up he nervously wiped his face with his handkerchief, forgetting that he had just polished his shoes with it. He couldn't figure out why Karoline was so amused by his appearance. She wasn't so amused to discover how obsessed he had become with the postures of social status. America was great for allowing poor Norwegians to rise in status, but people became so obsessed with success that they sacrificed everything else to it. Previously thrifty Norwegians bankrupted themselves to buy clothes and houses to give themselves the appearance of higher status. Karoline was content with her simple Norwegian values. Lars was reluctant to marry her right away and suggested that if she worked as a servant in a fine home, she would learn the ways of fine Americans.

On May 17, the Norwegian Fourth of July, Karoline was wearing a Norwegian flag ribbon while serving tea to a guest in the house where she worked. The guest scolded her for disloyalty to America and those who had sacrificed so she could enjoy freedom. Karoline replied firmly that in Norway women had the freedom to vote, and she had given that up in coming to a country where women were regarded the way only criminals and mental patients were regarded in Norway. In her spare time, Karoline started a group for the enjoyment of Norwegian music, reading, food, and games.

Lars tried to hide his Norwegian origin. When Lars and Karoline were out walking and an American came by, he switched from talking in Norwegian to English. He still read the *Decorah-Posten*, but in public he carefully hid it inside an American newspaper.

I thought I'd stop reading at dusk, but the big Viking Realty sign came on just above my head and provided enough light by which to read—read about a Norwegian family buying an impressive house they couldn't afford.

But it was time for me to join the party. There were now hundreds of people milling in the street, admiring the old cars, eating, drinking beer, and greeting friends. The live music was starting, a four-man black vocal group from Seattle called the Main Attraction. They had performed at the college last night, and the bar owner happened to see them and asked them to perform at the street party. They were clearly amused at the idea of having a party for the paving of a street. The leader enthused: "The street really does look brand new!" He told the crowd: "You may not have heard of our group, but you have certainly heard our music, as we were the voices behind the California Raisins."

A murmur of recognition and excitement went through the crowd. A murmur of dismay went through Waldemar Ager in his grave.

In Ager's day, being fashionable in American society was a matter of clothing or language. Being fashionable might be assessed annually by the changes in the Sears catalog. Since Ager's day American society has devised far more powerful tools to mold our tastes. Every minute of the day, from every direction, Madison Avenue uses every psychological tactic to define our values, our role models, our momentary desires, our life goals. The way we become happy or important is by buying things. Fads generated by commercials sweep through the nation on a frequent schedule. Then the commercials themselves become fads. On an almost regular schedule, a jingle or a slogan or a joke or a character or an event in a commercial enthralls the nation. Everywhere people repeat the slogan to one another, proving that they are trendy. A year later, no one would be caught repeating such an out-of-date slogan.

Such was the fame of the California Raisins. They started on television as a few clay animation figures dancing across a breakfast table to the tune of the pop song "I Heard It through the Grapevine." They became instant cultural icons. They soon showed up as dolls, jewelry, posters, bumper stickers, kids' lunch boxes. They were almost everywhere. Now they had arrived right outside the door of the greatest fortress of Norwegian culture. They had landed like anti-Vikings ready to storm a castle.

One of the most famous and dignified of Norwegian Americans had already been conquered by Madison Avenue. When Walter Mondale was campaigning for the Democratic presidential nomination in 1984, his aides were desperate to find a way to diffuse the growing appeal of his rival, a young, handsome, trendy guy with some catchy slogans. One aide told Mondale that he could discreetly label his rival a phony by adopting the latest television commercial fad, the slogan of a fast food hamburger chain. The aide tried to describe the commercial, in which an old lady deflated the pretensions of rival chains by staring into her open hamburger and asking "Where's the beef?" Mondale didn't get it. What did hamburgers have to do with debating political philosophies and policies, with deciding the leadership and future of the nation? The aide told him it was a national phenomenon; at work and school and home, everyone was saying "Where's the beef?" The old lady was even on the nighttime talk shows. The aide stationed himself in front of the television in Mondale's hotel suite to spot the commercial and show it to Mondale. Mondale still just didn't get it, but his aides finally prevailed. When a baffled Mondale first tried the line in public, he goofed it up, and it came out more formally: "Where is the beef?" He was amazed when his audience roared with gleeful approval. His line instantly made it onto the national news and apparently convinced a lot of people that Mondale himself was a pretty trendy guy after all. Mondale made the slogan into the punch line of every speech; his rival never recovered momentum. Another innocent Norwegian had been assimilated and was now an agent for the culture of superficiality. Unfortunately for Mondale, his rival in the fall election had been a Hollywood actor and a television pitchman and knew far more than him about style and catchy slogans.

If Walter Mondale couldn't withstand the seduction of Madison Avenue, then what chance remained for a crowd of small-town Iowa beer-lubricated Norwegians on a Saturday night when the Luther College football team had been humiliated by tiny Martin Luther College from highfalutin Minnesota and the only thing left to celebrate was tidy pavement, and some famous American icons had come all the way from Seattle to bless that pavement?

The music started. *In the jungle, the quiet jungle, the lion sleeps tonight.* They were smooth. *In the jungle, the mighty jungle, the lion sleeps tonight.* The dancing started. The first dancers to come forward were dressed very formally. They had come straight from their wedding. The bride and groom swung merrily. They would have a unique honeymoon story to tell the future of Norwegian America.

In a store window down the block were two elegant wooden chests made by a local artist. She had painted them with rosemaling, the traditional Norwegian flower decoration. On top of one chest was an old painting depicting a bride in a traditional folk wedding dress stepping into a large wedding boat crowded with friends and family who would row her to church, an ancient Scandinavian tradition.

The whole street broke out in dancing and foot tapping. The only Norwegians who weren't moving were the plastic models inside Vesterheim wearing their quaint folk costumes, their silly old wedding dresses. Right outside the holiest shrine to Norwegian tradition, hundreds of Norwegians in jeans and T-shirts were being assimilated. Even here in Decorah, protected behind its Norwegian ecological niche hills, they were being assimilated right before my eyes. I felt like I was in a *Star Trek* movie in which the Borg was implacably assimilating individuals and whole species into its collective mind and proclaiming to earthlings: RESISTANCE IS FUTILE. YOU WILL BE ASSIMILATED.

Except that here the entities being assimilated were the Borgs, and the Tollefons, and the Rölvaags, and the Knutsons. The California Raisins beamed with delight.

Not quite everyone was under the spell of the California Raisins. I had noticed that in the next block a group called the Nordic Trio were scheduled to perform. I went to check them out. As they were getting out their instruments, it appeared that there were actually four performers. I asked the lady next to me why they were called the Nordic Trio if there were actually four of them. She replied that her husband was one of the performers, but she didn't know why they were called a trio; it had always been that way. I asked her if they played Norwegian folk music, and she said, "Not particularly." The first song they played, with two fiddles, a guitar, and a keyboard, could have been some old Norwegian tune. A few dozen people were listening, but then the Nordic Trio were standing right next to the giant cookie, and most of these people were just waiting in line for a cookie. Only one person, a little girl, was dancing. When the Nordic Trio started in on a rickety rendition of the country standard "Your Cheating Heart," I headed back to the California Raisins. They were good.

The crowd seemed quite happy at being assimilated. They probably would have danced all night, but before long it started to rain. The California Raisins excused themselves and scrambled to pack up their sound equipment. We weren't going to hear them sing "I Heard It through the Grapevine." I suspected that this rain was no coincidence. Waldemar Ager was right after all. God really was a Norwegian.

I returned downtown the next morning to finish assimilating Ager's novel.

Henry Nelson became a college football hero and ended up marrying the rich Yankee's daughter. His mother was so proud of him, though of course she was too low class to get an invitation to the wedding.

Mr. Omley proudly married off his daughter Sophie to an up-and-coming Yankee bank clerk. The clerk seemed to know all about the enthralling world of American capitalism. The clerk innocently advised Mr. Omley to invest in an Arizona mining stock. It turned out to be a scam. Omley lost a fortune and had to move out of his house. In his despondency he became ill and died. At the funeral, the local newspaper reporter asked Sophie about her father's birthplace in Norway. She didn't know its name. Her husband later left her.

Lars watched the furniture store decline because the Norwegian owner wouldn't keep up with the latest fashions and because a Jew opened a rival store nearby and catered to modern Yankee tastes. The Norwegian customers, wanting to be like the Yankees, all started going to the Jew's store. Lars spread the rumor that the Jew was a shyster and that the best Yankee families in town shopped in Lars's store, so the Norwegians started returning. The Jew, to co-opt his competition, offered to hire Lars for more money. Lars's boss, badly in debt, had been paying Lars in IOUs, and when Lars tried to redeem his IOUs and leave, the boss took poison and killed himself. Lars took over the old store and used every shabby tactic he'd learned to turn it into a success. He started with a big sale to take advantage of all the publicity generated by the owner's suicide. Lars was struck by how fine the owner's daughter looked dressed in formal black, and he married her.

Karoline returned to Norway and became a respected nurse and married a compassionate doctor.

On the final page, Ager summarized his verdict on the American melting pot: "Some danced themselves into the great melting cauldron, others went calmly and quietly. . . . Others again marched to a full orchestra. . . . Some still went into it thoughtlessly and simply in laziness. . . . But Lars was among those who prepared his own unraveling and melted down by ridding himself of his best qualities first. And this was only natural, because the melting pot was precisely for the spiritually stunted."[2]

When I was hungry for lunch, I checked out the menu at a cafe crowded with young people in Luther College sweatshirts. I was about to go in, but then my conscience tugged at me. I headed down the street to the Norwegian cafe at Vesterheim. A handful of older folks, probably tourists, were there. I examined the traditional Norwegian buffet. There was fish and fruit and crisp bread and other things that looked really healthy. I headed back up the street to the crowded cafe. I didn't even ask if they had Knutson's soda. I ordered a hamburger and French fries and a Coke.

Resistance is futile. You will be assimilated.

14

More Swedish Than Sweden

Many a girl showing up in Lindsborg, Kansas, has looked at her little dog and declared: "Toto, I have a strange feeling we're not in Kansas anymore." They are, in fact, in Sweden, or at least that's what the people of Lindsborg would like you to think. Within one block in downtown Lindsborg you can eat a Swedish meal, watch a woodcarver making Dala horses, shop for fine Swedish glass or plain Swedish groceries, and stay in a Swedish-style hotel. The hotel alone contrasts Lindsborg with the thousands of other small American towns whose hotels were abandoned long ago and proves that a lot of tourists are drawn to Lindsborg.

I was introduced to Lindsborg by my father when I was thirteen years old. My father was familiar with Lindsborg before he ever saw it, for his college, the University of Oklahoma, made a habit of taking talent from Lindsborg's Bethany College. Today two buildings on the University of Oklahoma campus, Holmberg Hall and Jacobson Hall, are named for former students of Birger Sandzén. Jacobson became the mentor of many path-breaking Native American artists. Even the sacred University of Oklahoma football field is named for a coach taken from Lindsborg. (The Bethany College football team is named, of course, the Swedes.)

My father and I stopped in Lindsborg on our way to the Southwest. Our summer road trip got a late start that year, for we had stayed home to watch Neil Armstrong and Buzz Aldrin walk on the moon. After my father's education was interrupted by World War II and a resulting career at Bell Labs, he got his Ph.D. at Purdue, where one of his engineering classmates was Neil Armstrong, and when my father was at MIT, one of his engineering classmates was Buzz Aldrin. One year after the first moon landing, the astronauts marked the anniversary by being reunited with their command module, *Columbia*, which had disappeared on a tour of the country. The *Columbia* happened to be in Missouri, so one year after setting down on the moon, Armstrong and Aldrin set down at the airport in our town, Columbia, and I got to see them too.

Lest you think I am digressing, I should explain that Aldrin is Swedish. One of his Swedish grandmothers had an appropriate last name: Moon. Aldrin wasn't the only Swede on the first moon landing, for there was also the Swedish Hasselblad camera. NASA tested American cameras to record the greatest triumph of American technology but rejected them as unreliable technology. So it was a Swedish camera taking photos of a Swede on the moon. Unbelievably, in the biggest public relations goof-up in NASA history, NASA assigned the camera to Armstrong and didn't think of trading it off to Aldrin, so the world doesn't have a single photo of the first man on the moon actually standing on the moon. All of the photos are of Aldrin. When the Swedish post office issued a commemorative stamp, they cheated and showed the Swede holding the Swedish camera. The headquarters of the Hasselblad Corporation is on the Gothenburg waterfront, overlooking the dock from which Aldrin's grandparents sailed for America on a voyage that turned into a voyage to the moon.

Many years later I was on another summer road trip, this time in Sweden, when Buzz Aldrin again juxtaposed himself with Lindsborg, Kansas.

I was heading for Trondheim, Norway, planning to arrive on the day it started celebrating its one thousandth anniversary. In the Middle Ages, northern Europeans who couldn't make pilgrimages as far as Jerusalem found a substitute in Nidaros, the medieval name for Trondheim, where King Olav had become a saint and his relics at his cathedral worked miracles. A five-hundred-mile pilgrimage route started in Karlstad, Sweden, and followed the Klarälven River northward. Even Norwegians, unable to trek through fjord country, headed inland to Sweden and then north. I decided to follow the old pilgrimage route.

While in Karlstad I stopped by the Emigrant Register, a major Swedish emigration research center. On the wall they had Buzz Aldrin's family tree, including photos of the old Aldrin family home. It was in a hamlet so tiny that the librarian had to check several maps before we located it. It was only slightly off my pilgrimage route, so I decided to go find it.

Along the way, I ran into Lindsborg, Kansas. But let me finish the Aldrin story first.

I found the Aldrin hamlet of Stjärnfors. The main feature of the hamlet was an old mill. It turned out that only three weeks earlier the mill had been opened as a museum and art gallery. I was the very first American to visit. The curator told me they were planning a Buzz Aldrin exhibit. She said that Aldrin still had cousins in the area, and during the moon landing they had sat dumbfounded to think that this was their cousin walking on the moon. The Swedish Aldrins were iron workers, as were many people in the area. The museum held many iron ornaments, including iron cemetery crosses. The curator gave me directions to the Aldrin house.

I headed out of the hamlet. The pavement turned into a gravel road. I thought I had turned onto the right road at the right pasture, but after awhile I wasn't so sure. Fortunately, I came across three women walking their dogs, and they set me right. They told me that no one was living in the Aldrin house at the moment, as it was being repainted inside, so it was fine if I wanted to stop and look around.

The Aldrin house was a typical Swedish house, red with white trim and a tile roof, with a flagpole out front in a birch tree yard. I walked up to the window and peered in. It was a typical Swedish house inside too, except for its emptiness and sheet-draped furniture. It was a typical Swede who had walked on the moon.

Just so I won't irritate any Norwegian Americans who were looking forward to the big party in Trondheim, I'll briefly finish my pilgrimage. In a little town near the Norwegian border I stopped at a museum and found a strange scene: the exhibits were blocked and covered by sewing machines, work tables, big rolls of fabric, and women so frantically sewing away that no one even looked at me. They were trying to finish a very long tapestry to be presented to the city of Trondheim in a few days. Over several years they had embroidered sections of it in their homes, and now they were putting it all together. The tapestry was meant to be a modern answer to the Bayeux tapestry. It depicted scenes from the old pilgrimage, and as I looked over sketches of it, I recognized some of the places I had been, and I felt I was carrying on a noble tradition. Thirty thousand pilgrims a year once made this trek. Many churches and facilities sprang up along the way, and some traces of them remained. One evening I strolled away from my lodge, the Pilgrim's Inn, and found the stone floor of a medieval church by the river where pilgrims used to camp. A stone marker was carved with medieval messages. In a park just up the hill, a dance band was playing songs from Glenn Miller and the Beach Boys.

I did make it to Trondheim, where a stone Saint Olav on a pillar presided over the crowds and a pop concert in the city square and an oratorio about Trondheim history in the cathedral. I liked the feel of a one-thousandth anniversary celebration, and I planned to attend the next one that came up in America.

But back to Sweden. Driving along, I'd noticed on the map that the next town was Munkfors. Since the highway crossed the river there, I guessed that this is where the monks forded the river. At the edge of town was a sign welcoming me to Munkfors, but I didn't look quickly enough to finish reading the rest, and all I saw was "Lindsborg, Kansas." Puzzled, I turned around and went back. Munkfors was the sister city of Lindsborg. I decided to investigate.

I found the tourist office and asked a woman about the Lindsborg connection. She told me that many of the pioneers of Lindsborg came from the Munkfors area. There were still many family ties between the two towns. Sometimes the two towns sent representatives to each other's celebrations. In fact, this woman had ridden in the parade of Lindborg's Svensk Hyllningsfest, their biannual celebration of Swedishness. I asked her what she thought of Lindsborg, whether as a Swede she felt right at home there. I wasn't aware I had said anything amusing, but clearly she was amused. Well, she said, of course Swedes take much pride in their American cousins, but it was just so odd to travel to the most modern country in the world and find the most old-fashioned Swedish customs. Modern Sweden is thoroughly international in its clothing styles, music, dances, and food, and you'd have to look a long time in Sweden to find some of the customs paraded so proudly in Lindsborg. But her affection for Lindsborg was obvious when she summarized: "Lindsborg is more Swedish than Sweden."

This was a surprising idea for me. I had attended a Svensk Hyll-ningsfest, along with many thousands of Swedish Americans from far and wide, and I had supposed that the Swedish costumes, music, dances, and food I saw there were the essence of Swedishness. But now that I thought about it, standing here in a thoroughly modern down-town, without any artificially attached nineteenth-century Swedish ar-chitecture in sight, without any Swedish folk art in sight, with pizza and hamburgers more plentiful than Swedish meatballs, I saw that she was right.

Another thing missing in downtown Munkfors was Swedish folk music broadcast from loudspeakers, like you could hear in Lindsborg and in Kingsburg, California. I had a good idea what I would find in a music store in Munkfors, and it wasn't Swedish folk music. I had re-searched this subject more extensively than I'd wanted to in Karlstad, where I went into a music store searching for a copy of *Kristina från Duvemäla*. I failed to notice that next to the sales counter was a special rack for the top ten CDs in Sweden, and Kristina was sitting right there. As I surveyed the racks I saw that rock and roll was the biggest section and that most of the bands were the same ones you would find in Britain and America. There was also a large jazz section, with plenty of familiar names. There was a lot more country music than I would have imagined, and when I say country, I don't mean the country of Sweden. I was looking for the musical soundtrack section, and when I found it, I saw plenty of Broadway and London hits. But no Kristina. I spotted a Swedish music section, but it didn't hold Kristina and seem-ingly not much Swedish folk music, at least judging from the instru-ments on the covers. I returned to the rock section and looked under ABBA. Right next to ABBA was Ace of Base, another reminder of the big success of Swedish rock groups abroad. I'd heard somewhere that next to America and Britain, Sweden had exported more rock records than any other country.

Thinking about Lindsborg, I couldn't think of anywhere in town where you could buy American rock and roll or even Swedish rock and roll. But you could find lots of Swedish folk music. I know there are many Swedish Americans who are very fond of this music, especially if they grew up with it, but I have to confess it doesn't do much for me. I know I'm in good company in saying this. I once walked into a Swedish gift shop at opening time, and when the owner saw she had a customer, she took out the country music tape she was enjoying and put on a tape of Swedish folk music. Once in the gift shop of the American Swedish Institute in Minneapolis, which has lots of Swedish folk music for sale, I overheard one clerk asking the other clerk why she didn't have any music on, and the other clerk replied, "I'm just so tired of this Swedish stuff." Yet Lindsborg just wouldn't be as charming if the loud-speakers were broadcasting ABBA or Roxette.

I had previously discovered that American jazz was thriving in Scandinavia. The first time I stayed in Stockholm, a hotel around the corner from me was hosting the International Duke Ellington Conference, which included many jazz concerts in the largest halls in Stockholm, featuring several Swedish big bands. In Helsinki I attended a jazz festival featuring a very Nordic-looking group called the Harlem Jazz Camels. No white American band would ever dare call themselves the Harlem Jazz Camels, but the Nordics thought it was totally cool.

It was also totally cool for Scandinavian kids to wear American jeans and T-shirts and baseball caps, though these kids couldn't locate the cities whose teams they boosted or define the exact nature of a Red Sox or a Knick. The plentiful American logos I saw in Munkfors were quite a contrast with Lindsborg, at least during Svensk Hyllningsfest. Of course, most of the time Lindsborg kids wore Michael Jordan T-shirts like everyone else. But Lindsborg closets held a thousand Swedish folk costumes, which, as kids grew up, were traded between families and passed down to new generations. When old costumes wore out, new ones were sewn to match the design of the old. Each Swedish province has its own design of folk costume, and the costumes in Lindsborg reflected the varying origins of people's great-grandparents. Yet it seems that over 130 years, some mutations have occurred. Later that year I attended another Svensk Hyllningsfest. The Official Swede was a woman from the Swedish embassy. I asked her what she thought of Lindsborg, and she said with perplexed amusement: "I don't know where they got some of these costumes. I've never seen anything like them in Sweden. Maybe these were the costumes back when their ancestors emigrated." Perhaps it was the folk costumes in Sweden that had mutated and the Swedish American costumes that were frozen in time, like Shakespearean dialects in Appalachian hollows. I talked with another Swedish woman in the crafts tent who was selling embroidered flowers representing each Swedish province. Rolling her eyes in mock horror, she said, "You would never get Swedish teenagers to dress like that! Lindsborg is more Swedish than Sweden."

If I had looked around Munkfors I suppose I could have found some Swedish food at the risk of branding myself a tourist. Once when I was in Oslo I noticed a poster in the window of McDonald's advertising a McLak, which I guessed was a baked cod burger. Only in Norway, I thought. I went in and ordered one, only to find it was a special order, perhaps a downright eccentric order, requiring me to stand there for five minutes while a dozen Norwegians got their cheeseburgers and fries. American food too has conquered the world, although I've never understood why hamburgers, frankfurters, and French fries, with their obvious nods to Germany and France, are considered so American. The Egg McMuffin is now an American folk food, though it's made of English muffins and Canadian bacon. But I suppose McDonald's is a tribute to e pluribus unum. I suppose there are kids in Italy who go to Pizza Hut and assume that pizza is an American food.

You can find lots of Swedish food in Lindsborg and not just at festival time. For many Scandinavian Americans, traditional foods are a matter of nostalgia, reminding them of what grandmother made for them with love, or a matter of ethnic pride. Yet many of the foods patriotically consumed at Scandinavian American festivals were simply the foods of nineteenth-century peasants, which peasants ate only because they couldn't afford anything better and which they abandoned as soon as they got the chance.

By now the reader should have spotted a contradiction. If I am uninspired by Swedish folk traditions, then why do I keep going back to Lindsborg and Svensk Hyllningsfest?

I'll admit I'm less interested in Scandinavian folk culture than in "high culture," not just the great names like Ibsen, Sibelius, Bergman, Munch, and Hamsun but their current successors, who offer not only interesting glimpses into Scandinavian life but views of the human condition as perceptive as anyone's, maybe more perceptive. When it comes to symbols of Swedish America, coffeepot water towers are less satisfying than a photo of Buzz Aldrin on the moon. Yet I would be the first to agree that holding a Bergman film festival during Svensk Hyllningsfest would violate the spirit of it. Scandinavian American festivals are not, after all, about modern Scandinavia. Modern Sweden is an urban, well-educated society proud of its world leadership in technology, business, and culture, and it doesn't want to be represented by images of nineteenth-century peasant backwardness. But this was the life of most Swedish immigrants to America. This was the life they settled into in America. Cut off from the evolving culture back in Sweden, they were left in a time warp. After Lindsborg was founded on the remote prairie right after the Civil War by Swedes from the Bishop Hill area, it was under little pressure to change. Yet even if Scandinavian Americans realized that their folk customs were anachronisms to modern Swedes, they would say it doesn't really matter, for these were the traditions of their great-grandparents, and this is their way of honoring them.

Yet once again, Scandinavian Americans have been outmaneuvered by Scandinavian culture. Some of the customs that Swedish Americans practice under the impression they are carrying on the customs of their great-grandparents were actually unknown to their great-grandparents. There have been times in Scandinavian history, especially the 1890s, when a concern for national identity has led intellectuals to draw upon folk traditions to create new art and new customs. Some of the greatest names of Scandinavian high culture such as Edvard Grieg, Carl Larsson, and Hans Christian Andersen won their status by celebrating folk themes. New folk customs were also created such as the festival of Saint Lucia, the Christmas girl with candles on her head, which had old roots but which mutated into something new. Some of these intellectually-minted folk customs crossed to America with new emigrants and were incorporated into Swedish American traditions. So at today's Swedish American festivals, you can see customs almost extinct in Sweden alongside customs that never existed for Swedish American pioneers.

Yet none of this means that such festivities should be dismissed as fake or foolish. Scandinavian Americans have simply tried to create their own version of Saint Patrick's Day, which was a minor religious event in Ireland until Irish Americans transformed it into an ethnic celebration with such success that everyone in America gets into the spirit of it. Saint Patrick's Day can only be judged fairly by the role it serves within Irish American culture. Scandinavian American festivals, whatever their hybrid origins, are valid if they validate both our Old World roots and our New World branches.

When I stopped looking at Lindsborg like an anthropologist and looked at it with my blue eyes, it succeeded in its purpose of validating an identity that might otherwise be forgotten.

People who visit Lindsborg at nonfestival times may be puzzled by a large white circle painted on the red brick downtown intersection. If you are feeling like Dorothy in Oz, then this circle might just remind you of the spiraling start of the yellow brick road round which Dorothy danced off to see the wizard. And in truth this circle is there to guide dancing. During the festival Lindsborg shows the depth of its dedication to its heritage by presenting a very elaborate set of folk dances in this circle. Virtually every child in town is involved, and behind the scenes virtually every adult is involved. They practice the dances for months. The dances have been researched from century-old texts. The dances are called Swedish Folk Games, for each dance presents a theme or a story. The first grade class starts out, incredibly cute, with a dance portraying a hide-and-seek game. The second grade does a boat-rowing dance. The third grade does a carousel dance. The eighth grade gets to do a traditional Maypole dance. When Lindsborg kids reach high school, they are eligible for another folk dance group, which has regularly traveled to Sweden and won rave reviews there. When high school students graduate, there's an adult folk dance group, which has toured America. The funds for these tours are raised by the community. A whole town has united to uphold a demanding tradition. The festival dances, which go on for hours, also persuade me that it is possible to resist the Great American Assimilation Machine. Considering how much memory of Scandinavia has been lost in a few generations, it sometimes seems inevitable that within another few generations, with mobility and intermarriage and mass culture, all identification with any Old World origin will be completely washed out. While this might be a triumph of democracy, it would also be a loss, especially if we are all melted down to the mediocrity of Franchise America. A festival day in Lindsborg can leave you believing in the opposite fate, that America will manage to take the best part of every culture and marry them all into something extraordinary.

A century ago, identity loss and assimilation into American culture was an issue only for immigrants to America. Now it has become an issue for the whole world. Through the power of the media, the Great American Assimilation Machine has reached into the remotest villages in Africa and Asia. In Europe, movie theaters and television are dominated by American shows. The world must like what it sees, for it is doing its best to imitate America. Even in the Third World, it's not just an image of affluence that fascinates people. Africans and Asians see a democratic, law-ruled society where blacks and Asians can be full participants. Europeans see an open, energetic society unruled by its past where anything seems possible. Yet European intellectuals worry that the glitter of American pop culture is a Trojan horse that carries some unhealthy social values. In the affluent society they also see a cult of conspicuous consumption. In the open society they also see a rootless society. In the democratic society, where a black or an Asian can be an FBI agent, they also see that his or her days are immersed in insane violence. Today European intellectuals often sound like midwestern Lutheran pastors a century ago, warning against losing one's soul to American culture.

For many years I had a front-row seat to study America's media-driven assimilation of the world. I lived two blocks from the University of Missouri School of Journalism, the world's first school of journalism and, it likes to claim, still the best. Many people seemed to agree, for brilliant students came there from all over the world. Some of them were already established journalists in their home countries, and they came to Missouri to catch up on American techniques or simply to have a chance to observe American society firsthand. Since I was a writer type and used the journalism library as my own study, and since foreign students were curious about Americans and New Yorkers were curious about those exotic midwesterners, it was easy enough for me to be accepted into the journalism community. They were a fascinating group, and since many were astute and well-connected observers of their own countries, I caught a lot of insights into foreign cultures. But I caught even more insights into America. Again and again, things I took for granted about America would be cast into new perspectives when foreigners pronounced them either bizarre and appalling or miraculous and enlightened. The journalism school was one of America's most powerful connections with the world, for better or worse. I'd sit and watch Third World students poring over advertising trade journals, knowing they were going to inflict Madison Avenue's worst tricks onto their defenseless peasant societies. But there were also Third World and

Communist nation students who became so intoxicated with our freedom of the press that they went home determined to enlighten their people.

I received some of my first insights into Sweden by befriending a Swedish couple who came to the journalism school. Dan was studying film, and Cecilia was an established journalist checking out American ways for a year. I helped them check out American ways by taking them on a couple of road trips around the state, one of which included the Truman Presidential Library, where they somberly studied and discussed the panel listing Truman's justifications for dropping the first atomic bomb. I learned some things about Swedish society just from the ways they reacted to American society. For example, Cecilia was baffled and appalled by television commercials from profit-minded rival hospitals trying to sell birth as a product for pregnant women. Her reaction told me much about health care in Sweden. Cecilia was an especially good window into Swedish society, for her father was a member of the Swedish cabinet.

The first time I visited Sweden, I was unprepared for the extent of Americanization I found. The tourist guidebooks show you pictures of elegant old architecture, not close-ups of their store windows filled with American product logos and American celebrity faces. Nothing symbolized the American invasion of Stockholm better than a face I saw staring at me from posters in video store windows, a face I'd last seen in the University of Missouri journalism school library. I should explain that the journalism school is also famous for its dropouts such as Tennessee Williams and George C. Scott. At the time Dan and Cecilia were there, an advertising major was doing his best to follow in this illustrious dropout tradition, and he succeeded brilliantly, and now Brad Pitt's face was seducing defenseless Swedish girls into worshiping Hollywood. I wasn't so naive as to have expected Ingmar Bergman's face in video store windows, but still, I was baffled and appalled to be greeted by an advertising dropout from my own block.

When it was time to visit Dan and Cecilia, I couldn't help noticing a few signs of Americanization in them too. In America, Dan had bought a largish American car, which might have been the right size for American highways but which didn't work so well in Stockholm's narrow medieval streets. I was staying at a hotel, built in 1647, at the end of a narrow dead end street. My rented Saab tucked into the odd corners okay, but Dan's American car couldn't fit, and because of the crowds of Swedes attending the International Duke Ellington Conference, it was hard to find a parking place nearby. Seduced by America, Swedes no longer fit into their own city.

It was gracious of Dan and Cecilia to make time for me, since within the last week Cecilia had given birth to both a baby and a book. On the morning after I arrived in Stockholm, she was on the television news shows being interviewed about her book. As they made dinner for me, I listed all the Stockholm museums I had spent days in, and Cecilia said that now I probably knew more about Swedish history than Swedes did. Dan told me he was using his filmmaking skills to make a few commercials, which didn't used to be allowed on Swedish television. He got out a video and showed his commercials to me. They were very professional and smart, very American, in fact. When I said so, I felt a strange sense of guilt, as if I was now an accomplice in the Americanization of Sweden. My guilty feeling was irrational, and not just because Dan wasn't making commercials for profit-minded hospitals. Yet my guilt was quite real, and when I wondered about it later, I wondered if it wasn't a flashback to the last time, the only time, I had felt guilty about an American kind of event that happened to Sweden.

You see, I grew up in a society where political assassination was a normal event. One day when I was seven years old I was home from school watching television when the program was interrupted by the announcement that President Kennedy had been shot. I knew enough about American history to know this had happened before, but I was surprised that it was supposed to happen now, with me watching. Soon the announcement came that the president was dead. The agitation of the announcer made it clear that this wasn't supposed to be happening. But it did go on happening. It happened throughout my youth, a dozen prominent deaths or assassination attempts over the next seventeen years, and I accepted it as normal, like tornadoes or plane crashes. When Robert Kennedy and Martin Luther King Jr. were assassinated, I was sad but not at all surprised. As the years and the shootings went on, I developed a certain despair about it, like you'd have for a terrible disease. My despair was only deepened by the inevitable commentators who were in denial about there being any disease, who dismissed it as just another case of a sociopathic loner, not meaning anything about our great country. America seemed to have far more than its fair share of sociopathic loners, and I had studied the historical record enough to recognize that our assassins fit a remarkably consistent pattern. They were almost all the youngest sons of bullying fathers, leaving them with a simmering anger against authority, which crippled their ability to fit into school, work, or marriage. Even when they tried over and over to belong to something, they couldn't find any roots or kindness, and their growing anger sometimes took on political clothing and sometimes remained nakedly personal until they took it out against a symbol of all authority and society. A nation of strangers breeds a lot of strange behavior.

The one thing I had never really felt after an assassination was guilt, but I finally felt real guilt when John Lennon was killed by an outcast who had sought his sense of belonging through the world of media celebrity. Twice in quick succession, the next being the celebrity-mad would-be assassin of President Reagan, America's attempt to find belonging through images on screens mocked us violently. I think I felt guilt for Lennon because, while Americans grow up knowing that the rules of the game may include assassination, Lennon was a foreigner who never agreed to play by our rules and in fact tried to improve the rules a bit, and in exchange for his gift we inflicted our sickness on him. No, it wasn't irrational for me to feel guilt over Lennon's death.

What was strange was that when Sweden's prime minister, Olof Palme, was assassinated on a dark Stockholm street, possibly by a sociopathic loner, I felt guilty. I felt the familiar old despair and also guilt. I rebuked myself for the irrationality of these feelings, for after all, this wasn't an American event. But then I realized one valid reason for my guilt. I felt guilty because I had developed strong antibodies against the shock of assassination, while the Swedish people had no immunity at all. They were completely vulnerable and helpless. The assassination wasn't simply another confirmation of what they had always known about their society. It was a contradiction of their core identity as a people, too great a contradiction to even believe. The whole country was stunned with disbelief and had no idea how to deal with it.

And then I started wondering if this might actually be an American event after all. In filling the world's headlines and televisions with assassinations for twenty years and in filling the world's movie screens with images of alienation and violence, perhaps we were infecting the rest of the world, seducing its darkest impulses. All I really knew for sure was that Swedes were now learning what it was *really* like to be Americans, to watch leaders suddenly and inexplicably disappear, to watch trustworthy streets turn ominous. Sweden was being Americanized, and I hoped Swedes never learned what it was like to have such thick antibodies that they wouldn't be surprised by assassination. It was an ironic symptom of societal health that Swedes were so emotionally sick about it. The truth is that I actually admired them for being able to be so shocked, but of course I could never actually say so perverse a thing, and I felt guilty for even feeling it.

Perhaps few Swedes felt more dislocated than Dan and Cecilia, who were far from home, unable to satisfy their urge to go home to share in the mourning, and surrounded by oblivious Americans, surrounded by streets full of people who just went on smiling like idiots. Even their news-conscious American friends who tried to express sympathy didn't come close to understanding their devastation. At the same time, Dan and Cecilia were more intimately involved in the event than most Swedes, for in talking with her cabinet minister father on the phone, Cecilia was hearing details that wouldn't appear in the Swedish newspapers such as the most personal reactions of Palme's cabinet ministers and friends.

As I have said, making friends with foreign journalists offered me glimpses into the deepest soul of a people.

The Swedes who founded Lindsborg actually knew a lot about the deepest soul of America. Some of them had barely arrived in America before they enlisted in Lincoln's army, and they fought in some of the greatest and most terrible battles of the Civil War such as Shiloh. One of the first three Swedes to arrive from Illinois in the future Lindsborg also had an intense introduction to America. Very soon after Johannes Holmkvist and his fiancée, Lena, arrived in Springfield, Illinois, from Sweden, they went to get married, Lena wearing a wedding dress made from her mother's tablecloth. But when all the church bells in Springfield started ringing that day, it wasn't for them. The bells were joined by the ringing of a train bell and whistle that had haunted every town the train had passed through. Through the towns of half a continent, through the fields and woods, through the mountains and river valleys, through the lilac meadows, through the night pursuing a falling western star, the desolate whistle had blown, and everywhere people had gathered along the tracks, people holding torches in the night, people holding American flags and battle flags, people holding photographs of President Lincoln, people playing dirges, people in uniform saluting the man for whom they were supposed to die, strong people with tears flowing, traumatized by something that wasn't supposed to happen in America and that surely could never happen again.

When the funeral train pulled into the Springfield station, Johannes and Lena Holmkvist were in the crowd that met it, and they joined in the procession to the cemetery, Lena still wearing her Swedish tablecloth. She had also married a nation, and like any newlywed she was learning its deepest secrets. Johannes and Lena stared into the faces of Lincoln's longtime neighbors and closest friends, who were more intimately hurt than most Americans. They stared into the faces of cabinet members who had kept vigil over the dying Lincoln, who had seen not newspaper headlines but blood. They marched amidst the flags and the photos, the blackness and the dirges, they marched with the lilacs that with every returning spring for a lifetime would be picked from the dooryard and laid down in still-traumatized memory. Johannes and Lena had become real Americans.

The memory of that day still survives in Lindsborg, for Johannes's and Lena's great-grandson Thomas would write the pioneer history of Lindsborg, the book from which I've taken their story, a book on sale in Lindsborg shops alongside Dala horses.

The year after my second Svensk Hyllningsfest, I spent another weekend in Lindsborg. It would have been a quiet weekend, with nothing special going on, except that a busload of Swedes was in town on their tour of Swedish America, so a small contingent of Lindsborg folk dancers and musicians performed for them on the sidewalk downtown.

I was out at the Lindsborg historical park when the Swedes arrived there. The centerpiece of the park is the Swedish pavilion from the 1904 St. Louis World's Fair. The fair commemorated the one-hundredth anniversary of Jefferson's Louisiana Purchase, and the fair's enormous success, drawing 20 million visitors, set St. Louisians thinking about a more permanent memorial to the Louisiana Purchase. The result decades later was Saarinen's Gateway Arch.

After the fair, the people of Lindsborg claimed the Swedish pavilion, which looks like an old Swedish manor house, and reconstructed it in town, where for years it served as the art studio for Bethany College. I assume that Birger Sandzén painted many of his works inside it.

When I stepped inside the pavilion, I found a man working over an architect's table and blueprints. He explained that he was a historic preservation specialist who had a contract not just to fix up some of the pavilion's sags but to restore some of the original features that had been altered over the years. He also filled me in on the hot gossip in Lindsborg. This morning there was going to be an estate auction at a farmstead in a nearby town. The farm belonged to an eccentric bachelor farmer who never had electricity or running water and who only occasionally took a bath in town. Yet on his walls the farmer had original paintings by Birger Sandzén, Thomas Hart Benton, and Grant Wood. Those paintings could have bought the farmer not just electricity and running water but a whole new house. The art world had been notified of the auction, and dealers from Santa Fe and San Francisco had come out for it.

Then the busload of Swedes arrived, and I watched them wander around the pavilion. When they were finished, they lined up for a group photo in front of the pavilion. Since it looked like they were going to take turns taking photos and thus take turns being left out of them, I volunteered to be the photographer. The next thing I knew, I had a pile of twenty cameras at my feet. It took me awhile to take the photos, for on each camera I had to find a different button and sometimes fiddle with the focus. Then I had to frame the Swedes in front of the pavilion. Then I had to cap the lens and set the camera down carefully in the grass. I did notice, by the way, that most of the cameras were Japanese. None of them were Hasselblads.

As I framed the Swedish pavilion over and over again through the cameras, I saw something that none of the Swedes could see. I saw President Teddy Roosevelt walking up to the door of the pavilion. President Roosevelt came to dedicate the St. Louis World's Fair with a rousing speech about American national destiny and the importance of maintaining our pioneer virtues. Then he visited the Swedish pavilion, among other places. In his youth, Teddy Roosevelt became an admirer of Scandinavians. He was so inspired by Longfellow's *The Saga of King Olaf* that he committed it to memory. Roosevelt decided that he preferred the Nordics over the worldview he saw in Greek and Roman mythology. He felt that the fate-obsessed Greek and Roman gods stacked the deck against humans a bit too often. For Roosevelt, human effort, bravery, and toughness were the greatest virtues, and he felt the Nordics honored those virtues better.

I imagined more than Teddy Roosevelt walking up to the door of the Swedish pavilion. After he entered, I saw a phalanx of Secret Service agents station themselves at the door and start scanning the crowd for assassins. The last time an American president had visited a world's fair, he had been assassinated. It had been only a few years since President McKinley had exposed himself to the crowds at the Pan American Exhibition in Buffalo and been assassinated, making Vice President Roosevelt into the president. If the Secret Service had pleaded with Roosevelt not to visit the St. Louis World's Fair, he was not the kind of man who could act cowardly. He had long ago rejected fate in favor of bravery. But the Secret Service took extraordinary precautions to insure the president's safety. They lined the fairground avenues with thousands of soldiers and policemen. The chief of the Secret Service sat next to Roosevelt in his carriage, and agents hung from every handle. They kept the presidential train steamed up and ready for a quick escape.

I saw the Swedes standing in the grim gaze of the Secret Service agents looking for assassins. The Swedes stood there smiling, oblivious. Even when I was switching cameras, the Swedes barely relaxed their smiles. They just went on smiling like idiots.

When I was finished with the photography, the Swedes came up to collect their cameras and to thank me. I said I was glad I could help give them a souvenir of Lindsborg. They uttered various pleasantries, and I suppose it was inevitable that one woman would say with amusement: "Lindsborg is more Swedish than Sweden."

I smiled at her, smiled like an idiot.

But to myself I thought gravely: No. It's not. You don't know what you are talking about. Even here, even in the Swedish pavilion, you can't hide from the sickness in the land. Even wearing a Swedish tablecloth that has been piled high with Swedish folk foods and heard the lacework of Swedish fiddles, you are marching in a very American parade. No. Lindsborg isn't like Sweden at all.

15

By the Shores of Gitche Gumee

W*hen you* cross the border from Wisconsin into the Michigan Upper Peninsula, it's obvious that you have found the heartland of Finnish America. It's obvious from all the motel signs boasting about their saunas. Elsewhere in America, saunas may be a luxury found only in resorts, but in the Michigan Upper Peninsula (the U.P.), even modest motels feel obligated to offer them. Americans may think of the sauna as something Scandinavian, but it is more specifically Finnish, and for Finns it's not a luxury but a necessity for health. Finland is a damp place from all its lakes and fens, for which the country is named, so Finns are vulnerable to all the ills of a cold, damp climate. Most homes in Finland have a sauna, and it has become the center of family and social life, even the place where the children are born and the elderly die.

It is symbolic that the name Finland was given by outsiders two thousand years ago and is still used only by outsiders. The Finns themselves call their nation Suomi. This means "swampy," the same thing as Finland, but that outsiders won't honor the Finns' own name for themselves is symbolic of a national history of having identities imposed on them by their neighbors the Swedes and the Russians. Even when Finland finally became an independent nation in 1917, its struggle for identity went on. For the 300,000 Finns who immigrated to America before 1917, the struggle for identity went on in America. The Finns' hunger for a distinct identity may have something to do with why the

U.P. periodically threatens to secede from lower Michigan and become the fifty-first state. Taxes have something to do with it, but I doubt it's a coincidence that the U.P. is full of people who spent eight hundred years wanting to be free of Stockholm and Moscow, alongside which Detroit is equally alien. In Detroit too you can find recognition of the different culture of the U.P., for there are lots of jokes about the U.P.'s country bumpkins.

The Finns came to the U.P. partly because they got a later start than most immigrant groups, and the U.P. offered the only farmland left in America. Yet this land was quite marginal for farming, so many Finns ended up becoming miners or loggers. Whatever the U.P. lacked as farmland it made up for in timber and minerals, including one of the world's richest lodes of copper. Logging was a familiar Finnish occupation, and the U.P.'s climate was familiar too. Many other Finns settled in northeast Minnesota, which also combined timber and a world-class mineral lode, although in Minnesota it was iron.

It was an uncanny coincidence that the Finns chose to concentrate not just in the U.P. but along its northern shore with Lake Superior. This was the very site that Henry Wadsworth Longfellow had chosen, decades previously, for his *Song of Hiawatha*, his American version of the Finnish epic, the *Kalevala*. Oops, I guess I've just offended Longfellow, for I hear he was quite touchy about suggestions that he plagiarized the *Kalevala*. When I arrived in the U.P., I wasn't qualified to take a position in this controversy, for I had never read *Hiawatha*.

A century ago such an admission would have been disgraceful. In every schoolhouse in America, *Hiawatha* was as standard a text as the Declaration of Independence. Virtually every child in America had been required to memorize and recite "By the shores of Gitche Gumee, / By the shining Big-Sea-Water . . . " *Hiawatha* was turned into dramas and cantatas and statues. Longfellow was hailed as the American Homer, and his name was chiseled above college columns alongside Virgil, Dante, and Shakespeare. Today, this seems a curious anachronism. Yet Longfellow and *Hiawatha* served for America the same need that the *Kalevala* served for Finland, the need to establish one's own identity.

For the Finns, the nineteenth century was one long identity crisis. I guess I can claim that Scandinavians wrote the book on the subject of identity crisis, for it was the psychologist Erik Erikson (Danish roots,

German born, American career) who coined the term "identity crisis" and brought the concept of identity into prominence. At a time when psychologists and sociologists barely spoke each other's lingo, Erikson spent his career exploring the interface between the individual and society. He was especially intrigued by how an individual's struggle to formulate a set of values and goals for himself could coincide with the needs of a society, producing a solution and a leader in a time of social crisis. His books on Luther and Gandhi won a large audience (and a Pulitzer Prize) and made Erikson a guide during America's identity crisis of the 1960s.

Finland's identity crisis started in 1809, when Sweden ceded Finland to Russia. Though the Finns had never been delighted about being ruled by the Swedes, at least the Swedes had been polite about it and had schooled the Finns in Western culture. Much about Finland had become Swedish. To this day, street signs in Helsinki are in both Swedish and Finnish. Yet these signs reveal why the Finns never became Swedes. Even a casual glance reveals that the two languages are sharply different. The Finns originated as a tribe in the northern Urals who migrated westward, or at least this is what some scholars say. It seems symbolic of Finnish identity confusion that scholars don't even agree on where the Finns and their language came from. According to the Urals origin theory, part of this tribe headed farther south and became the Hungarians. Linguists can trace the common roots of Finnish and Hungarian, but the two peoples can no longer hold a conversation. Centuries of intermarriage with the Swedes lessened the Finns' eastern features, but they never forgot their uniqueness. When Russia took them over, the Finns knew they didn't want to be Russians, but they were no longer sure what it meant to be Finns. By the 1890s this question had become a crisis, for the Russians were planning to absorb Finland completely, leaving it just another Russian-speaking province. It was a symptom of Finnish identity loss that the Finnish nationalist movement, led by intellectuals, was conducted in Swedish, which could not even be understood by peasant Finns.

I don't know if Elias Lönnrot had an identity crisis, but he certainly behaved like it. It takes some sort of demonic need to set a man tramping thousands of miles through the remotest bogs and woods trying to find oral folk poetry. When Lönnrot gave the world the *Kalevala*, he presented it as an ancient epic he had rescued from obscurity. Modern scholars are more inclined to say he imposed classic epic form onto more random raw materials. But what mattered was that the *Kalevala* potently answered the national identity crisis. The epic was rooted on the Finnish landscape. It involved a mysterious object called the *sampo*, whose function as a mill connected it with modern mechanical Finland yet whose magical functions connected it with the tribal shamanistic past. It featured a cultural hero named Väinämöinen, who endured many challenges to bring his people what they needed to live. Väinä-möinen was the fictional parallel of Lönnrot, who performed the same task for Finland. The *Kalevala* was mined by both political and cultural leaders for its rich lode of Finnishness.

Culturally at least, America in 1850 was similar to Finland. We had long been part of another nation. Since Americans weren't under polit-ical pressure like the Finns, we were more sluggish about seeking our own cultural identity. We just went along imitating British forms and subjects. Even those who realized that this was inappropriate for a frontier democracy weren't sure what a real American literature would look like. When Longfellow read the *Kalevala*, he saw the answer. America too had tribal peoples with rich shamanistic legends. For-tunately, Longfellow only had to tramp to the Harvard library, for the explorer Henry Rowe Schoolcraft had made detailed reports of the lore of the natives of the Great Lakes area. Their name for Lake Supe-rior was Gitche Gumee. Longfellow made Hiawatha into the equiv-alent of Väinämöinen, a cultural hero who endured many challenges to bring his people what they needed to live such as corn, writing, the ca-noe, and the arts of peace. Longfellow became the American equiv-alent of Lönnrot, a cultural hero. The American founding fathers had been so eager to declare a cultural Declaration of Independence that they considered replacing the English language with Hebrew, but na-tional identity is not something that can be legislated; it requires myth-ological genius.

But at some point, the parallel between Longfellow and Lönnrot be-gan to diverge. Today the *Kalevala* is alive and well in Finland. It may be even more alive in America, where Finnish Americans still feel an urgency about Finnish identity. The *Kalevala* is a central element of Finnish American groups and festivals. Meanwhile, *Hiawatha* long ago got sent to the literary dead letter office. No American literary work has fallen from such prominence to such neglect. Part of the problem was that the Native Americans in *Hiawatha* not only weren't the forebears of white America, they stood in the way of national destiny, and whites couldn't afford to get too sentimental about them. But more fatally for *Hiawatha*, America stood on the brink of the Civil War, industrialization, and world leadership, and for such a world, Twain, Faulkner, and Hemingway seemed better guides.

When I decided to explore the U.P. and Finnish America, I didn't feel very confident about my ability to do justice to it. I was pretty vague about Finnish culture or what had become of it in America. I had a sharp-enough focus on Swedish culture that I could look at, say, a Dala horse and know where it had come from and what it meant to Swedish Americans. But I could look right at the Finnish equivalent of a Dala horse and not even recognize it. I didn't want to be a dumb tourist in Finnish America, accumulating places but not insights. Then I recalled what Lönnrot had done with his too-random raw materials. Maybe I too could find meaning by imposing epic form on my raw materials. To be more precise, maybe I could take along my copy of the *Kalevala* and find some parallels between it and the lives of Finnish Americans.

Then I discovered that a U.P. writer, (Mr.) Lauri Anderson, had already shamelessly stolen my idea. I ran into a book called *Children of the Kalevala: Contemporary American Finns Relive the Timeless Tales of the Kalevala*. Anderson did succeed in giving the lives of his characters, his backwoods, pickup-driving, deer-hunting, beer-guzzling Finns, some of the dignity of the heroes of the *Kalevala*, but his characters didn't glimpse their own mythological stature and bumbled through life, often disastrously. They tried to uphold their Finnish heritage, but they had only vague ideas of what this really was, and they got it ridiculously confused with American pop culture. Anderson had the humorous and tender touch of a Finnish Garrison Keillor, yet his characters were burdened with far more pathos and disaster.

Heck, I decided, the *Kalevala* wasn't about Finnish Americans anyway. They are the American version of Finns, so maybe I should turn to the American version of the *Kalevala*. I had never read *The Song of Hiawatha*, so maybe I could take it along, if I could even find a copy, and see some parallels between the two American versions, the people and the poem. The fact that this seemed like a clever idea at the time and that *Hiawatha* is actually almost totally irrelevant to Finnish American life is a sign of how clueless I was.

But it seemed promising at first. I entered Michigan at the town of Ironwood, whose most notable landmark was a fifty-two-foot-tall, six-teen-thousand-pound fiberglass statue of Hiawatha. He is wearing a headdress and holding a peace pipe and extending his hand in wel-come. If only the Hiawatha statue was made of copper it would be a perfect Statue of Liberty, welcoming Finns to the U.P., proclaiming: "Give me your tired, your poor, your masses huddled in the sauna, your Saarinens, your Heikkinens, your Neimis."

On my way into Ironwood, I was also welcomed by "Little Finland," a Finnish museum and festival center established in 1970 to promote Finnishness. A sign explained that by 1900 the Finns had become the largest ethnic group of this area. One of the buildings was a log house done in a Finnish "fish tail" style, the logs taken from an old ore ship dock in Lake Superior.

Lake Superior is one of those midwestern natural treasures that Americans from the East and West never seem to discover. Yet a res-ident of the Maine coast would feel right at home on the Michigan coast, with its rocky yet forested shore and islands, its lighthouses, its coves and harbor villages. The steep granite Minnesota north shore of the lake holds cascades and waterfalls worthy of the Rockies. The lake itself has waves and storms worthy of the ocean yet also a hypnotic blue peace.

One part of the Michigan coast I had to visit was Pictured Rocks Na-tional Lakeshore. This was supposed to be the exact place where Hia-watha had lived. The Pictured Rocks are tall sandstone cliffs that had sinuous strata to begin with and then were carved by waves, rain, and wind into various shapes tempting to the imagination. I stood at an overlook and looked for Hiawatha pictured in the rocks, but I didn't see him. Maybe he was out hunting in the Hiawatha National Forest.

That night I opened up *The Song of Hiawatha* and tried to find the Pictured Rocks in it. The first line is "Should you ask me whence these stories?" Longfellow then goes into a prologue explaining *Hiawatha's* origin in Native American legends. It almost sounded as if he was try-ing to preempt accusations that *Hiawatha* had its origins in the *Kalev-ala*. Then he starts with a Native American legend of the creation of the world. No doubt it was just a coincidence that the *Kalevala* starts with a Finnish legend of the creation of the world. I didn't notice any description of the Pictured Rocks. Since I was skipping around, perhaps I missed it. Or perhaps since Longfellow hadn't actually been there, he was playing it safe by not describing anything too specifically.

I spent that night in Marquette, where a local television station produces a weekly half-hour show on Finnish American subjects and entertainment. The show, done partly in Finnish, is rebroadcast in Canadian towns that have large Finnish populations.

Downtown Marquette, on a bluff overlooking Lake Superior, is recognizable to anyone who has seen the Otto Preminger movie *Anatomy of a Murder*. The author of the original novel, Robert Traver, was the district attorney in Marquette. In wandering around downtown I came upon the former Nordic Theater, now a bookstore, where part of the movie was filmed. Out front in the sidewalk are the cement footprints and handprints of the stars, including Jimmy Stewart and George C. Scott. As I was driving around the U.P. I was listening to another of Traver's novels on tape, *Danny and the Boys*. It was set in a U.P. Scandinavian logging outpost during the Depression. Though Danny and his good-hearted buddies were down-and-out, they still had a lot of fun. It reminded me a lot of John Steinbeck's Depression-era down-and-out good-hearted rascals of Cannery Row. Come to think of it, Steinbeck's group was also led by a guy named Danny. I didn't check the publication dates to see whether Steinbeck had plagiarized Traver or vice versa. All I knew for sure was that the part of Steinbeck's story where Danny attended his own funeral, which Steinbeck probably plagiarized from the Mark Twain scene where Tom and Huck attended their own funeral, was later plagiarized by network television and turned into an episode of *Gunsmoke*, and they didn't even bother to alter the name Danny. And did I mention that Otto Preminger's movie *Carmen Jones* plagiarized Bizet, transferring the story from Spain to America? No, it was ridiculous to suggest that Longfellow or any writer would even think of plagiarizing other sources.

The next morning, I found that the folks in nearby Ishpeming were proud to acknowledge having plagiarized a Scandinavian idea. I saw Finnish, Swedish, and Norwegian flags flying outside the U.S. National Ski Hall of Fame. Inside, the exhibits explained that it was here in Ishpeming that Scandinavian immigrants had introduced skiing to America. Ishpeming was still famous for its ski jump, where major competitions were held. One museum exhibit showed replicas of four-thousand-year-old skis found in Sweden. Another exhibit showed how the Finnish and Norwegian ski troops of World War II had inspired the U.S. army to start a division of ski troops. The displays of honorees in the Hall of Fame were full of Scandinavian names.

Heading east, I knew I was in Finn country when the towns on the map had names like Toviola, Tapiola, and Nisula. At one point I turned off the highway for a gravel road detour to the Hanka Homestead, an old Finnish farm that was now a living museum run by the National Park Service. It turned out that the Hanka Homestead was closed for the winter, the gate locked, no one around. I went ahead and walked up the road to the old log house. I was surprised to read that it had been built in the 1920s, as it looked much older. But then, it had become a museum because it was representative of timeless Finnish ways. Around the house was a barn, an earth cellar, and several other outbuildings, all of sturdy wood construction. If there had been a ranger or historical reenactor around I could have gotten some insights into the life of Finnish pioneers, but I had to settle for peering through the window into the log house. This was symbolic of how I felt I was doing at discovering Finnish America: I was still an outsider getting a superficial view.

The Hanka Homestead was similar to a place I had visited in the Minnesota Iron Range. I had actually started my exploration of Finnish America by visiting a few sites in Minnesota. The hamlet of Embarrass had a larger set of old Finnish homesteads, many long abandoned and collapsed but now being restored. It included an old pioneer sauna. The sauna was often the first thing that Finns built, especially if they arrived just before winter. The Finns lived in the sizable sauna all winter and then built a house in the spring.

I had also stopped in the town of Virginia, Minnesota, and found Finn Hall, which was typical of many Finn Halls, the center of community life, used for clubs, speeches, dinners, music, and theater. A short walk away, I peered down into a massive open pit mine. Yes, Virginia, the Finns do claim that Santa Claus is a Finn, as he couldn't find such reindeer anywhere else but in Finland.

In the town of Finland, Minnesota, I found an important part of Finnish American history, though to the average traveler it appeared to be merely the town's general store. This store was one of the last remnants of a once-widespread constellation of cooperatives. The Finland cooperative was eighty-five years old, and the fact that it still existed was one sign that Finnish Americans were probably more committed to the idea of cooperatives than was any other ethnic group in America.

The co-op in Finland, Minnesota, rested on foundations built back in Finland. If winter already imposed a community bond on Scandinavians, the Finns were burdened and bonded by yet another occupying power, the Russians. When the Russians first acquired Finland from Sweden, they realized that the Finns were accustomed to a light if not enlightened rule and that to wean the Finns from the Swedes they'd have to step lightly. This weaning process included building a new Finnish capital, Helsinki, farther from Sweden and closer to St. Petersburg. Yet by the end of the nineteenth century the Russians were governing Finland for Russia's sake, culminating in drafting Finns into the czar's army. Since Russia governed from the top down, there remained room at the local level for developing a self-reliance that served Finns. The Finnish cooperative movement came to have nearly messianic hopes attached to it.

While some Finns fled to America when they received a czarist draft notice, others were exiled for political activism. Even if Finland hadn't been facing Russian annexation, the impact of abrupt industrialization generated much political stress. Even Finns who went to America for economic motives had absorbed some of the political energy in the air in Finland. Because the peak of Finnish immigration coincided with this period of political crisis, Finnish immigrants were more charged with political energy than most immigrant groups, and America gave them a new outlet for this energy. In America the Finns often found they were laboring in mines run by Boston czars. The Finns went right ahead with their agenda of economic self-reliance and political self-rule. One result was the cooperatives, and another result was a heavy Finnish involvement in the American labor movement. The Finns often became the strong core of the most radical union, the Industrial Workers of the World. It was a Finnish IWW that led an Iron Range strike in 1916, winning a wage increase. But out in Butte, Montana, the Anaconda Company fired four hundred Finns for being "known troublemakers." In Bisbee, Arizona, the Finns were marched away to jail at vigilante gunpoint. Though Finns made up only 0.1 percent of the American population, they made up 15 percent of the membership of the Socialist Party of America.

World War I brought another identity crisis for Finnish Americans. For Danish Americans, who angrily remembered the 1864 German annexation of part of Denmark and the flight of Danes to America to avoid being drafted into the German army, it was easy to put aside everything else, including radicalism and pacifism, to rally around the American flag. But Finnish Americans weren't nearly so thrilled about being allied with the czar. Back home, Finnish leaders like Sibelius openly hoped that a German victory would finally free Finland from Russian rule. When the IWW went right on holding strikes during the war, Finns found themselves being denounced as un-American. What was ironic was that after the Russian Revolution, Finnish American labor leaders found themselves being denounced as Russians.

Even worse, Finns discovered that American law defined them as worse than Russians. Back in 1775 a German anthropologist had classified Finns as Mongols, and this classification had passed into American texts and law, meaning that the Finns were subject to the same anti-Asian laws that barred the Chinese from gaining American citizenship. Over and over, Finns found themselves being denied citizenship and the rights and opportunities that came with it. Only in 1908 did a U.S. court declare Finns to be Europeans. Feeling the force of American racism only increased the Finns' identity frustration and political radicalism. Yet ironically, West Coast Finns were quite willing to support anti-Chinese laws to protect their own jobs.

Of course, the large majority of Finnish Americans ignored the IWW just like everyone else did and remained patient believers in the American Dream. It was a big embarrassment that a U.P. Finn, Gus Hall, was the longtime leader of the American Communist Party. In the 1950s some Finns were so worried about being tainted by the radical branch of the Finnish family that they forbade their children from wearing the color red. Yet I am intrigued by the possibility that the radicalism of Minnesota Iron Range Finns found a more persuasive voice in a later generation. To check out this possibility, let's visit Hibbing, Minnesota.

Hibbing's Scandinavian presence is evident in a museum to its second most famous citizen, a Swede named Anderson, and his local business that did good, the Greyhound Bus Company. Another Hibbing

Swede was celebrated in a song that did good, "Girl from the North Country," written about the true love of Hibbing's first most famous citizen, Bob Dylan. Now just so no one accuses me of trying to claim Bob Dylan as a Scandinavian, I'll state that I'm quite aware that he is Jewish and that this alone may be a perfectly sufficient explanation for his conscience about social injustice. Nevertheless, back in the 1960s a procession of pilgrims started coming to Hibbing only to be baffled that their guru could come from such a workaday mining town, site of the world's largest open pit iron mine. In the 1960s Hibbing and Dylan signed a mutual aid pact in which Hibbing would pretend it had never heard of Dylan and Dylan would pretend he was born in Greenwich Village with a silver harmonica in his mouth. It seems that this pact expired on the very day I happened to visit Hibbing. The whole state of Minnesota was talking about the prodigal son's return, at least to Duluth, where he was born and where he was giving his first-ever Iron Range concert that night. I overheard much talk about it when I had lunch at Zimmies, the Dylan-theme cafe in downtown Hibbing. Anyway, I would simply like to point out that Dylan's seemingly precocious talent for social protest, which to middle-class American kids seemed to come out of nowhere, actually came from a place with a tradition of protest as deep as a mine. If you listen really closely to Dylan's protest songs, you might just hear a trace of a Finnish accent.

That evening the Duluth television news, after the top story about Dylan's homecoming, carried a story about a Finn in a nearby Wisconsin town who was working on his own homecoming. He was painstakingly restoring his grandparents' homestead. He was doing much of the work by hand, cutting shingles out of cedar. He explained that this was his way of honoring his Finnish heritage.

If by the time I left the Hanka homestead I still felt like a television viewer of Finnish America, I wasn't worried, for I was approaching the mother lode of Finnishness. The town of Hancock was supposed to be the Lindsborg or Decorah of Finnish America, with a Finnish museum and college.

The name Hancock, and the name of its main street, Adams, was a pretty good clue that the town was developed by a Boston-based mining company. Hancock sits on the Keweenaw Peninsula, the thumb that sticks north from the U.P. into Lake Superior. The peninsula is rich in copper. On the north side of Hancock, on Quincy Hill, tourists can ride the largest steam elevator ever built, down nearly two miles into the ground. The reason tourists and not miners are riding it is because the last Keweenaw mine closed in the 1970s, unable to compete with the open pit mines out west. Even when the mines were running, the average family lived modestly, often in company housing, and now times were harder. Downtown Hancock couldn't be mistaken for Solvang. But it did have street signs in both English and Finnish.

That night, staying in the Copper Country Motel in downtown Hancock, I tried to attend to *Hiawatha* again, but the contrast between a romantic Native American life in the woods and a miner's life in a rundown company town made my project seem pretty silly. At least Longfellow fit in with the Boston theme.

In the morning I had breakfast at the Kaleva Cafe. The motel desk clerk told me that when the old-timers gathered there for coffee, you could hear them speaking in Finnish. I only heard American talk about the World Series. I came back to the Kaleva Cafe for lunch and tried something called a pasty under the impression it was an old Finnish folk food. It's sort of a stew wrapped in dough, like an egg. The local Finns did indeed eat it, but I heard later that they took it from local Welsh miners. The pasty was a miner's trick, for you could heat it in the morning, wrap it up, and tuck it in your lunch pail, and it would still be warm at lunchtime. Now there were drive-thru pasty places.

Down the street was a Finnish gift shop, not very fancy, but they did have some quality imported Finnish things of glass, silver, and fiber. There were many CDs of Finnish folk music, but the music I bought bore a picture of a reggae band playing beneath a palm tree on a desert island. This was a local group called Conga Se Menne, and the music was all reggae, but the performers and themes were all Finnish. I listened to it as I drove around town and decided that my favorite song was one about saunas and snowstorms, sung with Jamaican accents. Sometimes identity confusion can be fun.

It was another mark of identity change that the Finnish-American Heritage Center was located in a converted Catholic church. The sacred vault was now a hall for Finnish music and lectures. There was an art gallery for Finnish and Finnish American artists. Downstairs was an archive of old Finnish books and immigrant letters and documents. Hey, they had a copy of *Hiawatha* in Finnish. I wondered if the Finns who read it found it oddly familiar. There were disappointingly few exhibits about Finnish America.

I asked the lady at the desk some questions, and before I knew it I had stepped on some tender spots of Finnish identity. I said something about exploring Scandinavian America, and she snapped back: "We're not Scandinavians." Thinking about it later, I realized that the Finns had waited out seven hundred years of Swedes trying to make them Swedish, and even when the Finns fled to America and built a church of Finnish identity, in walked an imperialistic Swede who tried to claim them. Geographically, of course, the Finns share the Scandinavian subcontinent; in social policy, technology, and culture, the Finns are still happy to learn from the Swedes; but when it comes to their basic identity, the Finns just want to be shown some respect. Now that I had revealed myself to be a Viking vandalizing the church, the lady at the desk switched into Finnish Identity Defense Mode. When I asked if there were Finnish sites farther up the Keweenaw Peninsula, she answered: "Everything is Finnish." I had done my tourist homework well enough to know this was hardly true, but I was beginning to realize it wasn't my role here to argue. But then I blundered again. I asked if there were any scholars at Suomi College who specialized in Finnish subjects. She answered defensively: "Everyone is interested in Finnish subjects."

Since there are larger ethnic groups that don't have their own college, Suomi College is a source of great pride for Finnish Americans. Yet any Suomi teacher who walks onto the campus of the flagship Norwegian or Swedish colleges, which are well endowed and nationally prominent, can't help but feel an identity crisis coming on. For a century Suomi had remained a two-year college, and it was only now establishing some four-year programs. With its weak economic base and small enrollment, only four hundred students, Suomi had long struggled just to survive. If it wasn't for the ethnic pride that supported it through the Depression, the mine closings, and every other challenge, Suomi might have closed long ago. When I was there, Suomi College was planning to change its name to Finlandia University. There was a trend for small midwestern colleges to rename themselves a university, and while the colleges would like the public to believe that their new name is a badge of sophistication, the truth is usually that this is a public relations strategy born out of financial desperation. But Suomi College was also changing its first name, and this change involved a uniquely ethnic motive. Suomi administrators found that many prospective students or financial supporters who no longer spoke their ancestors' Finnish no longer recognized that the word Suomi had anything to do with Finland. For a college that owed its survival to its Finnish identity, this lack of recognition was a serious matter. Yet the name change was also a paradoxical admission that Finnish Americans were now so far from Finland that they had to adopt the outsiders' name for Suomi. At least Suomi had also sought to honor its Finnish identity by establishing the Heritage Center.

As I wandered around campus, which architecturally was a typical American college in having started with an elegant, hand-crafted stone building and gradually devolved into Baby Boomer Bland, I came across something that was very Finnish, although not everyone would have recognized it as such. I recognized it because I have a friend back in Arizona who is one of the country's leading weavers of Scandinavian-style textiles. Traditional Scandinavian weaving involves a tighter weave than usual, requiring a special loom. Joanne's living room was full of looms, one of which was historic, acquired from the Cranbrook Academy of Art in Detroit, which reached international prominence under the direction of Eliel Saarinen, the father of Eero Saarinen, the designer of the Gateway Arch. Joanne regularly led weaving tours of Scandinavia, focusing on all the sites of interest to weavers, and she traveled America teaching workshops on Scandinavian weaving. Weaving had a special importance to Scandinavians, who needed sturdy and warm clothes, bed covers, rugs, and drapes. In the twentieth century, Scandinavian weaving had become a fine art, moving, like Navajo rugs, from the floor to the wall.

In the Suomi College art building I came upon a big room full of looms. Since there was no one present, I went in and looked around. One of the looms was very high tech, incorporating a computer console. I had never seen anything like it, and no wonder, for I soon learned there were few like it in the country.

I went in search of a weaver and found Elizabeth Leifer, who was in charge of a very ambitious weaving program. She was Australian by birth and accent and had spent many years in the Boston art community. Having a few Bostonian street names around town hadn't made it easier to adjust to Hancock. In Boston she had come to admire Scandinavian design, and not just in weaving, and she had expected to find a lot of it in a Finnish town. Instead she found a town so poor that people could barely afford to buy a bath mat from Sears. They were too busy trying to survive to care about fashions in art. A few people had family heirlooms brought from Finland, but these were of basic peasant design.

But now Suomi College was plugged into modern Finland, both technologically and artistically. The state-of-the-art loom could implement designs that were too intricate for mere memory to pull off. The college had established a link with a Finnish university, bringing accomplished weavers to campus, exposing both faculty and students to the most avant-garde developments in Scandinavian weaving. Yet the program wasn't designed to amuse artists. Weaving remained an important trade, offering good jobs to those who could keep up with its technological advances. For a century Suomi students had come there to learn practical skills like nursing. The weaving program was actually part of the business department. At most colleges, throwing management professors and avant-garde artists into the same department would be unthinkable. But this was Suomi College's solution to achieving its seemingly irreconcilable goals: preparing students for practical jobs and promoting Finnish heritage. I thought it was brilliant. It would be as if St. Olaf College had a contract with the Fortune 500 companies to supply them with a steady supply of Ph.D. bards who could recite and explain the Viking sagas. Maybe these Finns weren't so mixed-up after all.

As I left Leifer's office and walked back down the hall, I glanced at the names on the doors out of curiosity to see if there were many Finnish names. Then I saw the name Lauri Anderson. It was the writer who had plagiarized my idea of viewing Finnish America through the *Kalevala*. I knocked on the door, and when no one answered, I asked the guy across the hall if Ms. Anderson was around, and I learned that Lauri was a guy's name and that he had gone home for the day. I took the liberty of calling him up at home, and he said if I had time, I could stop on by. He lived just up the hill from the campus.

I found his house and started our conversation by observing that he seemed to have taken on a thankless literary task, for the simple folks he wrote about weren't likely to buy his books, while educated Finns weren't likely to appreciate his image of Finns. Anderson said that in fact he had received hate mail over his three books, reflecting a sharp division in Finnish America. The large majority of Finns were working class, struggling in a bleak economy, taking simple pleasures like fishing and drinking. During the workweek they were sober and sturdy workers, but come the weekend they would lubricate their reserved personalities with too much alcohol. And then there were the uptown Finns, who had managed to rise above the status of their immigrant grandparents, who were now insurance salesmen or schoolteachers, who attended the Lutheran church faithfully and never drank, and who abhorred the image of the uncouth, drunken Finn. The uptown Finns had written most of the memoirs of Finnish America, and they would have you believe that being Finnish consisted of baking Finnish Christmas cookies just like Grandma did. I thought this was true of other Scandinavian groups too. Anderson had stirred up still-smoldering embers of immigrant sensitivity about being accepted as successful Americans. He thought that Finns were still more sensitive about this than other immigrant groups, for Finns had settled in an area where economic opportunities were more limited. Even here, Finns had started out at the bottom of the immigrant pecking order, not being welcome to sit with the Welsh in the mining lunchroom, their kids being teased for their odd names. Thus today Finns still have an inferiority complex, and they compensate for it by boasting about the glory of being Finnish. This combination of hunger for assimilation and pride in Finnishness has led to a rather contradictory state of Finnish identity.

I asked him how the college fit into this. He said that much of the faculty had been drawn there out of identification with their Finnishness. But there wasn't much room for teaching Finnish subjects in the classroom, although you could learn the language. About half the students were Finnish, but for them it was just the local college, good for getting a job. Some of the students came from families so poor their houses were almost bare of furnishings. Perhaps one or two students in his class would have some interest in their Finnish heritage.

I spent the evening in the college library. I found an old book about Schoolcraft and Longfellow by a U.P. non-Finn named Osborn. He said, "I have lived for years with Finns as neighbors in the more undeveloped regions of Michigan. . . . I found these Finlanders most agreeable and always dependable when sane." He went on to explain that the Finns' fondness for drink "tends to increase the percentage of insanity among them." Osborn was an admirer of Schoolcraft and was trying to claim him as the inspiration of Longfellow's *Hiawatha*. Osborn vigorously denied that there was any Finnish influence on Longfellow. I ended up wondering if Osborn admired his neighbors a bit less than he admitted and couldn't stand the thought that a people of drunken insane miners could deserve any credit for the American epic of the Boston Homer.

I also skimmed through a couple of Finnish American histories, but at closing time I still felt that I had only skimmed through Finnish America itself. Yet I still had waiting for me the most important research tool of all. The Copper Country Motel had a sauna. Of course.

Finally, I thought as I approached the sauna, I would get to the heart of Finnishness. I guess Osborn hadn't convinced me of the irrelevance of Longfellow to Finland, for I brought along *Hiawatha* for one last try. But this was my big mistake. No sooner had I stepped into the sauna than my glasses fogged over. I felt like an idiot. I was lucky the sauna was empty this late at night, for if any Finns had seen my foggy glasses, they would have laughed. I felt that my attempt to get to the heart of Finnishness had just been declared a ridiculous failure. All my studying hadn't taught me the first thing about it. I would never get beyond seeing Finnish identity with a dumb outsider's fogged glasses.

But maybe the sauna was working its magic after all, for I then had a revelation. It wasn't a sign of failure that I was confused about Finnish identity. The Finns themselves were confused about Finnish identity. They had been confused about it for eight hundred years. Trying to escape that confusion by coming to America had only worsened their confusion. Confusion about identity was the very essence of Finnish identity. I had known their deepest secret all along.

As if to confirm my revelation, the sauna then handed me the greatest treasure of the *Kalevala*: the sampo! The mysterious object of all striving and grief in the *Kalevala*, the sampo. When it got too hot in the sauna, I went, since there was no snow outside to jump into like a good Finn, into the adjacent shower, and right there on the wall was an object that said Sampo on it. Or at least this is how it looked without my glasses. Maybe it actually said Shampoo. Shampoo and Body Soap. But at this point I no longer had the authority to argue with the sauna. If confusion was the essence of Finnishness, then I would indulge in it, and I did. I spread the sampo all over me. For a century, scholars had been arguing about the true nature of the sampo; in its uncertainty, it was the perfect symbol of Finnish identity.

I made several rounds between sauna and shower. Since I actually could read without my glasses, I picked up *Hiawatha* and went to the concluding section. "By the shores of Gitche Gumee" it started. I was, in fact, sitting just up the hill from an inlet of Lake Superior.

The Song of Hiawatha concludes with the end of tribal paganism and the coming of Christianity. Then the hero sails away in a boat. That sneaky Longfellow! The *Kalevala* too concludes with the end of tribal paganism and the coming of Christianity, and then its hero sails away in a boat. Well, of course if Longfellow wanted to create an American epic, he could never admit that it was just another copy of European literature. But if Longfellow had just been more honest, he could have gotten credit for being a seer, for anticipating real history in transporting the Finns to the U.P. and getting their identity further mixed up with American identities.

I at least wasn't confused anymore. It was all perfectly clear. Here I was sitting in downtown Hancock, where the street signs were in both English and Finnish, by the shore of Gitche Gumee, sitting in a sauna, anointed by the sampo, reading the Boston Homer, with a catchy reggae tune about saunas and snowstorms going through my head.

You couldn't get much more Finnish than this.

16

Home Run

A *third of* a century after I sat beneath Eero Saarinen's Gateway
Arch in St. Louis and watched the Beatles, I had another occasion to sit in the Cardinals' stadium and look at the arch. This
time I had a better chance to consider the meaning of the arch. I returned to the stadium night after night, although it wasn't as if I was
undistracted from contemplating the arch, for the packed stadium was
gripped by a mania it hadn't seen since the Beatles.

I arrived at the stadium well before sunset and watched the sunset
light play upon the stainless steel, dull-mirror arch. Sometimes the
arch matched its rainbow shape with rainbow colors. The arch faded
into the darkness in about the same way a rainbow fades away, but the
arch didn't entirely disappear. Even though the arch wasn't directly lit
by floodlights, the lights from the city kept the arch a vague presence
in the night.

I suppose if I was to continue the rainbow metaphor, I could bring in
the pot of gold. It really was a pot of gold, or at least a pot of rich topsoil, that drew millions of immigrants through the gateway to the West.
Though this vision of wealth played many tricks on Americans, it also
rewarded us richly. But it wasn't just a dream of wealth that was symbolized by the arch. At its root it was the oldest, most passionate dream
humans ever had, a dream expressed in both the Book of Revelation
and *The Communist Manifesto*. It was the dream that humans could
escape an imperfect world and start all over again and do a lot better.

Never before in human history had this dream been given an actual new continent to play with. It was this dream that inspired the founding fathers to dream up a form of government that expected more perfection from its citizens. Even when the American Dream was only a lust for wealth, it managed to remain a democratic lust, open to all.

For me the arch is the most powerful symbol of American history. Whereas the Jefferson Memorial in Washington, D.C., represents a person and an idea, the arch, which is officially part of the Jefferson National Expansion Memorial, proves the enormous energy unleashed by that idea, first just the energy of Lewis and Clark and then the energy of millions who were convinced to give up the home of all their ancestors and seek a new home for all their descendants.

Just a few weeks ago a monument to Saarinen had been dedicated in the museum underneath the arch. For years there had been a theater there showing a film about the conception and building of the arch. Now the theater entrance held a large relief mural showing Saarinen at an architect's table building a model of the arch. The mural was made of brick, which was kept soft while being carved, by the Nebraska sculptor Jay Tschetter and then fired. The technique of brick murals went back to Babylon, and it seemed quite appropriate here, at the junction of America's Tigris and Euphrates Rivers.

On my walk to the stadium, I passed another Scandinavian-built monument to America. It was across from Union Station, once the world's largest train station, the hub of hundreds of daily trains connecting East and West like zippers. This monument was a fountain designed in the 1930s by Sweden's great sculptor Carl Milles. It was called *Meeting of the Waters*. The Mississippi River was symbolized by a twelve-foot-high classical god riding a dolphin, escorted by four tritons. He was meeting his goddess bride, the Missouri River, who was escorted by four nymphs. I walked around it several times, trying to like it, but I found it a weak comparison to the arch. Perhaps it was those Art Deco fish spewing jets of water out of their mouths in a potentially disgusting way. Or perhaps it was simply that classical gods belonged in Europe and were ridiculous impersonating Huck Finn's river. Yet I understood that Milles was attempting the same thing as Saarinen, to find a grandeur that could express the American continent. And I did notice that all the jets of water formed silver arches.

Europeans weren't the first people to build a great city at the junction of these two great rivers. On the opposite side of the Mississippi, Native Americans built the largest city in what became the United States. The centerpiece of Cahokia was the largest earthen mound in North America, with a base larger than the largest Egyptian pyramid. Hundreds of smaller mounds surrounded it. Cahokia was the center of a culture that spread far up and down the two rivers, and it was located here for the same reason St. Louis was, because this was the transportation hub.

Standing atop the big mound at Cahokia offers the most provocative view of the arch. From here the arch is fifteen miles away and small. In a similar way, history puts things into a more distant perspective. From here you can feel the long sweep of history, the rise and fall of civilizations, for here in one spot are two great monuments to two different civilizations, one of which has vanished. Cahokia seems to have fallen due to its own flaws, before Europeans arrived. In a remarkably short time after the first white explorers showed up here, a massive migration swept through, built a society, and then built a monument to remember its migration. From atop the Cahokia mound, you don't see the daily struggles of millions of pioneers, only the fall of one society and the quick appearance of a new one. In the summer heat and humidity the arch can seem to waver, like a mirage, as if the migration and nation it represents couldn't possibly have sprung up so quickly.

Yet when you are sitting in the stadium with the arch and corporate headquarters towering above you, American society seems the only possible reality. The arch seems to symbolize the brave canvas arches of the wagon trains heading west.

But perhaps after this week, the arch will remind me of something else. The steep, powerful, skyward climb of the arch is kind of like the trajectory of a Mark McGwire home run.

I hadn't been to a St. Louis Cardinals game since I was a kid and my father took me to see the championship team of Bob Gibson and Lou Brock. But some old, deep loyalties seem to have been tapped this year by the nationwide enthrallment over McGwire's pursuit of the home run record. When I got to St. Louis, McGwire was only a few days and a few home runs away from tying Babe Ruth and Roger Maris, and the excitement in the stadium was massive.

Ordinarily, I am not inclined to grant much sociological significance to sporting events, but by the time I crossed Sammy Sosa's path a few weeks later and saw him hit home runs number sixty-four and sixty-five, I was persuaded that the great home run chase of 1998 could serve as a good marker by which to measure a third of a century of American history or all of it.

There was good historical reason for viewing baseball as a test of democracy. For several generations, through the largest influx of immigrants into America, playing baseball served as a ritual of assimilation. Kids who couldn't speak each other's languages, kids with rival religions, kids from countries with differing social values formed in their sandlots and brick streets a society where all could participate and anyone could win. The key to this sandlot society was a set of rules that was the same for everyone. It didn't matter where you had come from or what your father believed or how much he earned; all that mattered was what you could do. For kids who were eager not to be seen as Italians or Norwegians but to be accepted as real Americans, proving themselves in this uniquely American game acquired an importance that transcended the usual emotions of sports. Kids realized that they were training for a larger society, and the most important lesson they took into that society was how to play by a set of rules that was the same for everyone.

Of course, there were also plenty of sandlot arguments over whether the Italian kid, the Norwegian kid, or the black kid should be allowed to play at all.

When I had last sat in this stadium, all America was locked in a passionate and ugly debate over the purpose of our country, over who should be allowed to participate in our country. The symbols of that debate were all around me. The arch symbolized Thomas Jefferson, who had declared that all men were created equal. But only two blocks behind the arch and centrally framed in postcard images of it was the dome of the old courthouse, where a slave named Dred Scott had dared America to include blacks in that equality and been refused. A few miles down the Mississippi River was a fort also named for Jefferson where troops had rallied to Lincoln's renewed call for equality. A hundred miles up the Missouri River, in Jefferson City, James Earl Ray was plotting his escape from the state prison and declaring that someone should kill Martin Luther King Jr. St. Louis hadn't burned in the riots that scarred other cities, but frightened whites were fleeing to the suburbs. This national argument was occurring inside the stadium too.

Cardinals outfielder Curt Flood became a new Dred Scott by filing suit against the practice of players being traded like slaves. It was a former Cardinals manager, Branch Rickey, who had integrated baseball by hiring Jackie Robinson for the Dodgers, and Rickey was fully aware of the powerful symbolism of his act.

It did not require much of an eye for symbolism to notice that in the last third of a century America had not only made a new commitment to its democratic ideal but had made an enormous leap toward accepting it emotionally and achieving it in society. This was obvious in the fifty thousand largely white faces that surrounded me one day in Milwaukee County Stadium. There were several visible reminders that Milwaukee was a German city, first in the name of the baseball team, the Brewers, and then in the German costume of the team mascot, and then in the entertainers costumed as giant sausages. Repeatedly, I watched a stadium full of Germans all stand up, reach their arms high, stomp their feet, raise their banners, and scream hysterically for their hero. I couldn't help thinking of a stadium in Nuremberg. But this time the Germans were screaming for a black man, an immigrant, the descendant of slaves, screaming for him to beat their own team, to humiliate their own pitcher, to keep pace with a white guy in a contest for American hero. Whenever the Brewers' pitcher threw an unhittable pitch, his own fans booed him like a traitor. And when Sosa connected for a home run, the crowd went berserk.

Back in St. Louis, under Saarinen's open door to a better life for all, there was the same color blindness. There were a lot of blacks in the stadium, the descendants of slaves bullied to tote that bale on the wharf of Ole Man River a few blocks away, and they were cheering for a red-haired Irishman. When the PA speaker announced that in a game elsewhere Sosa had hit another one and pulled within one home run of McGwire, the blacks booed along with the rest of the crowd, and one black man sitting behind me joked that Sosa was like a bad cold: you just couldn't shake him off. Then McGwire hit one, and everyone was happy again. No one even noticed the significance of sons of England cheering for an Irishman.

McGwire rounded the bases, and as he touched home plate he touched fists with his son Matt, who was serving as the Cardinals' bat boy. Matt was ten years old, the same age I had been when I last sat in this stadium with my father.

I was to see four of McGwire's home runs.

Something else set me thinking of my father while I was watching Mark McGwire run home. That summer there was much talk about the year 1927. That was the year Babe Ruth amazed the nation by hitting sixty home runs. If the truth be told, the people of St. Louis weren't so pleased with Ruth's feat. In 1926 the Cardinals, under manager Branch Rickey and the home run champion of 1922 and 1925, Rogers Hornsby, had defeated Ruth's Yankees in the World Series. In 1928 Ruth and the Yankees would slaughter the Cardinals in the World Series. But in the meantime, in 1927 St. Louis had produced a hero who eclipsed even Babe Ruth. 1927 was the year that Charles Lindbergh crossed the Atlantic in the *Spirit of Saint Louis*. 1927 was a good year for heroes in America. As I sat so close to the Mississippi River, I thought of how, far upstream in Minnesota, sitting on the bank of a much smaller Mississippi, was the boyhood home of Charles Lindbergh. My father had been taken there as a kid by his father. But I still hadn't been there. It seemed an essential stop on any tour of Swedish America. So I decided it was time to visit Lindbergh's home.

That fall, Charles Lindbergh's daughter Reeve had published a family memoir. She was crisscrossing the Midwest on a book tour, and I crossed her path several times but never on time. The morning I was leaving St. Louis, she was to appear·that evening at the St. Louis History Museum, which featured a large collection of medals and official gifts Charles Lindbergh had received all over the world and loaned to the museum in 1927 for a ten-day exhibit that was so overwhelmed with visitors it never ended. When I arrived in Little Falls, Minnesota, the site of the Lindbergh home, I was a bit too early, but the local bookshop had already set up for Reeve's visit.

Reeve Lindbergh never visited her father's boyhood home until a year after he died. She drove there from halfway across the country because she missed him terribly and thought the house might remind her of him. As a child she had heard him tell stories about the house, but not until years later did she realize that the house actually still existed. When she approached the house, she found it a plausible match for the stories she remembered, but it didn't connect with her own experience of her father. As she toured the house and saw her father's toys and boys' adventure books, she still didn't feel the presence of the person she had known. Then she entered the kitchen, where on the stove was a black iron skillet just like the one her father had used for cooking for her. In her memoir she recalled: "Immediately, unmistakably, without any warning at all, my father was there with me in the room. His presence was a blow that almost doubled me over, in sharp recognition and sharper grief. I could see him, I could hear him. . . . He was here. I had found him. I burst into tears."[1]

Reeve Lindbergh returned to her father's home many times more whenever she missed him and wanted to feel his presence. She always felt her father come alive in this house. She never quite understood why this house spoke to her more strongly than places where she and her father had been together, but such is the strangeness of memory.

Reeve could no longer turn to her mother, Anne Morrow Lindbergh, for memories of her father, for her mother had lost her memory.

I wouldn't have even noticed a black iron skillet, but in other ways I too felt Lindbergh's presence in the house. Like Reeve, I felt it not so much in his childhood possessions but in things that evoked his actions. I felt it in the axe marks in the wood floor just inside the door where Lindbergh had cut wood when it was too cold to work outside. I felt it in the turtle shell into which he had carved his name; he had turned the turtle loose, and the empty shell was found in the woods long after he became famous. I felt it in the duck pond he had built with cement in the yard, signing his name and his dog's name in the cement.

Unexpectedly, I also felt my father's presence in the house. This was less logical than feeling Lindbergh's presence, but, as Reeve Lindbergh had discovered here, memory works in strange ways. My feeling my father's presence wasn't an idea planted in me by Reeve's experience, for I only bought her book in Little Falls and hadn't read it yet. Perhaps my experience was nudged by my focus not on Lindbergh's possessions but on his actions. My father too had acted here.

As I toured the house, I could almost see my grandfather standing here, so proudly showing his sons how a grandson of a Swedish immigrant could become an American hero. I know that this visit was important to my grandfather, for I have the journal he kept on that 1932 trip, and while many cities or landmarks inspired only the listing of their name, he devoted an entire page to Lindbergh's home. Of course, for my grandfather, the name was "Lindy." He described the setting of the house in a woods on a steep bluff 250 feet from the Mississippi

River. He described the house right down to the size of the furnace. Perhaps he noticed that on a bookshelf was a multivolume history of Sweden in Swedish. When Lindbergh's father gave those speeches in the U.S. Congress denouncing the oligarchs, he reportedly spoke with a Swedish accent. There wasn't much of a Swedish accent to the house, but in coming here my grandfather was trying to impress his sons with their heritage. The next year he would take them to St. Louis to see Lindbergh's trophies.

I was a bit late for the lesson, sixty-six years late, but I was sure my grandfather would be pleased with my coming here, with my own attempts not to forget. As the guide described Lindbergh's boyhood in this house, it helped evoke my father, for he too had been a boy when he had been here. As I looked at the back porch where Lindbergh had slept so he could hear the murmur of the Mississippi River, on which he loved to raft like Huck Finn, I could imagine my father identifying with the spirit of another boy. Perhaps it was here that an impression was made that would lead my father, decades later, to visit Sweden and lead me to visit here now, completing a circle.

The year after my father visited Lindbergh's home, Lindbergh made his own pilgrimage of remembrance to Sweden. He and his wife, Anne, slipped into Sweden unannounced and spent several days exploring Stockholm. Anne was astonished at how the Swedes behaved toward her husband. They recognized him readily enough and were clearly delighted to see him, for he had become a national icon in Sweden too. But the Swedes thoroughly respected his privacy. There were no crowds mobbing him like he was their property. Even the press photographers were a lot less aggressive. Anne wrote to her mother: "Charles and I have walked through a park here, recognized but not bothered! It is heady wine. . . . They respect our wanting to go about quietly. We can go into any good restaurant with less trouble than at home (with no trouble at all, in fact)."[2] She wrote to her sister: "I could live here forever."[3] Then the Lindberghs flew to southern Sweden and the village where his grandfather had lived. He found his grandfather's white house and barns and cobblestone courtyard. Across the road lived a man whose grandfather had been friends with Lindbergh's grandfather. The man gave Lindbergh some things his grandfather had left behind. The local community gathered in the courtyard and sang Lindbergh the Swedish national anthem. As Lindbergh was flying away, over the lakes and rivers and forests, he wondered "why my folks ever left that place?"⁴

Lindbergh's visit to Sweden was not simply an exercise in nostalgia. Lindbergh was looking for a new home. He was disgusted with America, with a society whose values he found grotesque, and he was ready to leave permanently. He considered settling in Sweden.

Four weeks before my father visited Lindbergh's home, Lindbergh's baby son had been found in a grave in the woods near the Lindbergh home in New Jersey, his skull cracked. Ten weeks earlier he had been kidnapped from his crib in the house, from beneath his Dala horse. Lindbergh was besieged by imposters trying to claim the ransom and by lunatics offering spurious help. The nightmare would never really end, because for the rest of Lindbergh's life men would keep showing up claiming to be his lost son. Lindbergh had won fame because he represented the best part of American mythology, but his fame drew upon him the worst part of that mythology, which sanctioned ruthless greed and emotionally rootless people. Lindbergh had already been appalled, like Greta Garbo and Jenny Lind, at the bizarre machinations of the Great American Fame Machine, and now Lindbergh too fled, first to England, then to France, and then he considered moving to Nazi Germany. The quality of innocence that had endeared Lindbergh to the American public did not serve him well when it came to politics. But Lindbergh was hungrily seeking a homeland that had a national dream greater than mere greed, and few leaders in history have more skillfully packaged a national dream than did Hitler. Lindbergh had attended the opening ceremonies of the 1936 Olympic Games in Berlin, a masterfully orchestrated pageant to Aryan vigor. Lindbergh imagined he saw a vigor and integrity lacking in America. When Hitler started vigorously invading his neighbors, Lindbergh fled back to America, where he used his still-substantial influence to discourage America from going to war against Germany. By such twists of fate, America nearly sabotaged itself: the worst part of American mythology nearly deprived the world of the best part, leaving the world without a dream of human equality.

My grandfather planned his visit to the Lindbergh home long before the kidnapping, but I am sure there were many visitors there that summer who came in response to it, who came not out of pride in Sweden but out of shock and bafflement about their own nation. I don't know what my father was thinking about his country as he followed his father through the house of an American god who still was powerless to protect his son from savagery.

It was in the wake of another act of savagery that shocked and baffled the nation that I visited my grandfather's house, the house where my father was born and raised.

When my grandfather first moved to Oklahoma City, he built a house on the south side of town in what was then the country. Loving engineering challenges, he built the house with his own hands, and from the pictures I've seen, it was an elegant job. I went looking for this house once, only to find that, like much of American urban memory, it had been erased.

When my grandfather started teaching at the new high school on the northwest side of downtown, he bought a house a few blocks away and added some touches of his own. When I was a kid my father drove me past the house once and pointed it out and told me a few stories about it. The neighborhood was a bit run down but still largely intact. Many years later I drove past the house a couple of times, but I never stopped. I thought of knocking on the door and taking a tour of my father's house, but I realized that in urban America one does not invite oneself into the house of total strangers, especially ones with signs warning No Trespassing and Beware of Dog.

A few days before I was to depart Arizona for a long visit with my father in his nursing home in Missouri, regular programming was interrupted for a special news bulletin. An explosion had rocked the federal office building in Oklahoma City. The building held hundreds of people, including a day care center full of children. The explosion was thought to be a bomb. Pictures showed one side of the building turned into a crater. A tornado of black smoke rose from it. Reports added that the whole neighborhood around the blast had been shattered, especially on the north side, where the blast had been focused.

At first I couldn't place any federal office building in Oklahoma City. But from news reports I figured out that it was on the northwest side of downtown. My father's house had to be only three or four blocks away and on the north side of the blast.

As I drove eastward through a New Mexico sparse with radio stations, I scanned up and down for news updates. The death count continued rising. It was indeed a terrorist attack. Buildings north of the blast were damaged beyond repair.

I hadn't been planning on going through Oklahoma City. I had been planning to cut through Kansas and stop in Lindsborg. But when I reached the exit to Kansas, I found myself going straight ahead. I needed to see what had become of my father's house, whether it had joined his memory in being obliterated.

When I reached downtown Oklahoma City, I had to detour around a large area that was barricaded off. Police were out waving traffic around. A lot of people had come to look. I could see the federal building with its wound, its collapsed floors, its piles of debris. I was surprised to see smoke still rising from it, but maybe that was just dust stirred up by the rescue operation. Cranes and bulldozers were working on the wreckage. The surrounding buildings showed much damage. I caught a glimpse of the old high school where my grandfather had taught, and all its windows were shattered. I parked and headed for my father's house. The sidewalks were thickly strewn with broken glass. My feet crunched over it.

A block away from my father's house, a parking lot was crowded with satellite dish trucks from all the national networks. Famous reporters were standing in the street, talking to cameras, with the federal building as backdrop. Thousands of people were watching the rescue operation and wandering around the neighborhood inspecting the damage. It was this, I guess, that emboldened me to walk right into the yard of my father's house and inspect it. I was just one of a crowd of people standing and staring at buildings.

I was relieved to see that my father's house was structurally intact. It was west enough of the blast that it wasn't in the main zone of concussion. Some of its windows had cracked but not fallen out. In the backyard I tried to spot traces of an underground clubhouse my father and his brothers had dug into the hillside. I looked at the old garage that had housed the valiant Model A Ford they had driven all over the country, including to Lindbergh's home. I wish I had found here, like Reeve Lindbergh, my own black iron skillet that evoked my father's presence, but I'm afraid that my strongest impression was of the obliteration of memory. As I was staring at the house, trying to see some reflection of my father, I noticed in the cracked window my own reflection. My own image was cracked. My image was vague to begin with, and because of the cracks, my few recognizable features were disrupted. I had sought recognition here, but I couldn't even recognize myself. But then, this is how the mirror of memory works. This is how my father saw me now. He would recognize me right up to the end, but through an increasingly distorted window.

I wandered around the neighborhood for a while. I examined the Emerson Elementary School my father had attended. I looked at other houses that had probably belonged to his friends. I looked at the faces of the other people wandering around, faces stunned and grim. I overheard snatches of conversation, people angrily wondering who could have bombed a child care center. In the media there had been vows of military retaliation against any nation involved in the bombing. When it became clear that it was America that had bombed itself, the result was a national soul searching rather similar to the soul searching that followed the killing of Lindbergh's baby.

Also rather similar was the etiology of both traumas. They arose from the inability of America to cohere as a people. They arose from a national mythology that placed far more value on self-interest than on the responsibility of people to one another. Those behind the bombing were believers in complete liberty, feeling no belonging to the American community. They chose the federal building as a target because it represented that community. While they were not motivated by financial greed, they shared with the Lindbergh kidnapper the same civic religion that made self-interest into a savage god.

As I looked at the bomb damage, I thought of how for half a century America had endangered the world with far more powerful bombs in the name of individualism and how the Soviet Union had threatened back in the name of collectivism. Both nations believed with messianic fervor that they were destined to create paradise on Earth and that anyone who opposed them was evil. Yet both nations were woefully immature and imbalanced. The Soviets could barely comprehend the idea of individual rights and democratic respect. In America, anyone who even tried to raise the subject of responsibility to the community risked being branded a traitor.

I was not drifting into impersonal history lessons as I thought such things. My father's best friend when he was growing up in this neighborhood had gone on to help invent the atomic bomb. My father and

Rossi were both scientifically minded. One time, they conceived the project of going to a different church every Sunday to decide if there was any rational basis for accepting one faith as true. They gave up after three weeks. Rossi was a true genius at physics, and he attracted the patronage of geniuses. His master's degree advisor was J. Robert Oppenheimer, and his Ph.D. advisor was Richard Feynman. Oppenheimer put Rossi to work on the atomic bomb. But when Rossi started to organize the atomic scientists into a union that might have a say over how their work was used, Gen. Leslie Groves, the director of the Manhattan Project, exiled Rossi into the army, against Oppenheimer's vigorous protests. When the McCarthy era started, Oppenheimer's defense of Rossi was one of the reasons Oppenheimer was officially branded as untrustworthy. Rossi was teaching at a famous private university at this time, and the bad publicity about him prompted the university to fire him. Other universities were too nervous to hire him. Rossi returned to Norman, Oklahoma, where he and my father had been college roommates and where their old biology professor, George Cross, was now president of the university. Cross was a strong defender of civil liberties who in 1945, before there was any civil rights movement to demand it, took it upon himself to integrate the university in a Supreme Court case that set the precedent for the integration of all higher education in America. President Cross had been fond of Rossi, and he wasn't fond of McCarthyism, so he decided to play a joke on Senator McCarthy. These were the years when the Oklahoma football team was the national champion under coach Bud Wilkinson. President Cross secretly hired Rossi to tutor the football team. When Senator McCarthy turned on his TV to admire the all-American champions proving the wholesomeness of American youth, he would never suspect that many of the players would have flunked out if not for the subversive he had blacklisted.

Now that I have disclosed how what might appear to be a mere sporting event can actually be a triumph of democracy, I think it's time to return to St. Louis in the days when Mark McGwire was closing in on the home run record, in the days when black outfielders no longer felt like slaves but could be fully accepted as American heroes. As I looked at the social progress since I had last sat in this stadium, at the growing of America into its democratic ideal, I felt a lot better about my country than I did when I was standing in Oklahoma City and staring up at an arch of wreckage. Anywhere else but under Saarinen's arch, I don't think I would have dared to hold up a mere baseball to answer the power of a bomb and the angry incoherence it represented. But the arch is a powerful symbol for me, a symbol, like the Statue of Liberty, of outsiders being welcomed in, and it set me thinking about the importance of symbols. As Branch Rickey knew, there is plenty of symbolism in a stadium full of people who define themselves not by race or class or gender or ethnic origin but by a set of rules that demands respect for everyone.

One reason the arch is a powerful symbol for me is because in it a Scandinavian immigrant took a distinctly Scandinavian design and rooted it firmly into American soil to speak for American history. The arch easily summarized my own Scandinavian American identity.

Eero Saarinen himself was rooted in America when his father, Eliel, became president of the Cranbrook Academy of Art in Detroit. Eero later taught at Cranbrook, and so did Carl Milles, who spent twenty years there. One day in 1942 Eero Saarinen and Carl Milles were astonished to learn that a house literally in Cranbrook's backyard had been purchased by Charles Lindbergh. Lindbergh was moving to Detroit to help Ford build airplanes for the war. Detroit was also where Lindbergh was born, for it was his mother's home. Lindbergh had come home. The Lindberghs became good friends with Saarinen and Milles. Anne started taking sculpture classes with Milles. This was only a few years after Milles had designed his St. Louis fountain and only a few years before Saarinen designed his St. Louis arch. (Did Saarinen sense the affinity between his silver arch and Lindbergh's silver *Spirit* soaring high?) Perhaps after his years in exile in Europe, Lindbergh too felt like an immigrant in America, seeing it with an immigrant's eyes, like his Swedish grandfather, like Saarinen and Milles both of whom were happy to celebrate America in steel and stone. Perhaps Lindbergh was able to see America through the brilliant eyes of Saarinen and Milles, and thus learn to celebrate it again. It isn't clear that Lindbergh ever really came to terms with his seduction by Nazi Germany. But it is clear that Lindbergh didn't settle there, or in England, or in France, or in Sweden. He realized that he belonged in America, and he came home. It is clear that Lindbergh was trying to prove that he belonged here, for he threw himself into war work, even flying combat missions in the Pacific. Not just exiles but mere vacationers discover that home is more appreciated after they have been away. I can't resist completing this train of thought with some more baseball symbolism. Unlike other sports, where the goal is to penetrate enemy territory, the goal of baseball is to return to where you started from, and when you come home, you are able to celebrate. Come to think of it, I am sure that T. S. Eliot must have been thinking of the home run when he penned his famous lines about how the end of all our exploring will be to arrive where we started and know the place for the first time.

Unexpectedly, I too had made a homecoming. In exploring my Scandinavian roots I had been prompted to look at America from new perspectives, from a distance much greater than that of the unhappy daily headlines. It came as a surprise to me how often I found, as I examined how Scandinavians have fit into American society, that they actually didn't quite fit in, that they were often uncomfortable with American values. As I came to have a sharper focus on Scandinavia itself and its values, I realized that many of my own discontents with America derived from my seeing it through Swedish eyes. I think it's true that my willingness to identify with Sweden derived partly from my perception that in some ways it was nobler than America. Yet as I wandered around Scandinavian America and crossed paths with Swedish tourists who were looking at America with fascination and admiration, I learned to look through their eyes too. I wandered into places I never would have sought out otherwise, into small prairie towns I would have dismissed, and because they were Swedish towns I gave them a second chance, and I even felt challenged to find something noble about them. And I did. And quite often, what I found to admire wasn't on the Swedish side but on the American side. I was reminded of why my great-grandparents had chosen to come to America in the first place. I was able to look through their eyes. I found that I had underestimated my own country.

Unfortunately, I underestimated my country one more time. I studied the Cardinals' schedule and tried to guess when McGwire would break the record, but the next tickets I bought turned out to be about a week late. But there was one advantage to watching the game on TV. The network producers seemed as fascinated by the arch as I was, for they kept showing it from the air, from the distance. It reminded me of the view from the top of the Cahokia mound. It put the commotion in the stadium at a farther distance, just enough distance that when Mc-

Gwire came home, it wasn't the athletic feat that struck me the most. Nor was it any history lesson, except for some personal history. I had taken McGwire a bit more personally because I too had played first base as a kid in the city league, and my father had always come to the games and, as with everything I ever did, paid his gentle attention to his son. So when McGwire came home what struck me the most, struck me not quite like a black iron skillet, not quite enough to make me burst into tears, was how the first thing he did was to give a huge hug to his son, who was the same age I had been when I last sat there under Saarinen's rainbow with my father.

NOTES

CHAPTER 2 | NIGHTINGALE ECHOES

1. Quoted in Allan Kastrup, *The Swedish Heritage in America* (Minneapolis: Swedish Council of America, 1975), 261.

2. Ibid., p. 251.

3. Quoted in Otto Robert Landelius, *Swedish Place-Names in North America* (Carbondale: Southern Illinois University Press, 1985), 24.

CHAPTER 3 | TIPPECANOE AND THE TITANIC TOO

1. Wyn Craig Wade, *The Titanic: End of a Dream* (New York: Penguin Books, 1986), 179.

2. Ibid., 217.

3. Ibid., 278.

4. Ibid., 235.

CHAPTER 4 | DOWN THE MYTHISSIPPI RIVER AND THE SAGA FE TRAIL

1. John F. Kennedy, *A Nation of Immigrants*, rev. ed. (New York: Harper and Row, 1964), 55.

2. Mark Twain, letter of September 6, 1899, to Reverend Joseph H. Twichell, quoted, without further reference, in Adolph Burnett Benson, *American Scandinavian Studies* (New York: American-Scandinavian Foundation, 1952), 339.

CHAPTER 6 | LISTENING POINT

1. Henry David Thoreau, *The Writings of Henry David Thoreau* (Boston and New York, 1906), 3:117.

2. Ibid., 5:82.

3. Ibid., 2:341.

4. Ibid., 3:304.

5. Ibid., 3:305.

6. Ibid., 4:247–49.

7. Wallace Stegner, *The Spectator Bird* (New York: Doubleday, 1976), 123.

8. Ibid., 24.

9. Jackson J. Benson, *Wallace Stegner: His Life and Work* (New York: Viking Penguin, 1996), 29.

10. Richard Etulain, *Stegner: Conversations on History and Literature* (Reno: University of Nevada Press, 1996), 4.

11. Sigurd Olson, unpublished memoir, quoted in David Backes, *A Wilderness Within: The Life of Sigurd F. Olson* (Minneapolis: University of Minnesota Press, 1998), 13, 14.

12. Sigurd Olson, *Runes of the North* (New York: Alfred A. Knopf, 1963), 70.

13. Ibid., 1.

14. Sigurd Olson, unpublished journals, quoted in Backes, *A Wilderness Within*, 159.

15. Robert Olson, personal communication, 1998.

16. Roger Tory Peterson, *Field Guide to the Birds* (New York: Houghton Mifflin, 1934).

CHAPTER 7 | TO SEE THE EARTH AS IT TRULY IS

1. Bill and Frances Belknap, *Gunnar Widforss: Painter of the Grand Canyon* (Flagstaff, Ariz.: Northland Press, 1969), 25.

2. Ibid., 25.

3. Helen Laird, *Carl Oscar Borg and the Magic Region* (Salt Lake City: Peregrine Smith, 1986), 5.

4. Ibid., 168.

5. Ibid., 169.

6. Ibid., 168.

7. Ibid., 155.

8. Emory Lindquist, *Birger Sandzén: An Illustrated Biography* (Lawrence: University Press of Kansas, 1993), 65.

9. Ibid., 41.

10. Ibid., 40.

11. Ibid., 107.

12. Ibid., 83.

13. Ibid., 82.

14. Ibid., 83.

15. Ibid., 84.

16. Ibid., 85.

17. Ibid., 88.

CHAPTER 8 | THE UNFORGOTTEN SPIRIT

1. This and the following quotes are from Janet E. Rasmussen, *New Land, New Lives: Scandinavian Immigrants of the Pacific Northwest* (Northfield, Minn.: Norwegian-American Historical Association, 1993, published with the University of Washington Press), 148–50.

2. Richard Nelson, this and the following quotes from personal communication, 1998.

3. Richard Nelson, *The Island Within* (San Francisco: North Point Press, 1989), xiii.

4. Ibid., 59.

CHAPTER 9 | ADVENTURES IN LEGOLAND

1. Pauline Peterson Mathes, *Bit of Sweden in the Desert* (Fresno, Calif.: Pioneer Publishing, 1991), 29.

2. Ibid., 199–200.

CHAPTER 10 | WITH LIBERTY AND JUSTICE FOR ALL

1. Quoted in Arnold Barton, *A Folk Divided: Homeland Swedes and Swedish Americans, 1840–1940* (Carbondale: Southern Illinois University Press, 1994), 316.

2. Robert B. Putnam, *Bowling Alone: The Collapse and Revival of American Community* (New York: Simon and Schuster, 2000), 294.

3. Eric Sevareid, *Not So Wild a Dream* (New York: Atheneum, 1946, 1976), 6–7.

4. Ibid., 515.

5. Theodore Roosevelt, *The Autobiography of Theodore Roosevelt*, Centennial ed. (New York: Farrar, Straus and Giroux, 1975), 101.

6. Jacob Riis, *How the Other Half Lives* (New York: Charles Scribner's Sons, 1890), 1.

7. Theodore Roosevelt, *An Autobiography* (New York: Charles Scribner's Sons, 1920), 169.

8. Penelope Niven, *Carl Sandburg: A Biography* (New York: Charles Scribner's Sons, 1990), 318.

9. Simone de Beauvoir, *The Second Sex* (New York: Alfred A. Knopf, 1957), 125.

10. Quoted in Deirdre Bair, *Simone de Beauvoir* (New York: Summit Books, 1990), 409.

11. Quoted in Earl Warren, *The Memoirs of Earl Warren* (Garden City, N.Y.: Doubleday and Co., 1977), 5.

12. Quoted in Carl Solberg, *Hubert Humphrey: A Biography* (New York: W. W. Norton and Co., 1984), 17.

13. Hubert H. Humphrey, *Political Philosophy of the New Deal* (Baton Rouge: Louisiana State University Press, 1970, publication of 1940 LSU master's thesis).

14. Quoted in Odd Lovoll, *The Promise Fulfilled: A Portrait of Norwegian Americans Today* (Minneapolis: University of Minnesota Press, 1998), 120.

CHAPTER 13 | MELTING POT STEW, WITH RAISINS

1. Waldemar Ager, *On the Way to the Melting Pot* (Madison, Wis.: Prairie Oak Press, 1995), 10.

2. Ibid., 198.

CHAPTER 16 | HOME RUN

1. Reeve Lindbergh, *Under a Wing* (New York: Simon and Schuster, 1998), 199.

2. Anne Morrow Lindbergh, *Locked Rooms and Open Doors* (New York: Harcourt Brace Jovanovich, 1974), 112.

3. Ibid., 109.

4. Ibid., 110.

For readers wishing to pursue their Scandinavian roots, there's a wealth of resources. The best place to start is the six major Scandinavian American museums in Seattle, Philadelphia, Chicago, Minneapolis, and Decorah and Elk Horn, Iowa. Aside from Seattle's Nordic Heritage Museum, which honors all five nationalities, these museums focus on one group, but they honor a larger Scandinavian identity, and their bookshops offer titles that span the nationalities and many subjects. Scandinavian gift shops and college bookstores usually offer Scandinavian-related books, but their selections vary widely.

Two attractively produced magazines, *Scandinavian Review* and *Nordic Reach*, offer views of life and culture in Scandinavia. A remnant of the days when immigrants were eager for news from home is *Scandinavian Press*, which focuses on recent events. Events in Scandinavian America are best covered by the *Sun*, out of Evergreen, Colorado, which includes extensive listings of upcoming festivals, shows, and lectures.

Scholarship on Scandinavian subjects is thriving, offering books on a crowded spectrum of subjects. The following list focuses on books related to the subjects in this book, on books more for general readers, and on books recent enough to be available.

The larger number of Swedish Americans gives them some advantages in resources, best typified by *Swedish American Landmarks* by Alan H. Winquist (Minneapolis: Swedish Council of America, 1995), a state-by-state, town-by-town travel guide packed with historical background.

For Viking history, the 2000 millennium of the Viking discovery of America spawned a major Smithsonian exhibit and a companion book, *Vikings: The*

North Atlantic Saga, featuring quality photography and the latest scholarship (Washington, D.C.: Smithsonian Institution Press, 1999). This anniversary also produced a fresh translation of *The Sagas of Icelanders* (New York: Viking Penguin, 2000). A good scholarly summary is *The Vikings* by Else Roesdahl, 2nd edition (New York: Penguin, 1998), and a more adventuresome look comes from W. Hodding Carter's description of building a Viking ship and crossing the Atlantic: *A Viking Voyage* (New York: Ballantine Books, 2000). The Vikings have often turned up in fiction, for better or worse, and the most worthy American contribution is Jane Smiley's *The Greenlanders* (New York: Fawcett Columbine, 1988).

For an overview of Scandinavian history, see *Scandinavia since 1500* by Byron Nordstrom (Minneapolis: University of Minnesota Press, 2000). A study of the origin, meanings, and impact of the *Kalevala* is *Kalevala Mythology* by Juha Pentikäinen (Bloomington: Indiana University Press, 1989).

The Scandinavian immigration has generated a vast scholarship, much of it focused on one aspect or community. The best overview of Norwegian immigration is Odd Lovoll's *The Promise of America: A History of the Norwegian-American People* (Minneapolis: University of Minnesota Press, 1984), complemented by Lovoll's *The Promise Fulfilled: A Portrait of Norwegian Americans Today* (Minneapolis: University of Minnesota Press, 1998). A good overview of Swedish immigration is *Swedish Exodus* by Lars Ljungmark (Carbondale: Southern Illinois University Press, 1979). A more personal view comes from two books by H. Arnold Barton, *Letters from the Promised Land: Swedes in America, 1840–1914*, 3rd edition (Minneapolis: University of Minnesota Press, 1990), and his personal genealogical adventure, *The Search for Ancestors: A Swedish-American Family Saga* (Carbondale: Southern Illinois University Press, 1979). Barton's *A Folk Divided: Homeland Swedes and Swedish Americans 1840–1940* (Carbondale: Southern Illinois University Press, 1994) traces the tug of war between ties that bind and fail to bind. Good overviews of Danish immigration are hard to find in bookstores, but libraries may have George Nielsen's *The Danish Americans* (Boston: Twayne, 1981) and Frederick Hale's compilation of immigrant letters, *Danes in North America* (Seattle: University of Washington Press, 1984). A compilation of letters and diaries from every nationality is *The Scandinavian American Family Album* by Dorothy and Thomas Hoobler (New York: Oxford University Press, 1997).

Immigration studies with a regional focus include William Mulder's *Homeward to Zion: The Mormon Migration from Scandinavia* (Minneapolis: University of Minnesota Press, 1957, 1985) and *New Land, New Lives: Scandinavian Immigrants to the Pacific Northwest* by Janet E. Rasmussen (Northfield, Minn.: Norwegian-American Historical Association, 1993). For the saga of Bishop Hill, see *Wheat Flour Messiah: Eric Jansson of Bishop Hill* by Paul Elmen (Carbondale: Southern Illinois University Press, 1997). For Lindsborg, see *Pioneer Cross: Swedish Settlements along the Smoky Hill Bluffs* by Thomas Holmquist (Hillsboro, Kans.: Hearth Publishing, 1994).

No other immigrant group has had its experience fictionalized by gifted writers such as Ole Rölvaag and Wilhelm Moberg. Rölvaag's *Giants in the Earth* (New York: Harper Perennial, 1991) is completed by *Peder Victorious* and *Their Fathers' God* (Lincoln: University of Nebraska Press, 1982). Moberg's novels, *The Emigrants, Unto a Good Land, The Settlers,* and *Last Letter Home,* are back in print in America thanks to the Minnesota Historical Society Press. Moberg also offered his perceptions about Swedish America in nonfiction form, *The Unknown Swedes* (Carbondale: Southern Illinois University Press, 1988). Nobel Prize novelist Halldór Laxness portrayed the Icelandic immigration to Utah in *Paradise Reclaimed* (New York: Vintage International, 2002). Even a great American author, Willa Cather, was inspired to adopt Scandinavian women as the strong heroines of two of her novels, *O Pioneers!* and *The Song of the Lark.* For a fictional encounter with contemporary Finnish America, try Lauri Anderson's *Children of the Kalevala* and *Heikki Heikkinson* (St. Cloud, Minn.: North Star Press, 1997 and 1995).

The best attempt to define Scandinavian character may be Åke Daun's *Swedish Mentality* (University Park: Pennsylvania State University Press, 1996). A more business oriented approach is *Modern-Day Vikings: A Practical Guide to Interacting with the Swedes* by Christina Johansson Robinowitz and Lisa Werner Carr (Yarmouth, Maine: Intercultural Press, 2001).

Scandinavian social policy has generated much discussion, much of it strictly for policy wonks. One popular discussion comes from the original prophet of the middle way, Marquis Childs, who half a century later revisited the subject in *Sweden: The Middle Way on Trial* (New Haven, Conn.: Yale University Press, 1980), assessing how his evaluation had held up. A more complete discussion is *Sweden: Social Democracy in Practice* by Henry Milner (New York: Oxford University Press, 1989).

Most of the individuals discussed in this book have recent biographies. For Sigurd Olson, see *A Wilderness Within: The Life of Sigurd F. Olson* (Minneapolis: University of Minnesota Press, 1997). The University of Minnesota Press is also keeping alive four of Olson's best books, *Listening Point, The Singing Wilderness, The Lonely Land,* and *Runes of the North.* Wallace Stegner's biography is *Wallace Stegner: His Life and Work* by Jackson J. Benson (New York: Penguin Putnam, 1996), and he costars with Bernard DeVoto in the intellectual biography *A Country in the Mind* by John L. Thomas (New York: Routledge, 2000). For Roger Tory Peterson, see *The World of Roger Tory Peterson* by John Devlin (Montreal: Optimun, 1977). Buzz Holmstrom has emerged from undeserved obscurity in *The Doing of the Thing* by Vince Welch, Cort Conley, and Brad Dimock and in *Every Rapid Speaks Plainly*, a collection of Holmstrom's river journals (Flagstaff, Ariz.: Fretwater Press, 1998 and 2003).

The continuing devotion to Gunnar Widforss is measured by how the only book about him, *Gunnar Widforss: Painter of the Grand Canyon* by Bill and Frances Belknap (Flagstaff, Ariz.: Northland Press, 1969), is now a collector's item worth hundreds of dollars. Easier to find are *Birger Sandzén: An Illustrated Biography* by Emory Lindquist (Lawrence: University Press of Kansas, 1993) and *Carl Oscar Borg and the Magic Region* by Helen Laird (Salt Lake City: Peregrine Smith, 1986).

Of numerous biographies of Charles Lindbergh, the one that won the Pulitzer Prize is *Lindbergh* by A. Scott Berg (New York: G. P. Putnam's Sons, 1998). Jenny Lind's American adventure is detailed in *P. T. Barnum Presents Jenny Lind* by W. Porter Ware and Thaddeus C. Lockard Jr. (Baton Rouge: Louisiana State University Press, 1980).

Eric Sevareid's biography is *The American Journey of Eric Sevareid* by Raymond Schroth (South Royalton, Vt.: Steerforth Press, 1995). Jacob Riis's autobiography is *The Making of an American* (New York: Harper and Row, 1966). An intellectual biography of Thorstein Veblen is *Thorstein Veblen: Theorist of the Leisure Class* by John Patrick Diggins (Princeton, N.J.: Princeton University Press, 1999). The most comprehensive biography of Carl Sandburg is *Carl Sandburg: A Biography* by Penelope Niven (New York: Charles Scribner's Sons, 1991). For Nelson Algren, see *Nelson Algren: A Life on the Wild Side* by Bettina Drew (Austin: University of Texas Press, 1989). Sissela Bok chronicled her parents' history in *Alva Myrdal: A Daughter's Memoir* (Reading, Mass.: Addison-Wesley, 1991). For Earl Warren, see *Chief Justice: A Biography of Earl Warren* by Ed Cray (New York: Simon and Schuster, 1997). For Hubert Humphrey, see *Hubert Humphrey: A Biography* by Carl Solberg (New York: W. W. Norton and Co., 1984). A period biography of Walter Mondale is *The Democrats' Dilemma: Walter F. Mondale and the Liberal Legacy* by Steven M. Gillon (New York: Columbia University Press, 1992).

Beyond the scope of this bibliography are plentiful resources covering genealogical research, language skills, travel in Scandinavia, Scandinavian crafts, modern Scandinavian culture, and children's literature.

INDEX

This book was set by Omega Clay using the typefaces
Berling and Signa Condensed. Berling was designed in
1951 by the Swedish typographer and calligrapher
Karl-Erik Forsberg. Signa was designed in 2001
by Ole Søndergaard of Denmark.